3RD EDITION

The Landlord's Troubleshooter

A Survival Guide for New Landlords

Robert Irwin

Dearborn™
Trade Publishing
A **Kaplan Professional** Company

This publication is designed to provide accurate and authoritative information in regard to the subject matter covered. It is sold with the understanding that the author and the publisher are not engaged in rendering legal, accounting, or other professional service. If legal advice or other expert assistance is required, the services of a competent professional person should be sought.

Vice President and Publisher: Cynthia A. Zigmund
Acquisitions Editor: Mary B. Good
Senior Managing Editor: Jack Kiburz
Interior Design: Lucy Jenkins
Cover Design: DePinto Studios
Typesetting: the dotted i

Library of Congress Cataloging-in-Publication Data

Irwin, Robert, 1941–
    The landlord's troubleshooter : a survival guide for new landlords /
Robert Irwin.— 3rd ed.
        p.   cm.
    Includes index.
    ISBN 0-7931-8601-3 (6x9 pbk.)
    1. Real estate management.   2. Rental housing—Management.
3. Landlord and tenant.   I. Title.
HD1394.I78 2004
333.5¢4—dc22

                                                        2004012320

Contents

PART THREE
REMOVING TENANTS

PART FOUR
RULES AND REGULATIONS

This third edition of *The Landlord's Troubleshooter* takes a big step forward by answering the most asked questions of first-time investors in rental property, including how to find good rentals . . . and dump bad ones. Of course, it also contains updated information and techniques that experienced landlords have come to rely on in previous editions. Thus, whether you're picking up this book because you're just starting out as a landlord or because you have 100 units, you should find it a helpful guide.

I've been asked how this book differs from the other tomes that are out there addressing the subject of being a landlord. My answer is that not only does it attempt to give you all the information you'll need, but in addition it uniquely draws on my own experiences during 30-plus years of being a landlord as well as on the experiences of the many people I've met in the field.

That's why this book is filled with stories, *Landlord's Tales,* of how rental property investors coped, or failed to cope, with common problems. That's why there are special *hints, rules,* and *cautions* to alert you to pitfalls. And that's why I've taken great pains to emphasize those areas most likely to demand your best landlording attention.

But most of all, this book should provide you with immediate solutions. It is designed to be a troubleshooter: You've got a problem, it's got an answer. And that answer is expressed in commonsense language.

Yes, feel free to read this book from cover to cover at your leisure. But if you want solutions to a specific question, also feel free to turn right to that issue.

What I've put into this book is what has worked for me and other landlords. It's a book of landlords' answers to landlords' questions. Use it to come out a successful rental investor.

MAKING MONEY ON RENTALS

1

ARE YOU READY TO BE A LANDLORD?

*Always be friendly with your tenants. Never make them
your close friends.*

Landlording comes on us in many different ways. In recent years many investors have become landlords to take advantage of skyrocketing real estate prices. Buying a property or two, renting it out for a time, and then reselling at a profit has become a model for success.

Others need to rent out their home because of a job change, divorce, or other personal situations. For whatever reason, they can't or won't sell and thus are forced into becoming a landlord.

Or sometimes a person who is old and ill may move into a convalescent home. Suddenly, the responsibility of taking care of the person's home is thrust on a son or daughter who doesn't want to sell the family home; but the property has payments. So it's time to be a landlord.

Or . . . ?

Whether it was your choice to become a landlord or you involuntarily fell into it, chances are you're now reading this book because "You are the one!" You need to quickly and accurately learn how to deal with this new job.

In this chapter I'll cover how to develop an attitude that allows you to be a winning landlord. (Surprising to many newcomers, attitude is critical when it comes to success in this endeavor.) In subsequent chapters you'll learn which properties make good rentals, how to find them as well as dispose of the bad ones, and the nuts and bolts of being a good landlord.

It's All in the Way You Look at Things

This is a tale of two landlords, Jim and Julie. What they have in common is each owns one rental house. However, they are worlds apart in their attitude and therein lies the difference between success and failure. First, Jim.

Jim is new to landlording and approaches it strictly as a business. He has rules. He'll follow them and expects the tenants to follow them as well; it's just that simple.

Jim rented his older house to a couple with two children. The couple paid their rent on time for two months. Then, one night at eight o'clock, they called to say that one of the kids had accidentally smashed the glass on a slider (a large glass door that slides open and closed). A shard of glass had cut the girl on the arm, and she was in the emergency room receiving stitches. However, it was winter and with the glass at the back of the house gone, wind and cold were coming in.

Jim said he was sorry about the girl but that the parents should have been more careful in watching her. As for the glass door, the tenants broke it, so it was clearly their responsibility to fix it. That was spelled out in their rental agreement. Jim said he expected them to replace it immediately and not bother him. Then he hung up.

The tenants moved out within a week. They had left a piece of plywood covering the hole in the glass door. Jim had it replaced and took the money out of their security deposit; he then called his lawyer to pursue the tenants for abandoning the property without giving proper notice.

Within weeks Jim was threatened with a lawsuit. The tenants not only wanted all of their security deposit back but were suing Jim because he had rented an unsafe property. They wanted all their daughter's medical costs paid plus damages.

Preposterous, Jim said . . . until an examination by his insurance carrier revealed that the sliding glass door had standard plate glass that cracked into dangerous shards when broken. Safety plate glass was required on all modern structures, but because his was an older home, it wasn't up to current standards. The insurance company eventually paid off the tenants with a handsome settlement and immediately canceled Jim's policy. Further, Jim's lawyer advised him to give back all the security deposit and not fight the tenants on the issue of the broken window. Jim threw up his hands in disgust and quickly sold the property without a profit.

Moral?

Update older properties? Check out the glass on sliders? Treat your tenants better?

The answer is yes to all of these, especially the latter. Tenants are people, and although we expect them to pay their rent, we must also be ready to come to their aid in a reasonable way. What would it have hurt for Jim to call a glass company to come immediately on the tenant's call and repair the window? It would have helped satisfy the tenant, and Jim still could have deducted the cost from the security deposit. Further, he could have told the tenant that he would contact his insurance carrier about the daughter's medical costs, which were minimal. Finally, he could have come down to see that the family was OK.

Jim, however, wanted to keep his rental property at arm's length— the same way he might treat a stock investment. He didn't want to become involved.

Julie, on the other hand, had a different attitude, experience, and results. She owned a duplex (or duet), which is two units in one building. She bought it as an investment and immediately rented out both units.

However, within a few months, the tenants in one unit called a day before the rent was due to say that they were having trouble with coming up with the rent money. She immediately went down to see what the problem was.

As it turned out, the husband was the breadwinner. He was a roofer who had fallen off a roof. His ribs were bandaged, and it would be a month before he'd be back at work. The wife and three kids looked frightened. They said that the emergency medical payments had taken most of their cash, and they had little left.

Julie knew that getting the rent was the most important thing. She also knew that most people have some reserves to call on, even though they don't want to. However, she understood that her tenants were in a bad situation. She asked them when they would have the money. They offered to give her half the rent immediately (it wasn't yet late) and then pay the second half two weeks later.

Julie explained that this wasn't the way their rental agreement was written and that by accepting half a month's rent, she could be putting herself in jeopardy with her own mortgage and tax payments. But she agreed. She also came back later and brought the family groceries to help out.

Two weeks later, her second half of the rent came right in on time. Further, in this true story, those same tenants have been with her now for more than 18 years. She currently offers them a greatly reduced rent, and they take care of the maintenance of her more than a dozen rentals in the area as well as field most tenants' maintenance and repair problems for her.

Moral?

Allow late rent? Feed your tenants? Be a softy?

No to all of these. The moral is that when you're a landlord, it's not just a business relationship. You're dealing with the most important possession any family has: its home. And as such, you must let your humanity and your instincts have a say in what you do. Sometimes it's necessary to do something that's bad business but makes good "human" sense if you want to be a successful landlord over the long haul.

Dealing with People

When you become very successful at being a landlord, when you own 20 or 30 separate homes and apartment buildings, you *may* want to hire a management firm (see Chapter 5) to handle all of your rentals for you. (I say "may" because many self-made real estate entrepreneurs never trust anyone else to handle their property.) Until then, however, you'll find it necessary to deal directly with tenants yourself.

This usually means walking a kind of tightrope. On one hand, you'll need to know when to strictly adhere to the rules. On the other, you'll need to develop a sense of when to bend. You'll have to know how to gain people's confidence and sometimes how to insist that things be done only your way, which is to say that you must know your own mind. If you are easily manipulated by people, then your job as landlord will be made much more difficult. Because you will find that many tenants try to take advantage of you, you must be able to chart your own course and stick firmly to it.

If you are impatient with people, you'll quickly find that you're constantly in the midst of problems that seem to arise from the woodwork. And the more impatient you become, the more difficult the problems you're likely to find yourself facing.

Perhaps the best way to determine if you're likely to succeed as a landlord is to take a quick look at some of the major tasks you'll be expected to perform. Here is a list of those tasks—a landlord's duties:

- Buy suitable properties (unless they are thrust on you, as noted earlier)
- Determine appropriate rental rates and security deposit amounts
- Find tenants who want to rent your property
- Screen tenants to eliminate those who won't pay or are likely to damage the property, while observing antidiscrimination laws
- Obtain tenancy agreements and make sure tenants sign them
- Collect rents from tenants
- Pay expenses involved with investment property ownership
- Handle all repairs and maintenance of the property
- Deal with tenants who are slow payers
- Evict tenants when they won't pay
- Clean up after tenants leave and make the property presentable for the next tenants
- Sell the property

From this list, it should be evident that being a landlord is actually divided into several distinct types of jobs, each of which requires different skills. These are discussed in the following sections.

Working with People

This type of job includes finding tenants, persuading them to rent, collecting money, and dealing with tenants' problems. If you love talking and working with people, this will be the best part of being a landlord.

H *i n t*

You want to be friendly with tenants, but you don't want to be their best friend; otherwise, you won't be able to do the harsh things that a landlord sometimes must do.

Working with Property

This runs the gamut from fixing a leaking faucet to putting in a new water heater, or from cleaning up a dirty apartment after tenants leave to dealing with ants, spiders, roaches, and rats that may occasionally infest your property.

As a first-time landlord, your cash flow is likely to be small or negative (the property operates at a cash loss), which means that you're unlikely to have the financial resources to call in contractors, plumbers, electricians, and other professionals to deal with the physical aspects of owning a rental. Thus, most new landlords find they are handling property problems themselves. (As time passes, rents go up and you acquire more properties; then you'll find you do have the money to hire out solutions to property problems but not usually at first.)

Working with Numbers and Paper

There are such basics as keeping track of expenses (mortgage, taxes, insurance, maintenance, repairs, advertising, and so on) as well as tracking and depositing rental payments.

But there's also more. You'll want to know which items are repairs/maintenance and which are improvements for tax purposes. You'll want to calculate the smallest amount you can spend on advertising to obtain tenants, how you handle security deposits (whether the money is yours or the tenants), and how to deal with local and state government agencies.

Resources

Of course, as a new landlord, you have resources available to you, which usually means developing a team. That doesn't have to be done overnight but instead can be done over time. As the need arises, you'll want to avail yourself of different types of professionals and organizations, as shown in the following list of landlord resources:

- **A good agent**—to help you find good rental property, initially rent it up, help determine rental rates, and clue you into local and state requirements. Often a friend in the business will help or perhaps someone you've dealt with before.

- **A good accountant**—to show you how to set up and maintain your books as well as explain and deal with tax matters. Many computer software programs are also available that will help with this.
- **A good attorney**—to help you obtain a good rental lease agreement, deal with evictions if necessary, and handle any other litigation that might be necessary. As you get to know more people in the field, a few names will keep coming up: lawyers who specialize in landlord-tenant issues.
- **A good handyperson**—to take care of your basic maintenance and repair problems in a prompt and inexpensive way. Again, word of mouth is often your best source. Also, talk to neighbors and other landlords to find out which repair people they use.
- **A good peer service**—to keep you informed of what's happening out there to other landlords. You may want to join a local association as well as the National Apartment Association (http://www.naahq.org), which can provide you with this type of help.

The National Apartment Association (NAA) serves more than 20,000 independent rental owners (those with fewer than 50 individual rental units and often without full-time onsite employees) through their membership in one of NAA's 164 affiliates. By joining a local affiliate, members receive a monthly magazine devoted to the apartment industry, access to the NAA Web site (http://www.naahq.org), and members' only information about federal, state, and local legislative and regulatory issues; the industry's largest annual education conference and trade show; NAA's annual income and expense survey; and discounts on all publications and education materials in the NAA Resource Library. In addition, local affiliates may provide special forums and education opportunities specifically designed to meet the needs of independent rental owners.

NAA also provides education on all facets of apartment management, including leasing and maintenance, and a continuing education program to assist with professional development. It also sends out regular bulletins on critical industry issues such as mold, lead-based paint, and terrorism awareness. For information about NAA or how to join a local affiliate, call NAA at 703-518-6141 and ask for the membership department.

- **A good educational service**—to help you learn more about being a landlord. You may want to consider the Institute of Real Estate Management, which is part of the National Association of Realtors (http://www.irem.org). It provides classes in landlording to its members.
- **A good property management firm**—to help when you're large enough to afford it, have property at a distance, or simply don't want to deal with it yourself. Chapter 5 discusses finding this resource.

Are You Up for It?

This short chapter takes a quick look at what's involved in being a landlord. Chances are you're going to be able to say, "Yes, that looks doable."

However, it's important to be realistic. Perhaps you have good people skills that will enable you to work well with tenants and good management skills that can handle the paperwork and numbers. But you're all thumbs when it comes time to cleaning out a drain. If that's the case, recognize this fact early on and expect to hire someone to handle that aspect of dealing with your property.

Or perhaps you're great when it comes time to fix things—you're a regular handyperson—and you're adequate when dealing with people. But if you never do your own taxes and keeping track of money is a mystery, then be prepared to hire outside help for these aspects of landlording.

On the other hand, if you're not naturally gregarious and are easily manipulated and threatened by people, then perhaps you might want to hire a property management firm to deal with all your personal interactions with tenants. However, it will be expensive. And at least when starting out, hiring a management firm won't be as good as dealing directly with tenants yourself.

Take stock of yourself. Remember that few people have all the necessary skills. They still manage to be good landlords, however, by recognizing their weaknesses and hiring professionals to help in those areas.

You don't have to be perfect to be a good landlord. But especially when you're first starting out, it's really helpful to be willing to listen, to learn, and to change your mind as necessary to fit the new situation you're entering.

2

IDENTIFYING GOOD RENTAL PROPERTY

Never buy rental property more than an hour away from your home
or in an area where you would be afraid to go to collect rents.

You can rent out any habitable house—True. Any habitable house makes a good rental—Not true!

Although any house can be a home and/or a rental, not every house makes a good rental property. Indeed, some properties should never be rented out—they are simply unsuitable!

In this chapter we're going to take a look at what makes a property a good rental . . . and what you should avoid when looking for a rental investment. If you already own a property that turns out to be a rental "dog," this chapter may convince you to sell or trade it. Here's a list of what makes a good rental:

- Location
- Size and layout
- Features
- Yard
- Rental market
- Financing
- Age

Location, Location, Location?

Certainly everyone's heard that these are the three most important things when buying a home to live in. But for a rental?

Yes, once again these are just as important. With a home you're presumably looking for a neighborhood with few rentals in it. The reason is occupant-owners' pride of ownership, which typically translates into better upkeep of the yard and landscaping, quieter enjoyment of the home, fewer cars on the streets, and so on.

A perfect neighborhood for an owner? Yes, and also a perfect neighborhood for a tenant. Tenants enjoy living in this type of environment as much as owners do. Further, when it's time to sell, you'll be able to get more for the property and sell it more quickly.

But what about apartment buildings? Often dozens or even hundreds of apartment buildings are built in a group. Does the rule apply here?

It certainly does. Consider that you buy a ten-unit apartment building in a neighborhood that has 50 similar ten-unit buildings. What are your chances of snagging a good tenant?

Yes, tenants are more likely to know about this area of town. But on the other hand, their feelings toward it may be that it's less desirable. After all, a neighborhood of apartment buildings means that there's going to be high density along with associated cars, motorcycles, noise, children, adults, and so forth. Further, your units will be competing with nearly 500 others for the same tenants. You can expect it will be harder to rent and harder to resell.

The best environment for a small (or even a large) apartment building is in a neighborhood of mainly single-family homes. This helps lower the density and creates a more desirable place to live.

Remember that tenants tend to be temporary occupants. Where there are lots of rentals, tenants are constantly moving in and moving out. The more tenants you have in a small area, the more unstable the neighborhood tends to be. (That's part of the reason why most lenders will *not* make loans available to condominium owners when more than 25 percent of the units in the condo association are rentals.)

R *u l e*

Buy rental property with as few other rentals around as possible.

In addition to avoiding other rentals as much as possible, additional location considerations you should look for are shown in the following list of the signs of a good rental location:

- Within commuting distance of a large workforce, such as an industrial or commercial park, factory, or similar source of jobs
- Good access to freeways, mass transit, airports, and other means of getting around
- Close to shopping, both for groceries and other essentials
- Good schools, although this is more likely to influence long-term tenants as well as buyers when it's time to sell
- Good-looking neighborhood—a nice place to live

The speed with which you are able to rent your property and the quality of the tenants you get are often determined in large part by how good the location of your rental is.

Too Big, Too Small?

Some homes are too big to make good rentals, and others are too small. How do you know the difference? Think of it in terms of the number of occupants.

If you have a house with five or six bedrooms, who is typically going to want to rent it? Of course, the answer is a big family with lots of children. (Or, alternatively, sometimes two families who want to cut the rent by sharing a home.)

The trouble here is that even though children are delightful, crowding lots of them into a home can result in lots of wear and tear on the property. And today you cannot refuse to rent a home to families who have children except by limitations on the size of the house and the number of people occupying it.

C *a u t i o n*

Some landlords attempt to restrict the number of children by limiting occupancy to two people per bedroom. This might be construed as discrimination on the basis of familial status, because two parents may otherwise choose to keep a child with them in a bedroom. Your restriction would have a disparate impact on tenant applicants. If you ask a city zoning department how many people can occupy a home, they will typically answer three to four per bedroom. Think how many people that is in a five- or six-bedroom home!

Three bedrooms are plenty. You expand your potential tenant base with four bedrooms, but you can, of course, expect a lot of the tenants to be kids.

There's also the matter of the number of bathrooms. Some smaller, older homes have just one bathroom, sometimes for three or even four bedrooms. This is simply an untenable situation for most families. Inevitably, two (or more) people will want to use the bathroom at the same time. And if some of the occupants are teenagers, bathroom time can be even further extended.

Therefore, a home with only one bathroom is far harder to rent than is one with two or more bathrooms. Furthermore, you're far less likely to get long-term tenants in a home with only a single bath. So how many bathrooms are enough? Two is absolutely the minimum. After that, it's not usually critical unless, of course, you have five or six bedrooms.

The layout of a home is also important. A home that has a mudroom or an entryway where people can shed dirty shoes (or at least clean them) before coming into the main entrance goes a long way toward keeping your carpets clean and in good shape. A similar entrance from the rear or the garage also helps. Entrances from the garage to the kitchen (often through a utility room) are also desirable, as they keep short the distance that tenants must carry groceries (or kids); and they also help when it's time to resell or rerent.

Tenants are likely to accept lots of stairs in a home, but at resale time a single-story home is becoming increasingly more desirable. Homes with a master suite that can be isolated from the rest of the house are also popular with both tenants and subsequent buyers, as are rooms that can be made into offices.

Best/Worst Features

An example of a case where better is sometimes worse is a $2,500 front door with etched glass. You'll be very happy with the door until a tenant accidentally puts a foot through the glass. (Although you can charge the tenant for fixing the door with regular glass, you may not be able to charge the tenant the full amount for expensive etched glass.)

Or you may have absolutely marvelous granite countertops in the kitchen that cost you $15,000 to install. But when a tenant moves out after six months, you *might* find scratches cut into the countertops and stains that won't come out. (It's not true that you can't cut or stain granite—you can, but it's just harder to do than it is with other surfaces.) You may want to charge the tenant, but how much are you going to get for a scratch or a stain when the only real way to fix it is by replacement?

Perhaps a house has magnificent off-white Berber wool carpeting. If you were living in the house, you'd take off your shoes to walk on the carpeting and insist guests do likewise. Would you reasonably expect similar treatment, however, from a tenant? Expect lots of dirt and spots that won't come out when a tenant leaves. And tenants may protest if you try to charge them anything for carpet damage, arguing that it's only reasonable for white carpeting to more easily get dirty.

You get the idea—often those special features that add value and class to a home whose occupant is the owner can be the kiss of death where the occupant is a tenant.

Possibly one of the biggest mistakes landlords can make is to judge a rental house in the same way they judge a home to live in, at least in terms of features. With a property you'll occupy, the more elaborate, expensive, and desirable the features, the better. With a rental, the more basic, sturdy, and cleanable, the better.

All around the Yard

All of us want a big yard until we get it; then most of us discover that it's nothing but work. Unless you plan to have a gardener on

R *u l e*

Try to go with the most basic and easily replaceable, easily cleaned features for a rental.

a regular basis for both the front and the back of your rental, look for a property with a very small yard.

The yard has to be big enough to hold only a few chairs, a table, and a barbecue. (That's the size of the yards in most condos.) Anything bigger means lawns that need mowing, shrubs that need trimming, and, of course, watering for everything. (Don't think you can get around this by paving over a big yard—that's just an opportunity for kids to fall and get hurt on hard pavement.)

Big yards mean lots of water bills for you. (If you ask the tenants to pay the water charges for a large yard, expect a lot of dead plants. After all, why should they pay good money to grow your landscaping?) Also, don't expect tenants to do the mowing and trimming that you might do if you lived there. It makes little sense for them to take as good care of the yard as you would yourself.

Pools and spas are a definite no-no for two big reasons. The first reason is liability; a pool/spa in a home you occupy is a huge liability, which is why, if you have one, you also undoubtedly also have (or should have) a locked, minimum five-foot-tall fence all around it. And you watch anyone who uses it like a hawk.

A pool and/or spa in a rental is an enormous liability. A tenant or a member of the tenant's family could accidentally be injured or drown. A gate could accidentally be left open and could become your fault. The tile could be slippery, the water contain bacteria, the children using the pool unguarded, and on and on. As the owner, expect to be included in any liability issue.

A diving board, slide, or similar device is an impossible liability. Should you be unfortunate enough to obtain a rental with one of these, my suggestion is that you immediately have it removed. The danger of someone's being seriously injured or killed on any of these devices is too high.

The other issue with a pool/spa is upkeep. Who's going to clean and maintain the proper chemical balance? Your tenants? Why should they? (Would you, if you were a tenant?) Even if your tenants agree to do the upkeeping, are they capable of handling the sometimes complex tasks involved?

A tenant might think he or she is doing a good job until you get a phone call asking you to please come down and take care of the yellow-green water in the pool. (A pool/spa left uncared for can result in permanent damage to the plaster and the equipment.)

If not the tenants, a pool service? If you're there all the time, you can keep an eye on the service to make sure it's doing a good job. A tenant, however, is likely to just assume things are going well . . . until you get that phone call about the ugly water. Besides, a pool service can be expensive.

The Volatile Rental Market

It's possible to find a property in what appears to be a great location with no issues regarding size, features, or yard . . . and still realize it's a bad choice because of the local rental market. Some areas simply don't have a large population of tenants. In others, the tenant population may be looking primarily for inexpensive homes or, alternatively, for expensive ones.

Yes, there will always be someone looking to rent in any area. But as with buyers, the more tenants, the better your chances of hooking one. It's sort of like fishing. You have a better chance of hooking a fish in a lake stocked with trout than in one that's been fished out or has no native fish.

It's important, therefore, to take stock of the rental market in the area in which you will buy (or already have bought) a rental. There are lots of ways of accomplishing this. You can always become a "pretend" tenant yourself. For a weekend or two, check all the local rentals in your price range and area advertised in the newspaper, and go to see many of them. You'll see what's available and how much they would cost. Along the way you can talk with landlords to discover how easy it is for them to find tenants or if they are desperate because there are no tenants. You can also see the different price ranges of property available.

These are red flags denoting a poor tenant's market:

- Landlords advertise a free month's rent (or more) to move in
- Landlords offer bonuses (appliances, cash, TVs, etc.) to move in
- A large number of rental ads in the local newspaper
- The same rentals are available week after week, month after month

You can also do a more scientific study of the local rental market to see what it's like. Call the local chamber of commerce and planning

R *u l e*

Jobs are the key to rentals. The more jobs an area has, the higher the demand for rentals should be.

commission to check out the economic climate of the area as well as plans for new business development that will provide jobs.

Talk to and ask an agent to provide you with the rental inventory statistics for your area. These are usually available as a computer report that should state the number of rentals listed (agents handle rentals as well as sales), the average time it takes to find tenants, and how this report compares with those of previous years. Ideally, you want a rental market where the rent-up periods are less than a month. Local universities may also have available studies about the local economy and trends.

Finally (or first, if you're computer savvy), check the Internet. There are dozens, perhaps hundreds, of sites that deal with rental housing information. The best keyword I've found to use is "rental statistics" or a variation such as "rental housing statistics." Most of the sites are for a particular area of the country, such as Denver or Puget Sound, although a number of them provide national stats. The federal census department (http://www.census.gov) and commerce department (http://www.commerce.gov) also provide many useful tidbits of information.

Getting Financed

Financing is, or should be, a major determinant of whether a property will make a good rental. To understand why, consider this comparison of two different types of financing on the same home. We're talking about a home priced at $200,000 whose potential monthly rental income is $1,400.

Property #1 financing. The owner obtains 100 percent financing and gets a 30-year loan at 7 percent with payments of $1,331 monthly. Add in taxes, insurance, maintenance, repairs, and vacancy allowance of $400, and the monthly payment goes up to $1,731. Because the monthly rental income is only $1,400, this property will have a monthly loss (negative cash flow) of more than $300 a month. This is the owner's out-of-pocket money needed to cover cash expenses every 30 days.

Property #2 financing. The owner obtains 90 percent financing (putting 10 percent down) and gets a 30-year loan at 5.5 percent with payments of roughly $1,000 a month. Add in $400 for other expenses and this property breaks even. It has no negative and costs the owner nothing each month.

The difference, of course, is the financing. By putting some money down, the owner of Property #2 was able to secure a lower interest rate on a smaller loan. In the process the monthly payments were reduced to the point where the income from the property could handle the expenses.

The type of financing available is often determined by the property itself. Older properties may not be able to get financing as attractive (a low interest rate) as more modern ones. The credit-worthiness of the borrower is also an important factor, which could mean that buying a lower-priced property could help an investor get a better loan deal with less credit.

The financing you can get on a particular rental often makes the difference between a positive or a negative cash flow property. It should definitely enter into your consideration of what to buy.

Age Counts

Finally, there's the age of the unit to consider. Newer properties simply tend to make better rentals. The reason, quite simply, is that there's less to go wrong with them. With an older property, you're likely to have constant headaches from the operating systems. Water heaters will go out, furnaces will break, roofs will start leaking, air conditioners will poop out, and on and on.

Although all of these mishaps can also occur in a house you own, as an owner you expect to pay for these mishaps out of your personal funds. When they occur in an investment property, you suddenly start seeing red ink bleeding through your books. You always hope the property's income will cover its expenses—after all, the property is a business. You're not owning it for the pleasure associated with a personal residence.

But as expenses add up and overwhelm income in older homes, it's a different story. Here it becomes a losing proposition, and you'll rue the day you didn't buy a newer home.

This doesn't mean that *all* older properties make bad rentals. If older properties have been properly renovated—that is, someone has gone through and updated their systems and kept up with their maintenance—then they may operate for years without a costly repair. On the whole, however, younger properties tend to fare best when it comes to rentals.

The Bottom Line

From location to age, each property is different and each will make a better or worse rental. If you're in the market to buy a rental property, be sure to check it out from the perspectives considered in this chapter. That could make a huge difference in your state of mind and state of finances down the road.

On the other hand, if you already own a rental property and an analysis based on what I've discussed here suggests that it isn't going to make a good rental, consider ditching it. You may be able to sell for a profit. Or if that's not possible (or if tax considerations are an issue), consider doing a tax-deferred trade out of the property and into another one. Consult your real estate agent and tax advisor as well as Chapter 4 for more information.

3

GETTING MORE MONEY FROM YOUR RENTALS

You can't always get the rent you want. But you can always get the rent the market will bear.

How do you turn a negative cash flow rental into a positive cash flow property? One of the quickest ways is to increase the rent. Get enough income from the property, and I guarantee that your negative cash flow problems will go away.

Raising rents, however, is a tricky issue. How do you do it without losing tenants? Can it even be done at all? Isn't it something you should really take into consideration *before* you buy the property?

I'll look at answers to these and other questions in this chapter.

The Only Way for Rents to Go

From a landlord's perspective, there is only one direction rents should go: up. Unfortunately, the rental market in any given area is always changing and not always for the better. Some years it's tight, with more tenants chasing fewer rentals. Other years it's loose, with more landlords chasing fewer tenants. The truth of the matter is that you can only charge what the market will bear. Charge too high a rental rate and you'll have a vacancy. As a result, you must *judge* the market carefully.

Sometimes to keep a good tenant in a bad market, where there are just too many rentals, you will actually want to lower your rates. Do it.

You will astonish the tenant and usually avoid the hassle of cleanup and the difficulty of rerenting with too many vacancies around.

On the other hand, you should do a thorough evaluation of the market in which your rental property will be before you buy. Here are some suggestions on how to go about doing this.

How to Determine the True Market Rental Rate

Whether you're considering the purchase of a rental, renting out for the first time, or thinking about raising rents, you should always first check out the market. You can do this in a variety of ways, but the simplest place to start is the local paper where rentals are advertised. Let's say yours is a single-family home with three bedrooms, two baths, and a fireplace. Now check the paper for three-bed/two-bath homes with a fireplace in the same area as your rental. It's usually best to do this with the Sunday paper near the end of the month, because usually more rentals are shown there.

Within just a few minutes you can get a good idea of what properties about the same size, location, and features as yours are renting for. If another property has a pool, deduct a bit from what you can get. If yours has a bigger yard or an extra family room, add a bit. No, the figures you come up with won't be 100 percent accurate, but they probably will be close to 90 percent accurate.

Now, as described in the last chapter, take an afternoon, become a pretend tenant, and go to see a half dozen similar rentals in your property's area. Within a very short time, you should be able to get a highly accurate sense of what the market is for your rental. Be sure to ask landlords how long they've had their house on the market and if there are any reductions, for example, for signing a year's lease. This should help you verify, or change, the conclusions you drew from checking out rental ads in the paper.

Another method is to call several local real estate agents whose offices specialize in the management of rentals. Describe the property. (You can say you're considering using a property management firm, which you may very well be doing.) Agents are usually happy to send someone over to check out your property and tell you what rent they think you can get. Check with three or four firms, and you'll have what is probably a highly accurate estimate of your true rental rate. These experts can also quickly let you know if there are any move-in bonuses that are common in your area such as gifts, free rent, or something else.

L a n d l o r d ' s T a l e

A few years ago, Hal bought an eight-unit rental property in Phoenix, Arizona. He had been told that Phoenix was growing at a phenomenal rate, something like 10 percent a year. Yet residential property was amazingly cheap. His plan was simple: Buy property, hold it a few years while renting it out, and then sell at a profit. (Does that sound familiar?)

What Hal didn't realize was that at the time, housing construction was also increasing. Far more homes were being built than there were buyers . . . or tenants . . . in the area. In other words, it was a terrible market.

Almost from the moment Hal bought the property, things began to turn down. The eight-unit apartment building he bought had been fully rented, but after taking it over, he realized that most of the tenants were nonpayers. The former owner had "doctored" the books.

Hal kicked out six nonpaying tenants and then tried to rerent the building. But he quickly found that in this highly competitive market, other landlords were offering one or even two months' free rent. Some were offering free TVs or microwaves to anyone who would move in. Some were offering to rent without cleaning or security deposits.

Hal, on the other hand, figured out how much income he would need to cover his expenses, divided by eight, and asked that much for each unit. For the two currently occupied units, that meant a rent increase. By the end of the month, the two remaining tenants moved out.

Hal now had a completely empty eight-unit apartment building that stayed empty for five months. At that time, Hal bailed out of the market, selling the building to an investor who just took over for the mortgage amounts, resulting in Hal's losing his equity. The new investor cut the rental rate, filled up the building, and hung on to it for four years until the market turned around. Then he was able to get hefty rent increases and eventually sold the building for a good profit.

The moral of the above tale is simple: *Don't be stubborn when it comes to the market.*

Yet another method is to join the local rental property owners association (NAA—see Chapter 1) if there is one in your area. These organizations can sometimes give you lists of rental rates and can also often provide lease and other forms most suited to your area.

Thus, after a day or two of work, you should be able to quickly and easily determine the market rental rate for your unit.

Your property will rent for whatever amount the market will bear, and that amount has no relation to your expenses. One of the greatest mistakes a landlord can make is to try to fight the market. You want $1,000 a month, but the market will bear only $950. So you stubbornly hold out for your money. Eventually, perhaps four months later, you find some crazy tenant who's willing to pay your rate and you exult at your victory. But have you won or lost?

Consider that it took you four months to find this crazy tenant. That's $3,800 in lost rent that you presumably would have received by renting immediately at the market rate of $950 a month. But, of course, you're now getting $50 a month more at a rate of $1,000. The trouble is that it's going to take you 76 months, more than 6 years, to recoup the 4 months of lost rent. By renting immediately for $950, you might have been able to raise the rent $50 a month after one year.

Remember that it's a lot worse to have a property vacant than to have it rented full-time at a rate lower than you want. Your goal is to get as close to 100 percent occupancy as possible. If you drop below 90 percent occupancy, then you're probably charging too high a rental rate.

When to Raise Rents

Some landlords follow a rule of thumb whereby they raise rents every year a tenant stays in the property—kind of like a penalty for renting from them. The longer the tenant stays, the more the tenant has to pay. Of course, tenants rarely stay long with these landlords.

In my opinion, there are three conditions—*all* of which must be in effect—that you must meet before raising your rent:

1. You need to get more money from the rental. If you're in a negative cash flow situation, you may not survive long holding on to the property. Either you won't have the funds to continue or your will to stick it out will be worn down. Any rental property worth its salt should at the least break even. (That's after all considerations, including extra rental income from washing machines, Coke machines, extra car space, and so on as well as all write-offs, including depreciation.)

You need to raise the rents.

2. The market will bear an increase. You've done your homework and found out what other rentals are charging. You are charging less. You probably will be able to sustain a rental increase.

3. The tenants feel you are justified in raising rates. Your goal is not to have the tenants move out. Rather, your goal is to keep the same tenants, but only get a higher rental rate. To accomplish this the tenants must feel that you are justified in raising rates. The tenants will feel this way if you handle the increase in a civilized manner (with respect for the tenants' feelings); present a logical case that includes market analysis of other rental rates; and assure them there won't be another increase very soon. When they check it out and discover you're correct, they'll probably stay. Remember, as soon as you raise rents, every tenant will go out there and see what it costs to rent comparable units elsewhere.

The Cost-of-Moving Factor

You should be aware that tenants almost always consider the cost of moving. If you are charging the current market rate, you can often successfully raise the rents a bit more, depending on what it costs for the tenants to move someplace else. For example, let's say the typical costs of moving are $1,000. You might successfully raise the rent $50 a month on a year's lease, even though that's $50 higher than market rate. Over a year it only comes to $600, less than the cost of moving someplace else.

L *a n d l o r d ' s*
R *u l e*

Don't overlook the "inertia factor." Most people don't like to move. It's a hassle. The kids might have to change schools. As a result, your tenants may stay simply because it's easier than moving. Of course, increase the rents high enough and you'll drive any tenant out.

4

WHEN AND HOW TO SELL
A BAD RENTAL

An important rule of investing is knowing when to dump a loser.

Some of us are born stubborn. We're the kind of people who refuse to admit defeat in a baseball game even though our team is down ten runs at the end of the ninth inning; or people who work endless hours trying to turn around a client who's been losing money for ten years; or people who hang on to a stock they bought at $40 a share when it's now at 35 cents a share.

You get the picture. Such people will never cut their losses and run. They will always hang in there and tough it out. This can be admirable. Or it can be foolish. When it comes to rental property, it's important to know the difference.

When the Negative Is Killing You

Negative cash flow is the single biggest reason that a rental will be considered bad. Almost all landlords expect some negative cash flow, at least in the early days of property ownership. With high-priced properties, it's almost impossible to buy a rental that will immediately break even, let alone show a positive cash flow. Sometimes, however, that negative can become overwhelming.

It's important to remember that negative cash flow—paying out of your pocket each month to keep the property financially afloat—has a cumulative effect. And that effect can be different for each of us.

One person may be able to easily handle a $1,000 monthly loss both financially and emotionally year in and year out. Another may find a $50 a month negative cash flow emotionally devastating, even though the financial drain is minimal.

You'll know when the negative gets to be too much. It might be after you've owned a property for three years and had to continually pump money into it. One day you say to yourself, "That's it. I've had it. I don't want to spend another dime on this dog!" Now it's time to sell.

On the other hand, if after years you're still hopeful that you'll make a profit in the end, if the property is giving encouraging signs of life, such as allowing a rent increase and a more stable tenant load, then it's probably not time to sell.

Of course, there are other reasons that a property is considered bad, or unprofitable. Here are some that may prompt you to get rid of your rental:

- You have negative cash flow each month (already discussed).
- The property is located more than an hour's drive from your home, making it almost impossible to keep maintenance, repair, and rent-up costs down.
- You have a hard time finding and keeping tenants.
- The tenants you have don't pay their rent on time or at all.
- The tenants are constantly breaking things that cause you expensive repairs.
- The tenants you get stay only a few months and then move out, leaving a mess resulting in an expensive cleanup.
- You've had to serve three evictions on tenants in the property over the past two years.
- You dread thinking about the property. It gives you nightmares.
- You have fights with your spouse over the time and money you're spending on the property.
- Your health is being affected.

L a n d l o r d ' s   T a l e

Herb had heard that housing was inexpensive in Las Vegas. Even though he lived in Oregon, he flew to Vegas and arranged to buy a rental home. It was older property in a poorer section of town. He knew there were gangs in the area, and the area was subject to some vandalism, but the price was too good to pass up.

Herb held the property for more than a year. During that time the only tenants he could find were Section 8 (government subsidized), and the rent paid didn't cover his expenses. In two instances, the tenants moved out and left a mess. He had been assured the government would pay for repairs and cleanup, but he could never seem to get the money.

The property was vacant two and a half months the first year and was vacant again at the start of the second year of his ownership. Because he was so far away, Herb was relying on a management company to handle the rental for him. This was costing him $150 a month over and above his other expenses.

At one point, after a tenant moved out, Herb decided to fly down and do the cleanup himself. But it was the middle of summer and the temperature was over 110 degrees in the desert. The air-conditioning wasn't working, and Herb couldn't stand the heat. Besides, he had his regular job to attend to, so he flew home and told the management company to find a buyer at any price.

Herb sold at a substantial loss but was thrilled to get rid of the property. He later invested in Salem, the town where he lived; he got a good rental, which after a few years turned a positive cash flow, and Herb became a happy landlord.

The Property Will Tell You When It's Time to Sell

The bottom line is that a bad rental lets you know when it's time to bail out. There won't be nearly enough money coming in, and there'll be far too much aggravation going out. You'll know it's time to dump it.

When it's time, don't delay. The longer you procrastinate, the greater the financial and emotional toll. On the other hand, don't rush out blindly and give away what you've got. Even the worst rental is an asset and should be able to produce some kind of benefit to you on sale.

The Outright Sale

Once you've determined you want to get rid of a rental property, then chances are you can't wait to move fast enough. Years ago I bought a property for $55,000, kept it one very bad year, and sold to the first buyer, who offered me $45,000 to cash out.

I was thrilled at first. Then I began wondering if I couldn't have gotten a better deal? That was an important lesson about property for me. Thereafter, I never sold a rental hastily, no matter how bad it seemed.

An outright sale at a loss is not a terrible thing. From an income tax perspective, it may provide you a capital loss. This can be used to offset other capital gains and sometimes can be used to help offset other income.

Nevertheless, a loss is a loss. It's always better if you can find a way to turn it into a profit. Since the rapid run-up of real estate prices in most areas of the country over the past five years, even a rental that's lost money through negative cash flow may show a substantial capital gain upon sale. You may be able to avoid paying tax on this sale if you're careful.

The Tax-Deferred Sale

A section 1031 tax-deferred sale allows you to transfer the equity from one property to another without immediately paying taxes on the gain. This type of sale is ideal for people who have to sell and have acquired a capital gain. Instead of paying the capital gains tax on the sale for property held over a year (which currently is 15 percent but can be higher on recaptured depreciation), the seller can trade for another property of "like kind." (Like kind doesn't necessarily mean a house for a house. It could be a house for an apartment building; it means property held for investment purposes, not, for example, a rental for a personal residence.)

Sometimes a loss can turn into a profit in a trade. You have a rental you want to get rid of. Someone else has a rental he or she wants to get rid of. So you trade. But how can this help you? Aren't you trading your headache for someone else's?

Not necessarily. Consider, in the example above, that one of the basic problems Herb had was living in Salem, Oregon; yet he had purchased a rental in Las Vegas. To get out of Vegas, he sold at a loss.

On the other hand, what if someone in Vegas just happened to own a rental property in Salem or a nearby Oregon city? That person might be having just as much trouble with long-distance management as was Herb.

However, if the two traded properties, both headaches might go away. Both might end up with a better deal than either had before. Besides, in a trade the price can be "adjusted" to reflect the wishes of the parties somewhat more than reality might warrant. If you're a scrupulous trader, you might end up with a better deal!

Other Trading Options

We've been talking as if you had to find a partner in order to trade. But realistically, how likely are you to find someone in Oregon who wants to trade for a rental in Vegas and vice versa? Probably more likely than you might suppose.

But it doesn't matter because the government allows delayed, or Starker, tax-deferred trades. (The name *Starker* to identify these tax-deferred trades was the result of a win by T.J. Starker in a famous U.S. Court of Appeals decision in 1979 that approved delayed tax-deferred exchanges.) Here you basically just sell your property as if you were getting cash, but you put the money you receive from your equity in an escrow account you can't touch. Then you have 90 days to identify a rental property you will buy (trade for) and 180 days to complete the purchase. (You can also identify the property before the sale of your current rental.) Now, you simply go ahead and buy the property in the usual way, using the funds from the sale of your rental.

But it's not quite that simple. There are special rules to follow, such as not taking any money ("boot") out of the property as part of the sale.

And making sure all deadlines and other requirements are met. You'll definitely want a good tax accountant/attorney to help you with a trade.

Nevertheless, by using a tax-deferred sale, you can defer the payment of taxes on your capital gain into the future. And if you're shrewd, you may also be able to get rid of a property that's giving you all sorts of aggravation and trade for one that's much better for your situation.

Where the Grass Is Greener

The bottom line is that if you've got a rental that's giving you all sorts of problems, why not get rid of it? By doing so, chances are you'll immediately improve your financial condition and your mental health, you'll have fewer fights with your spouse, and you'll sleep better at night.

Remember that investing in rental properties is not a test of your determination. If it's bad, let it go. Chances are you'll soon find a much better property that will rent easier, make you more money, and let you sleep a whole lot better at night.

5

THE GOOD AND BAD OF PROPERTY MANAGERS

*Don't expect someone else to take care of your property
as well as you do.*

Many people who go into invest-
ment real estate are coming from other investment models, notably stocks
and bonds. In these fields, there is essentially no management; you simply buy your stock or bond, watch prices, and sell when you've got a
profit. Many would-be real estate investors hope to do that same thing
when it comes to property.

Of course, that's not possible. Residential real estate, in particular,
requires a hands-on approach to finding tenants, collecting rents, keeping the property up, and so on. Many readers may take to this like a duck
to water, but many others would prefer to have someone else handle all
these tasks for them. Harkening back to the model of stocks and bonds,
you might like to keep your hands off and hire a property management
(PM) firm to do all of the serious rental work for you.

Although I always suggest you at least give it a try when it comes to
managing your property (if for no other reason than you'll learn what's
actually involved), there are many good reasons to hire a management
firm to do it for you.

Reasons to Hire a Property Management Firm

Your property is far away. Your property may be at a sizeable distance from you, more than an hour's driving distance or 50 miles away from your home. For most of us it's a mistake to buy such a distant rental. We can't be there to rent it out. We can't easily handle maintenance or repairs. We can't pop right over when the tenant has a crisis. We can't be there "Johnny on the spot" when the rent's late. In short, we can't be a good landlord at a distance.

On the other hand, perhaps the only property you can get at a price that makes sense for renting is in the next county or state. Or perhaps you inherited the property. Or maybe it's your old home and you moved a long distance away to a new job. Or whatever.

If you want to keep the property but aren't close enough to manage it yourself, then you'd be wise to hire a property management firm.

You've got too many rentals. At some point you may become so successful that you have many rentals and just don't want to bother taking personal care of all of them. It's one thing if you own only a single-family home or even an 8-unit apartment building. But what if you have 25 units or more? You could wear yourself ragged trying to keep up with the tenants. In this case, a property management firm may very well pay for itself.

You're not comfortable collecting rents. Not everyone feels good about demanding the rent from tenants when it's due. It may cut across the grain of your personality to do this. If so, you may find that you're losing money because you simply can't be firm enough. If that's the case, then a PM firm is definitely in order.

You're not knowledgeable enough. Landlord-tenant relations is becoming an increasingly sophisticated field. Laws affecting rental housing are constantly changing. You may feel you don't know enough and don't want to spend the time learning to handle your own rentals. Again, a PM firm may be the answer.

From what I've just said, it may seem as though every investor should hire a property management firm! That's certainly not the case—there are excellent reasons for not doing so.

Reasons Not to Hire a Property Management Firm

High fees. Most PM firms charge 10 percent or more of your rental income for their basic service. Keep in mind that this is in addition to any charges that may arise for maintenance and repairs. The 10 percent is just the PM fee. (Some firms also charge separately for finding tenants during a rentup.)

Depending on your income/expense situation, PM fees could throw your property into a serious negative cash flow situation. As noted, most investors in the early years are very lucky to come close to breakeven, so taking 10 percent or more out for a PM firm will seriously throw these figures out of whack. In short, you may not feel you can afford to hire a property management firm.

High repair and maintenance costs. When you're taking care of a property, you *can* keep the costs down. When a washer goes out on a sink, it may only cost you 35 cents for a replacement and your time to do the repair. However, when a PM firm is in charge, the firm will hire someone and bill you for the service. That 35-cent repair could be $25 for a handyperson or $65 for a plumber. A couple of repairs a month can seriously eat into your cash flow.

In addition, some PM firms add a markup on the service performed. In other words, if the electrician sends a bill for $35, they may add on an additional $4 (or whatever) as their fee for handling the problem.

Lack of diligence or expertise. You naturally expect a PM firm to be on top of the situation with your rental(s) 24/7. After all, that's what you're paying it for. But that's not always the case.

However, a firm may simply not care very much. If a tenant doesn't pay on time, it may be a week before the firm shows up instead of going right down there the first day the rent is late. Then the firm may let the tenant go for another couple of weeks, and you could be out many weeks' worth of rent simply because the PM firm wasn't diligent in its collections.

Or, what could be worse, the firm could do something that was un-ethical or illegal. Although certainly rare, the firm could violate a civil rights law or a landlord-tenant law. And because the firm is your repre-sentative, you could be considered responsible. Presumably, you're hir-ing the firm for its expertise, but if the firm's members don't know what they're doing, they could land you in hot water.

Finding a Good PM Firm

If you decide to go forward with a property management firm, then it's vitally important that you thoroughly check out any you are consid-ering. Following are nine questions for you to answer:

1. **Will the PM firm handle all of my needs?**
   You should make a list of exactly what you want the PM firm to do for you. Don't assume that it knows what you want or that every firm does everything. Here's a list of typical services that you may expect the firm to provide. Be sure you show the firm your list and ask point-blank if it offers the service:
   - Rent up the property (including advertising and tenant screen-ing) according to your specifications (You'll set the rental rate, the number of pets allowed, and so on.)
   - Collect rents on time and forward the money to your account when agreed
   - Handle tenant emergencies without always calling you
   - Take care of repairs and maintenance at previously agreed-on rates
   - Make periodic inspections of the property to see that the ten-ants are maintaining it
   - Any other service you may need.

2. **Will the firm give me fee-for-service?**
   You may not want the PM firm to handle all of your rental duties. Rather, you may only want it to handle the initial rent-up. Or you'll handle rent-ups and only want the firm to collect rents. Will it do limited work on demand?

3. **Are the firm's fees clear and reasonable?**

   You can expect the firm to tell you up front what its charges will be. Be sure to ask about repair and maintenance costs. Does the firm have a markup? A handyperson to handle simple repairs inexpensively? Are there any extras?

4. **Does the firm have a regular real estate sales business?**

   There are pros and cons here. Many real estate offices operate a property management firm, not so much to derive income from it but as a potential source of listings. Presumably when you decide to sell, you'll list with it. This can be a disadvantage for you, however, as the firm may not be willing or able to devote full-time attention to your property.

   On the other hand, a company that also handles real estate may be in a position to let you know when deals that could benefit you arise. As one of its investors, you may be alerted to bargains.

5. **Is the firm licensed?**

   A property manager should have a real estate license or, in some states, a property manager's license. This should be on display, but it doesn't hurt to ask to see it if it's not. Of course, if you're concerned, you can always verify a license by calling or e-mailing your state's real estate division.

6. **Does the firm belong to recognized trade organizations?**

   At a minimum, it should belong to the NAA (National Apartment Association) (see Chapter 1). A variety of other organizations are also available. The National Association of Realtors' IREM (Institute of Real Estate Management) provides training and certification. Look for the designations CPM (Certified Property Manager) and ARM (Accredited Residential Manager).

7. **Does the firm carry insurance?**

   You want the firm to be bonded in case one of its employees scoots out with your rent. You also want it to carry some form of professional insurance in case it does something that injures a tenant. Of course, it should also carry the usual insurance, such as workers' compensation, liability, and the like.

   Even though it sounds pushy, I would ask to see the policies, which the firm should be able to provide. Look at the amount of coverage (I consider $3 million a minimum for liability and $1 million for errors and omissions) and the effective dates. You want to see a policy that's continuously and currently in force.

8. **Will it provide references?**

   Any good firm will. Don't just look at the list; make some calls. Find out if the people you talk with are current clients of the firm. Are they satisfied with the service? Do they have complaints? If they are former clients, why did they leave?

9. **Will the firm provide you with a copy of its client agreement?**

   Because this agreement determines your relationship with the firm, it's a good idea to take it to your attorney to check out. You should look for:

   - **Negligence clauses**—These sometimes excuse or hold harmless the PM firm for its own mistakes. You don't want such a clause.
   - **Cancellation clauses**—These sometimes stipulate that you can fire the firm only on giving it long-term notice (sometimes three to six months). You want to be able to terminate it immediately or at most with 30 days' notice.
   - **Time-sensitive actions**—You want the firm to be available to you and your tenant on a 24/7 basis.
   - **Pass-through and markup conditions**—All the monies collected for you should pass directly through to you. Any late fees should be yours, not the PM firm's. Also, there should be no markups on labor or materials.
   - **Extra costs**—Is there a separate charge for renting up the property? Real estate agents often charge a substantial commission or one or two months' rent as a fee. You want the PM firm to handle this as part of its costs.

An outside property management firm plays an important role—that of intermediary. The firm steps between you and a tenant and gives you some distance. Further, the firm is often better able to deal with tenants because it can always say, "Well, you know the owner insists that we raise the rent. What can we do? We're just the managers." Just as a real estate agent acts as a kind of referee between buyer and seller, the property management firm can act as a go-between for you and your tenants. It can tell a tenant something unpleasant, such as the rent's going up or a dirty house causes spiders. And if tenants get angry, it's usually at the

L *a n d l o r d ' s* **T** *a l e*

Sally owned a single-family house with a pool that she rented out to a lovely couple with two charming, small children. They seemed to be wonderful people, concerned with their environment, anxious about the condition of the house, eager to get their rent in on time.

But as soon as they moved in, they began complaining. The screen door didn't slide easily. There were ants in the house; then they found a big spider. The carpets weren't clean enough. The windows didn't lock properly. The pool-cleaning person didn't come often enough.

Of course, Sally responded to all of the complaints quickly, but often they were trivial. For example, she called an exterminator for the ants. Then she called him back for the spider. But he explained he wouldn't guarantee a spiderless house; the only way to keep spiders out was to get rid of all the cobwebs in the corners and elsewhere. Then she called a handyman to work on the windows and the sliding screen door, but he couldn't find a problem.

The tenants did pay their rent on time, and the house was an older one in a not-so-wonderful neighborhood, so Sally didn't want to lose them. But their weekly (or more often) calls became extremely annoying. Further, because the couple talked to her so often, she began to feel they were becoming overly familiar and were expecting favors—such as the time a few months later, for example, when they called to tell Sally their rent would be a week late but were sure she would understand and that they could count on her friendship.

Finally, Sally began to realize that these tenants, though probably not doing it consciously, were getting under her skin and keeping her from being a good landlord. The final straw was when she planned to raise the rent but realized she just couldn't make herself tell them. She had become an ineffective landlord.

So Sally hired a professional property management firm. It charged her 10 percent of the rental income but raised the rent the first month by 10 percent and so quickly paid for its cost. More to the point, the firm fielded all the tenants' complaints effectively, and for the first time in a long time, Sally could relax and no longer dread a ringing phone announcing a complaint from her problem tenants.

bearer of the bad news—the property management firm, not you, the owner.

When a tenant becomes too frustrating to deal with or a property gets too hard to handle, it may be time to call for outside help. In the long run it could not only make it easier for you to sleep at night but also save you money.

Property Management Firms and the IRS

You may have heard that to obtain the exclusion from the active/passive tax rules that apply to real estate, you must manage your property yourself and cannot use a PM firm. This is not necessarily true.

The active/passive rules basically state that to claim a deduction against your ordinary income when you have a loss on your rental (i.e., expenses, including depreciation, exceed income), you must be actively in charge of your rental. (You must also meet specific income requirements.) The rules are generally interpreted to mean that you must do such things as set the rental rate, determine the lease agreement to be used, fix the term of the tenancy, and so on. There's no reason that you can't do these things, spending the necessary number of hours the government may require actively managing your property and still use a PM firm.

Because the rules here are tricky, be sure you consult a real estate tax expert before taking a write-off on your rental property or doing anything that might result in tax consequences for you.

6

CONVERTING YOUR EXISTING HOME TO A RENTAL

What's good for an owner isn't necessarily good for a tenant . . . and vice versa.

There are many good reasons why you would want to convert your existing home to a rental. You may be buying a new home and be unable to sell your old one, at least at a price you want. Yet you must keep on making those mortgage payments on the old home. The obvious answer is to convert the old home to a rental.

Or perhaps you bought a home with the intention of moving in but circumstances changed, and now you can't, or don't want to, move in. Again, converting to a rental may be the answer. Or perhaps you see an investment opportunity. Buy a new home and keep your old one as a rental.

Whatever your reason, it's important to conduct an evaluation of your property. Is it really suitable as a rental? Some properties are more suitable than are others. In this chapter I look at some of the factors that determine how good a property will be as a rental. I also consider whether you really want to become a landlord.

Will Your Property Make a Good Rental?

Can't every property be rented out, you might ask? Every property certainly can, at some price and at some risk of damage. The problem is that some properties command smaller rental rates and offer greater risks. Let's look at some of the concerns.

The House with a Pool and/or Spa

You may feel that a pool or spa is a great advantage. I know that when I initially purchased properties as rentals, I thought a pool or spa was a big plus. A pool or spa meant I could always get more rent.

A growing number of homeowners and now landlords, however, realize the problems that a swimming pool or spa produce often far and away exceed the benefits. Thus, in many markets a pool or spa is not a plus but at best a wash and at worst a negative. Nevertheless, in Sun Belt states you can often rent out a home with a pool or spa more quickly and for more money than you can a home without either.

However, in my opinion, a pool or spa is always a negative for rentals, even with the increased revenue and speedier rent-up time it brings in. There are several reasons why (also mentioned in Chapter 2).

Liability. People, children, dogs, and cats sometimes have accidents in and around pool or spas. Fortunately, drownings seldom happen. But people falling in, skinning their knees or other body parts on tiles, injuring themselves while diving, and so on happens far more often than most of us realize. When we own or live in a home with a pool or spa, we can watch to be sure that adverse mishaps such as these don't occur. When we rent out, however, it's up to the tenants to be careful. And if they're not, it's likely we are going to be asked to pay the consequences.

To protect yourself from charges of negligence, at a minimum you need to have a fence completely surrounding the yard that the pool or spa is in. Even in an enclosed backyard, it's better to have a second fence surrounding just the pool or spa itself. This is to ensure that some small child doesn't wander out the back door of the house and accidentally fall in.

When I had pool-home rentals, I also always removed all diving boards, slides, and other accessories that actually make the pool or spa more fun to have. But there's simply too much danger of someone being injured on them.

Finally, you'll want to have adequate liability insurance. Many property management firms suggest a minimum of $300,000 to $500,000. I recommend a minimum of $3 million through a combination of standard liability insurance and an umbrella policy. (See Chapter 26 on insurance.) One problem is that in some areas it's difficult to get this kind of insurance for a rental.

Cost. No matter what anyone says, pool or spas are not cheap. Besides extra insurance, they require large amounts of electricity to run the pump and chemicals to maintain water purity. Depending on the condition of your pool or spa, the costs can be anywhere from $20 to $150 a month, offsetting much of the increase in rental income the pool or spa might bring in.

Upkeep. Someone has to clean the pool or spa, clean the filter, put in the chemicals, and so forth. A pool or spa service can easily run you $50 to $100 a month. And don't make the mistake of thinking you can have the tenants do this. Tenants are notoriously forgetful when it comes to remembering to add appropriate chemicals and clean the pool or spa regularly. Besides, do you really want the liability that attaches when a tenant pours such chemicals as acid and chlorine into water and accidentally burns himself or herself?

Repairs. Pools or spas don't repair themselves. They require that you hire someone to fix pump motors and clogged filters. Broken or clogged pipes, black algae growing into plaster, and cracks in the cement are just a few of the occurrences that can entail very expensive costs, particularly when you're not there to watch out for the pool or spa yourself.

In short, because pool or spas are a liability problem, are difficult and expensive to maintain, and have all sorts of costly physical problems, my feeling is that a house with a pool or spa is simply not suitable for renting out. It's better that you sell it now at a loss than to rent it out and end up paying thousands of dollars because of the pool or spa later on.

I realize, of course, that many property managers may scoff at such concerns. Many, in fact, do successfully rent out houses with large pools or spas. I can only offer that their experiences have been different from mine. In my book, having a pool or spa automatically disqualifies a property from rental status.

The Very Old House

Houses, in one sense, are like cars—they deteriorate over time. When a house is new—under 7 years of age—usually nothing or, at most, very little goes wrong. By the time it's a teenager, however, important areas begin causing trouble—water heaters, roofs, appliances. As a house gets into its 20s and 30s, additional problems arise with the heating/air-conditioning system, the plumbing, and especially the cracking in walls and ceilings from a settling foundation. A house that reaches the ripe old age of 50 to 70, however, may need the entire plumbing system replaced (converting from rusting galvanized steel to copper), perhaps a new electrical system (converting from a two-wire to a three-wire grounded system) in addition to a complete roof replacement, foundation repair, driveway replacement, and so on.

Yes, it's true that these expenses may occur whether you're living in the property or renting it out. However, if you're living in it, you can "nurse it along," making do with old and decrepit features. When you're renting out, however, you must be sure the property is habitable and meets minimum public health and safety standards (unless, of course, you want your specialty to become slumlord, a category not covered in this book).

When the air-conditioning or heating system goes out, a tenant wants it fixed immediately, and that could mean complete replacement. On the other hand, if you were living in the property, you might wear a bathing suit (in summer) or an extra sweater (in winter) for a few weeks until a less expensive repair part could be found. The same holds true for leaking roofs, electrical systems that go down, plumbing that stops up, and so forth. No tenant will put up with what you might put up with. All of which says that maintenance and repair costs mean it's more expensive to rent out an older house.

Again I recognize that many landlords disagree here. Some well-maintained, well-located older homes can indeed do very well as investment rentals. If there are minimal physical problems with a house of any age, it should be a good rental opportunity. My own personal experience with many older properties, however, has been that sooner or later they gave me very expensive headaches.

The Poorly Located House

Everyone knows that location is the most important aspect of real estate. What few realize, however, is that a great location for a home to buy or sell does not necessarily make for a great home to rent out.

Properties that are close to work sites, shopping, bus lines, and so on usually make good rentals. On the other hand, a property very close to any of these might make it more difficult to sell the house. A house located far out in the woods, however, may be an idyllic setting for someone buying a home and wanting a romantic location. But someone wanting to rent may not want the hassle of a long drive and the upkeep of a woodsy environment.

In general, single-family homes, apartments, condos, duplexes, and almost all other kinds of residential rental property do best as rentals in an urban or suburban setting that is clean, relatively crime free, and newer. Houses that are far out, are in higher crime areas, or have difficult access to freeways or bus routes do less well.

The High-Maintenance House

As a homeowner, you may be willing to spend several hours a week watering the lawn and shrubs. I can almost guarantee your tenants won't bother. If your house has automatic sprinklers, a drip, or other watering system, it's a big plus as a rental. If everything has to be done manually, it's a minus.

Big yards are great for big families, particularly when you live on the property. But if you're renting out, big yards attract big families, which means extra wear and tear on your property. Also, there's the matter of who is going to mow the lawn, trim the shrubs, rake the leaves—you get the idea. You do it yourself or hire an often expensive gardener.

Houses with big yards tend to be a minus for landlords. Either you're going to be fighting the tenants to get the work done or you're going to have to hire a gardening service, which can cost a substantial amount of money. (Hiring a gardening service, however, is a plus when finding a tenant and often allows you to charge a slightly higher rent—rarely, however, high enough to pay for the entire gardening service.) As noted in an earlier chapter, houses with big yards also tend to be costly in terms of water.

Summary

Try to avoid converting your residence to a rental if it has a pool or spa, is old and run down, is far off the beaten track, or is high maintenance. If you do convert with these negative features, you may end up with a substantial negative cash flow on the property.

On the other hand, if your home is newer, is well located, has no pool or spa or big yard, and is low maintenance, it may make an ideal rental.

7

BUYING AN
EXISTING RENTAL

*Never believe everything a seller tells you . . . always verify it
with the tenants.*

As you move forward in the role of
an investor, you will surely come across properties that are already
rented up—anywhere from single-family units to apartment buildings.
You may think that buying an existing rental filled with tenants is a plus.
For example, you buy a six-unit apartment building fully leased. You
don't have to worry about finding tenants; you just sit back and collect
the rents, right?

Maybe! Depending on how careful you were in your purchase, on
the terms of your sales contract, and on your own investigative efforts,
you could have purchased anything from a nightmare to a gold mine. In
this chapter we're going to consider some of the ramifications of buying
preleased properties.

Things to Consider before You Buy

There are a number of concerns you should address before con-
cluding a purchase. Typically, in the purchase of a business property like
a rental, you will insist on an investigative period (sometimes called a
due diligence period) during which you can check out the property. Following sections discuss some of the things to look for during this period.

Tenants' Files

Every landlord keeps a file on every tenant. A file includes such things, among others, as the amount of rent, the dates when rents were paid, deposits, and personal property of the landlord in the unit. Make sure that you get copies of these files so you have a basis on which to begin your investigation.

Who's Got the Deposits?

This is one of the biggest areas of concern. Chances are that every tenant in the property you're buying paid a deposit of some amount for some purpose to the former owner. But how big was the deposit and who now has the money?

If you're taking on a large property, say 100 rental units with deposits of $750 for each, you're talking about $75,000. That's serious money, not something you should leave to chance. Even if you're taking on just a single-family house that's rented out, there could be a $1,000 or more in deposit money somewhere out there. If you wait until after you make the purchase to go after the money, you may never find it and may, indeed, be responsible for ultimately paying it back out of your own pocket. The time to track it down is beforehand.

Be sure to get a statement from the owner about the deposit from each tenant, and then go to at least some of the tenants to verify the amounts. Also, be sure your purchase agreement specifies that the deposits the owner is holding will be transferred to you.

Who Has the Last Month's Rent?

The same holds true for the final month's rents as for the deposits. If the property is leased, chances are the tenant(s) has paid a last month's rent up front, and the old landlord received the money. But unless it's placed in escrow or otherwise handled as part of your purchase transaction, you may never see it.

L a n d l o r d ' s   T a l e

Sally was purchasing a 14-unit apartment house that was almost fully rented (one unit was vacant). She had a clause inserted in the sales agreement that the seller was to turn over to her all deposits and last month's rents, and that further she had the right to secure an inventory of the funds. However, the seller said there were no deposits and all the tenants were on a month-to-month basis so none had paid a last month's rent; hence, there was nothing to turn over. Further, although the seller had signed rental agreements with all of the tenants, he could not produce them, saying they had somehow gotten misplaced.

So Sally went door-to-door in the building introducing herself as the person who was buying the property and asking the tenants about rental agreements, deposits, and the final month's rents. Surprisingly, nearly all of the tenants had a copy of their rental agreement. Sally found that five of the tenants had leases and had paid the last month's rent up front. Further, all of the tenants claimed to have put up cleaning/security deposits of one kind or another. As the new owner, she would be responsible for one day returning these funds.

Sally inventoried the monies and then presented her inventory to the seller. It came to over $12,000. She said that was owed to her in cash as part of the deal. The seller said, "No way!" He at first disputed the claims of tenants about deposits and final month's rents, and then he said that tenants had indeed put up money, but the amount was much lower than the one Sally reported. In any event, he said he had spent it all and wasn't about to sweeten the sale by $12,000. Sally pointed out that he was obligated to come up with the money or they had no deal. After all, she wasn't going to pay $12,000 extra for the property just because he had spent the deposits and last month's rents.

Eventually they reached a compromise—partly in cash and partly in better terms on a mortgage the owner was carrying back. Sally got her building and took care of the deposits and the final month's rents.

The story about Sally illustrates a way to handle deposits and final month's rents when buying an occupied rental property. Of course, you could always buy blind and take your chances later on. However, sometimes with very expensive properties, as noted earlier, the combined deposits and other funds held for tenants can be as large or larger than the purchase's down payment! It's not something you want to just let go.

Personal Property Included in the Sale

Do appliances in the units belong to the seller or the tenants? If they're the seller's, you need a list of all of them. Then you need to verify with the tenants that the list is accurate. Refrigerators are usually the biggest bone of contention, because in many rentals they are the property of the tenant and not of the landlord. Be sure you verify the ownership status of all refrigerators (as well as stoves and furniture).

Paperwork

All rentals have some paperwork that usually includes tax statements, tenancy agreements, licenses and permits, service contracts, insurance policies, and utility bills. You should be provided with copies of all of these.

Analyze them carefully. They present a documentation of the property's rental history. They also suggest what your costs in the future may be as well as what problems you may run into. As with other areas, verify as much as possible with the tenants.

Giving Notice of a Change in Ownership

After the purchase, it's important to formally let the tenants know that you're the new owner and to inform them of the way you intend doing business. The best way to accomplish this that I have found is by a formal letter. Ideally, you would have a sign-off letter from the former landlord and a sign-on letter from you, the new landlord. The idea here is to let the tenants know what's happening and to reassure them that there is a continuity of management and their interests are protected. (See the end of the book for change-in-ownership sample letters.)

The former landlord's letter need only be short and sweet. It let's tenants officially know that the building has changed hands, that you are the new owner, and that you will be contacting them soon. I suggest you write it yourself and have the old landlord sign it; then you can mail it to the tenants. (If you leave the mailing to the old landlord, it may never get taken care of.)

You should include the following in the new landlord's letter:

- Introduction of yourself
- Indication that you have your own rental agreement you want the tenants to sign
- Indication that you are responsible for deposits and last month's rents and a request for the tenants to come forward with copies of their rental agreements, canceled checks, or other evidence of having paid in monies
- Indication of how you intend to collect the rent in the future
- Statement giving tenants your correct address and phone number so they know where to send the rent (if that will be your method of collection) and how to contact you

If possible, deliver these letters in person. That way you get to know the tenants, and they get to know you.

Changing Rental Agreements

One thing you most certainly want to do is begin using your own rental agreement with the tenants. However, you cannot simply step in and change rental agreements, because you may be bound by the agreement signed by the old landlord. With a lease, you have to wait until the lease term is up to change it . . . or offer the tenant some incentive—for example, reduced rent, a few free weeks, a better apartment—to change it sooner.

With a standard month-to-month agreement, you can usually change it with appropriate notice, normally 30 days in most states. However, the tenants must sign your new agreement before it becomes effective.

Sometimes a tenant refuses to sign your new agreement and insists on staying put under the former landlord's agreement. Perhaps there's a clause in yours that the tenant objects to. Your choices are either to change your rental agreement, which you probably won't want to do, or to ask the tenant to move. My suggestion is that if you value the tenant, you play it carefully and compromise as much as possible.

Persuading Tenants to Sign Your Rental Agreement

You may not have much information about the existing tenants. Therefore, before you have them sign a new rental agreement, you should have them fill out an information sheet. You can use the sample rental application form found at the back of this book, although I wouldn't insist on all of the financial information—after all, they are already living in the property.

You need to obtain the following information:

- Each tenant's rental term and type of agreement
- Number of tenants in each unit, names, ages, and pets
- Where tenants work and the types of cars they have
- Who to be called in an emergency
- Which personal property (appliances, wall coverings, and so on) belongs to them
- How much they have put up in a deposit/last month's rent as evidenced by a rental agreement, canceled checks, and so on

Early on, give a copy of your rental agreement to each tenant along with a date by which you want it signed (plus any other limitations imposed by local or state ordinance).

Once you have the information about the tenants, you can call—perhaps a week before you want the agreement signed—and ask them if they have any questions or don't understand anything. Finally, make a date to come and have a filled-out agreement (filled out by you) fully signed.

L *a n d l o r d ' s* **H** *i n t*

You can get information about existing tenants' finances in part by noting the bank and account number on the check by which they pay and keeping that information for future reference. (But remember, unless they authorize it in writing, you shouldn't do a credit check on them.)

Increasing the Rent

When buying a rental property, the buyer often has raising the rents in mind. After all, the value of such property is normally determined by the amount of income it produces. Raise rents and you've increased your equity, sometimes quite substantially.

If you feel that the market justifies rents higher than those currently being paid by tenants, I suggest you raise them as soon as possible, preferably within the first three months. (Of course, with leases you'll have to wait until the lease term runs out to raise the rent.) The tenants will understand that the rents are being raised as part of the change in ownership and will either accept it or move. If you've checked the market carefully, they'll quickly see that the rents are only being raised to realistic levels, and most will stay. Nevertheless, any time you raise rents, you always run the risk that some tenants will move rather than pay.

A Higher Last Month's Rent

With leases, the tenants will have probably paid the last month's rent in advance. However, you cannot raise the rent during the term of the lease (unless there is a specific clause in the lease allowing this). Further, the total amount of money to be paid over the term is usually specified. Thus, you can't increase the last month's rent for a lessee, even though other tenants may be paying more now.

Where this really becomes an issue is with a tenant who originally rented on a lease, stayed past the expiration of the lease, and is now on a month-to-month basis. That tenant, through several rent increases, may now be paying $1,000 a month, although he or she originally put up only $750 for the last month's rent. Can you now insist on the extra $250 when the tenant decides to move and the last month issue comes up?

It depends on how your original lease was written. But in any event, I can guarantee you that the tenant is not going to look with pleasure on coming up with that extra $250. In fact, most tenants will fight you tooth and nail over the money.

I suggest you calmly ask the tenant for the money and explain why it's owed you. However, if the tenant protests strongly, I then suggest that you compromise, accepting half, or write it off if only one tenant is involved and protesting. Sometimes the hassle just isn't worth it. Yes, it's important to be right but not if it causes you a heart attack in the process.

Getting Copies of Keys

Ideally, the former landlord was well organized and had a separate set of duplicate keys for each rental unit. In the real world, however, the old landlord may actually have been a complete dud when it came to keeping track of little things like keys and may only have had a master. In a worst-case scenario, the old landlord may have no keys at all to turn over to you!

Keep in mind that you must have keys to each rental unit you manage. There could be a fire or other emergency requiring your gaining immediate access to a unit. Without a key, your only recourse would be to break the door down. Thus, you have the unpleasant job of going to each tenant and asking for his or her keys so you can make a duplicate set. If a tenant is hesitant to give up the keys, you can point out why you need them and what you would have to do if you didn't get them. I can't think of a single tenant I've known who would rather have his or her door knocked down than give up a key. Nevertheless, should a tenant still refuse, you may have to get an attorney to press this issue. You can't compromise here—you *must* have keys to all your rental units.

8

CLEAN UP
TO RENT UP

Provide a clean rental and you'll get a clean tenant.

It's not up to the tenant to get the property into habitable shape. It's your responsibility as a landlord to provide a habitable rental. That means neat and clean. On the other hand, it doesn't necessarily mean spotless. Don't feel that new tenants are like guests coming into your house. You don't have to scrub and clean as if you're expecting your son's new bride to be spending the night.

Preparing the property so that it appeals to a prospective tenant is somewhere in between two extremes. In this chapter we'll consider what you can do, what you should do, and what you can forget about doing.

Must Dos

Perhaps the best way to primp up your property so that it appeals to a prospective tenant is to separate those areas that you must work on from those that you can forget. Let's consider the "must-do" areas first.

Entry. Clean or repaint the front door. Be sure the door handle is clean and the entry way swept. If possible, put a new floor mat down.

First impressions are critical. The first thing the prospective tenant sees is the entry, so make sure it looks great. A new coat of paint on the front door takes only a few moments, and it can make a world of difference.

Living room, dining room, hallways, bedrooms. Shampoo the carpet/polish the floors. Paint any walls that have marks on them. Clean the windows and window coverings.

In most rentals, carpets cover most of the floor space. A freshly shampooed carpet makes an entire room look fresh. On the other hand, a "lived-on" carpet looks dirty and worn even if it's fairly new. Good tenants like things clean, and a clean carpet is very important.

Walls that have marks on them look old, worn, and dirty and are a real distraction.

W *a r n i n g*

Beware of trying to *clean* walls. Unless it's a very superficial mark that can be removed by a gentle sweep of a sponge with Fantastic or other remover on it, leave a mark alone. If you scrub, you'll only succeed in digging into the paint and creating an obtrusive "hole." Even if you do get the area clean, chances are it will make the surrounding areas look dirtier by comparison. The correct answer is to repaint.

Paint the walls that have marks on them in any room. It only takes an hour or so per room with today's modern latex paints and washable equipment.

Dust and clean blinds, closets (including shelves), window sills, and baseboards. Dry clean draperies.

Kitchen. This is a vital area. If it's clean, prospective tenants will feel the whole house is clean (assuming you've haven't left a mess in the bathrooms as Hal did).

Be sure to clean the oven(s) thoroughly, especially any see-through windows. If you have an electric range, don't waste time cleaning the "spill catchers" under the heating units—replace them instead. They cost only a few dollars each and are readily available at most hardware or grocery stores. Don't forget to clean the stove hood.

Thoroughly clean the sink, dishwasher, and any other appliances. Be sure to wash down the walls (assuming they have washable gloss paint) and wash and wax the floors.

Be wary of any bad odors or lingering smells. Use of a pine oil cleaning agent and air freshener will usually take care of this.

Bathrooms. Clean the tub/shower, sink, and toilet. Clean around the base of the toilet as well. Wash the walls (assuming they have washable gloss paint) and wash and wax the floors.

As with the kitchen, be wary of any bad odors or lingering smells. Again, use of a pine oil cleaning agent and air freshener will usually take care of this.

If all of this seems like a lot, it is. Assuming that the tenant leaves the property relatively clean, you could still have a couple of good days of cleaning ahead of you.

Remember, a clean house attracts a clean tenant.

Hire a Cleaning Service

You don't like cleaning? I don't blame you; neither do I. In the old days (decades ago), I used to do the cleaning myself on all my rentals. However, in recent years I've found that it just doesn't pay. Usually for

$100 or so, I can hire a service that comes in and, often in half a day, cleans an entire unit far better than I can.

Worried about the extra cost? I build it into the monthly rental. I set aside $20 a month from the rent for one year and then use it to hire the cleaning service. Even if I had to pay for it out of my pocket, it's worth it to me not to feel that I'm a maid to my tenants.

Don'ts

There are also a number of things that you don't want to do. Those that follow will help you avoid wasting time and money on work that isn't necessary.

Don't wash walls except in kitchens and baths. Today, most residential rooms (with the exception of kitchens and baths) are painted with a flat white latex paint. If you go to a store to check out a can, it almost always is labeled "Washable." Don't believe that for a minute.

Over time walls get uniformly dirty and marked up in certain spots. When you look at a wall that hasn't been painted for a year or so, you'll see the marks, scratches, stains, and the like. But you won't see the overall dirt; it doesn't stand out because it's everywhere.

But just try to wash down the marks or spots on a wall painted in flat latex, and you'll see more dirt than you saw when you started. What happens is that where you washed is clean, whereas everywhere else now looks especially dirty; the overall dirt shows up by comparison. (This isn't usually the case with kitchen/bath walls that are usually small and have high-gloss paint. The dirt tends to uniformly come off these walls with just a sponge and mild detergent.)

Thus, unless you plan to carefully wash bedroom, living room, and dining room walls from floor to ceiling, any washing at all will only make matters worse. That's why I suggest never washing—paint instead. Painting walls, these days, is cheap.

Don't overscrub. I once hired a cleaning person who was so determined to get the kitchen sink clean that she actually scrubbed through the porcelain! You want the property to look clean, not operating-room sterile.

Don't install new when old will do. There may be rust marks in a dishwasher tray. Replace the tray, not the dishwasher. The tiles in the sink may have a few cracks. Clean and regrout, but don't replace them. The carpet has soiled areas and is worn in some walkways. Shampoo and use cleaners. Consider a runner to cover the heavily walked-on areas. The faucet leaks. Put in a new washer, not a new faucet.

What you want to end up with is a property that's clean, tidy, service-able, and profitable. Don't sink your profits into unnecessary repairs. Remember, the tenant is only renting it—not buying it.

Don't keep outmoded features. In bathrooms, sinks are important. You can replace a stand-alone or wall-hanging sink that looks old-fashioned and cheap with a modern cabinet and sink top for under $250. It will make the bathroom look brighter and more modern and will attract a better class of tenant.

An ancient chandelier hanging in the dining room can date the rental. A new, inexpensive one can modernize it.

Old, dark paneling can be depressing and steer potential tenants away. Installing modern light paneling or even painting over dark wood can make a big difference.

You get the idea. Many old-fashioned features can be quickly, easily, and inexpensively replaced. Doing so gives your rental a much more appealing look.

Who Pays the Cost of Rental Preparation?

Many landlords look at their job as having two functions only: collecting rents and denying tenant complaints. They tend to see rental cleanup and preparation as an extra, and, as such, they don't see why they should have to pay for it. From their perspective, either the tenant who moved out (and left the place dirty) or the tenant who's moving in (and wants the place clean) should pay for the cleanup.

The problem is that there's always going to be some clean-up work that can't be charged to the tenant who's leaving and some dirt that the new tenant won't tolerate: these are the responsibility of the landlord.

Carpets are perhaps the best example. Over the course of a tenancy, carpets are normally going to not only get wear and tear but are also going to accumulate dirt. It's not the tenant's fault. It happens. It happens even in your own home.

Should you ask the leaving tenant to pay for cleaning the carpet? I don't think so. If you do, the tenant is very likely to say, "I'll clean it before I leave." (Tenants do this to save the money you would deduct from their deposit if you pay for the cleaning.) Then the tenant typically goes to a local grocery store, rents a steamer, and essentially ruins your carpet. Yes, it might look superficially clean. But chances are the dirt has only been rubbed off the surface and deposited deeper into the pile. Often, within a few weeks after the new tenant moves in, the carpet is dirty again, and this time it's more difficult and expensive to clean.

I think it's better to just accept the fact that as a landlord, some costs must be borne with a tenant turnaround, and carpet cleaning is one of them. I ask my departing tenants to make sure the carpet is well vacuumed, and I charge them for any dirt or spots that can't be removed. But I then have the carpet professionally cleaned and pay for it myself. That way I know it's done right and won't need to be done again. It's just a cost of doing business.

Other areas that are the landlord's responsibility include any repainting that's needed as well as the replacement of any fixtures that are outdated. (Of course, you can charge the departing tenant for damage to walls, paint, and fixtures.)

Checking Safety and Security Features

Before you've finished preparing your property for tenants, you should make sure that all safety and security features are operating properly. These include:

- Smoke alarms (test in every bedroom and in hallways and main areas)
- Fire extinguishers (check to see they are full)
- GFI (ground fault interrupter) circuits (test to see they are operating, especially in kitchen, bath, and outdoors)

- Door locks (see that locks on all outside doors are working properly and are rekeyed)
- Window locks (be sure locks on all windows are working properly)
- Railings (test they're secure on balconies, entries, and patios)

It's a good idea to keep a record of when and how you checked the safety and security features of a rental should there ever be a problem in the future.

When Should I Show the Property?

A great rule of thumb to remember and guide you is that tenants have no imagination. If they see a dirty property, they'll always think of it as dirty. Thus, if you show your rental *before* you clean it, you could actually be driving away good tenants.

I prefer to wait until I have my rentals cleaned before showing them. If someone absolutely has to see one, I will show it during the cleaning process, always avoiding showing it dirty.

Yes, this may cost a few days of rental time. But on the other hand, I usually end up with a better tenant who thinks of the rental as a good place to keep clean.

Cleanup Checklist

- All previous tenants' possessions removed (don't do this until you have legal possession of the premises)
- Kitchen—all appliances working, countertops and floors cleaned, all drawers and cabinets emptied and clean, all knobs and handles in place
- Bathrooms—all plumbing working, countertops and floors cleaned, all drawers and cabinets emptied and clean, all knobs and handles in place
- Windows—no broken windows or screens, all operating properly with locks
- Doors—no holes in doors, all hardware working properly, locks rekeyed

- Carpets—clean with no spots (or if spots, noted); no threadbare areas (if there are, replace carpeting)
- Walls and ceilings—all clean and repainted as necessary
- Safety and security features—all in place and working
- Yard—lawn mowed, shrubs trimmed, sidewalk and driveway cleaned
- Garage—clean and empty
- Home systems—water heater, furnace/air conditioner, fans, and any other systems fully working
- Front—neat and clean; front door and front of unit repainted if necessary
- Washer/dryer—connected and working properly

Part Two

FINDING
AND KEEPING
GOOD TENANTS

9

HOW TO FIND
GOOD TENANTS

*You may have the best rental, but until you get the word out,
you won't have a tenant.*

How do you find just that right tenant you are looking for? For most people, the first and only answer is an ad in the local newspaper. Although this is certainly a basic method of getting the word out about your rental, there may be other, less expensive methods as well. In this chapter we'll look at all the possible avenues of locating just the right tenant for your rental.

Antidiscrimination Laws

Whenever you advertise a rental, you are subject to the fair housing laws. Although there may be additional local, state, and federal ordinances that affect you, the federal Fair Housing Act of 1988 provides that you cannot refuse to show a rental, cannot refuse to rent to someone, and cannot advertise indicating a preference on the basis of the following:

- Race
- Color
- National origin or ancestry
- Sex
- Religion

H *i n t*

Before undertaking to put your property up for rent, consult with a local real estate agent as well as a local attorney for specific antidiscrimination rules that may affect you.

- Physical disability (including chronic alcoholism, AIDS, AIDS-related complex, hearing/visual impairment, chronic mental illness, and mental retardation)
- Familial status

The law is quite clear. It provides that you cannot set different terms, conditions, or privileges for a rental; cannot provide different housing services or facilities; cannot falsely deny that a rental is available for inspection or renting; cannot refuse to make housing available; cannot deny a dwelling unit; and other similar conditions.

If you deny pets to tenants, you must be sure that doing so does not violate the federal Americans with Disabilities Act, which states that landlords cannot limit or discourage occupancy to tenants who have a companion animal required by a medical prescription. Note that this includes guide dogs but may also include other animals that have been medically prescribed for a variety of physical and emotional conditions. (See further explanations in Chapter 25 on discrimination.)

The Importance of Signs

Don't overlook or downplay the importance of a sign on the property. Over the years, I've probably gotten as many as a third of all my tenants simply from a sign stuck in front of the property (or put in a window in the case of a condo).

The reason a sign works so well is that prospective tenants who want to live in your area are often cruising it, looking for rentals. In many cases, in fact, as soon as you put out a sign—perhaps the first day—you'll have people stopping by to ask about the property.

The sign doesn't have to be fancy. It just has to get the message across. A typical rental sign may be as simple as this:

```
FOR RENT
555-3465
```

You may, of course, add additional information such as the number of bedrooms and the price, but I advise against advertising your price on the sign. The reason is that the people who see the sign are seeing only the outside of the property. (Unless you're there to show it, it's locked up.) You may eliminate potential tenants who think it's either too high or too low based on the way the outside looks. But they can't know the real value until they see the inside, and they won't do that until they call you and you show it to them. So advertising the price on the sign can work against you.

Besides, I think announcing the price on a sign cheapens the property. It's almost like saying that the price is the *only* reason to rent this property, not because of its design, size, cleanliness, or other outstanding features.

> **c a u t i o n**
>
> You want to make it perfectly clear, if you're in the process of painting/fixing up the property, that the way it currently looks is not the way it will look when you're ready to rent. Therefore, it's a good idea to put a date on the sign; for example, "Available 6/30." This also alerts tenants who have to move from their current house when they can move into yours. (See more on this below.)

The Neighborhood Flyer

The problem with using only a sign is that unless potential tenants happen to drive down your street, they won't see it. Unless your street is heavily trafficked, your sign alone won't do the job.

Whenever I have a rental, I create a very brief flyer describing the property and run off a hundred or so flyers at the local copy store. Then I hire a neighborhood kid to leave one at the door of all the nearby houses. (Be careful to instruct your delivery person not to put flyers in mailboxes—the post office won't tolerate anything in a mailbox that isn't properly stamped.)

This way, all the neighbors know the house is for rent and can send any prospective tenants by. Besides, the flyer can be handwritten or typed; copying costs only about $5 for a hundred, and usually $25 pays to get them distributed.

L *a n d l o r d ' s* **T** *a l e*

This problem with signs came home to me several years ago when I was trying to rent a house using a sign and a newspaper ad. After almost a month, I finally rented the property to a marginal tenant. (By then I was desperate.)

No sooner had the new tenant started moving in than a neighbor from the house behind mine (and on a different street) stopped by to say they saw the moving van and how sorry she was that she hadn't known my house was for rent. Her cousin and his wife were new in the area and were looking for just the sort of house I had. Her cousin had a great job, and the couple had excellent credit and . . . you get the picture.

From then on I made sure that all the neighbors know when I have a property for rent.

Typical Flyer:

FOR RENT!
[You can paste in a picture of the house for greater impact]
1234 Titus Street
3 Bedroom, 2 Bath
$750
Den, Fireplace, Repainted, New Carpets
Call 555-5465
Available 10/1

Putting the price on the flyer is a good idea. People can always call, but letting them know the price up front helps them learn if it's in their price range.

Timing: Don't Be Too Soon or Too Late

Timing is critical in finding tenants. Typically, rents are up at the end of the month or, to a lesser extent, on the 15th. That means tenants wanting to move from their current rental will be looking to move on or around the 1st (or 15th). Thus, they'll be shopping for a new rental a few weeks before that. (This is also critical when placing your newspaper ad, as we'll see shortly.)

Thus, it's a good idea to get your flyers (and your sign) out there early. You may want to get the flyer out by the end of the month to indicate the property will be available on the following 1st (or 15th).

Bulletin Boards

People read bulletin boards at supermarkets, pharmacies, and other neighborhood centers, so you may want to tack one of your fliers to a bulletin board. (Because some boards allow only 3¥5 cards, you may have to cram the information on one of those.)

Another and better source can be the bulletin boards at the housing or personnel offices of local companies. A number of major employers are often in the nearby area. Call and ask if you can hang a flyer on their board; most will be happy to oblige. (Sometimes it's a good idea to hang four or five flyers with a push pin. That way, someone interested can take one and leave the rest for other prospective tenants.)

One problem with bulletin boards, particularly in such public areas as shopping malls, is that you're also announcing your house is vacant to those who may only be interested in breaking in, having a party there, or stealing appliances, drapes, or whatever. These are probably remote possibilities in most areas, but in certain high-crime areas you may want to just forget the bulletin board idea.

Internet Advertising

In many areas today, services are available that offer online advertising, some of which are quite well known locally by tenants. It may therefore pay for you to put an ad on an online service. Some of these services not only refer tenants to you but also screen them in advance.

But be wary of services that act as agents and want substantial fees for finding tenants. It's one thing to pay 20 bucks to get your property advertised online, quite another to owe 5 percent of a year's rental for finding a tenant. Many areas also offer online bulletin boards that are essentially free. You just put up a notice about your property, and it remains there for a certain period.

You can find out about these services by contacting a local real estate agent, who may be able to recommend reliable ones. You may also simply want to do a search through a service such as Yahoo! or Google for rental housing. Be sure, however, to specify the area; you don't want to list your property on a St. Louis service when it's located in Boston.

Of course, you need a computer, a modem, and a provider (such as AOL or Microsoft Network). But having a gateway to the Internet today is becoming as common as having a phone or a VCR.

Yet another high-tech bulletin board is that found on local cable access channels. Sometimes as part of its public access service, one of these channels may allow you to list your rental for a week or so if you're a landlord with a single property. If your cable company provides this service, take advantage of it. It may give you only five seconds to flash a notice; but people watch these access channels, and the novelty of seeing a rental advertised could attract widespread attention and find you a choice tenant.

Listing with Agents

Landlords sometimes forget that real estate agents not only sell property but also rent it. Real estate agents, particularly those in big offices, often have a steady stream of calls from tenants looking for rentals.

Agents like rentals because they can sometimes convert prospective tenants to buyers and because they can sometimes convert landlords to sellers. Often an agent will take on your property and handle the rental for just the cost of advertising.

Some agents, however, may want to list your property on the Multiple Listing Service or other brokers' exchange, whereby one broker splits a commission with another broker who finds a tenant. This gives your property much more exposure, although it is probably the most expensive method of getting a tenant, because the typical fee is a full month's rent or more. That's right, you pay the agent (or agents) one month's rent to find a tenant for you.

Of course, the agent may also qualify the tenant and guarantee the tenant will stay put for a certain period. If the tenant moves out within six months, for example, the agent may refund a part of the fee or may find a new tenant for free or, at least, charge you a reduced fee.

In a tight market where there are few tenants and lots of rentals, you may want to consider this alternative. After all, you don't pay unless the agent finds a tenant.

Fee Lists

Some agents disseminate a list of rentals area by area. They charge prospective tenants a fee for the list, which is usually updated weekly. Because getting on the lists is often free for landlords, there's usually no harm in having your property advertised on these lists.

Newspaper Advertisements

By far the most widely used advertising medium for rental properties is classified ads in newspapers. On some Sundays in certain cities at the end of the month, rental ads may cover many full pages. That, of course, is the problem. Your ad is in direct competition with everyone else's in the newspaper. The other problem is the cost. Advertising your property in the newspaper can be very costly, perhaps the most expensive form of advertising you're likely to use.

Tenants, however, often look to the newspaper as their first source of information about rentals. Therefore, you will be hard-pressed not to advertise (unless your sign or flyer worked very well). Your goal, however, becomes effectiveness and, of course, keeping the cost down.

Effective Newspaper Ads

To get the biggest bang for your buck, you need to think like a tenant. What sort of advertising would a tenant read? Which paper?

Don't advertise in a big-city paper. It costs too much and covers too large an area. Just like buyers looking to purchase a house, ten-

H *i n t*

Less is more when it comes to classified advertising.

ants look for area first. They are often looking specifically within a single residential development, or perhaps even a much smaller area. Many big-city papers cover downtown and all the surrounding suburbs. If you're paying for advertising that's reaching people completely out of your area, you're wasting your money.

On the other hand, there are often smaller local papers, weeklies, journals, shoppers guides (given away free), penny-savers, and the like. These are typically aimed at a very small shopping area. Consider that you are looking for a rental in a specific area. Wouldn't you look in these first? To find them, check local grocery stores, which often carry them. Also, ask neighbors or your current tenant who is moving out. Any of these can usually tell you which are the more popular papers.

Don't be afraid to advertise in a small paper or one that's filled with ads and not many articles. These are often the very best sources of tenants for you.

How Big Should Your Ad Be?

Don't believe the old maxim that bigger is better. When it comes to rental advertising, bigger just means costlier, not better.

Think of it from the tenants' perspective. They are looking for the best, least expensive rental they can find. Someone who takes out a display ad is saying, in effect, "I can afford to place big, costly ads; therefore, it stands to reason that I have to charge more for my rental!"

Prospective tenants tend to look for the smallest ads. Therefore, those are what you need. I rarely place an ad in a paper with more than three or four lines. That's more than enough to get my message across.

How Often Should Your Ad Run?

Run your ad as often as possible. However, pick and choose when to run it. And change it frequently.

No, that's not as contradictory as it sounds. The idea is to run the ad when tenants are looking. As noted earlier, most tenants move around the end of the month, so most are already settled in by the first or second week of the month. Relatively few are looking then. Therefore, your ads will usually reach fewer prospective tenants during the first or second week of the month. Conserve your money. Don't advertise early in the month or else run a smaller ad. (If you have your act together, you'll rent from the first to the first and will advertise from the middle of the month *before* your property becomes vacant.)

The best time to catch tenants looking at ads is the middle to end of the month—the last two weeks of the month. (You can tell this is the case because rental ads are typically heavier then.)

But don't run the same ad for more than a week. If you don't catch a tenant by then, change the ad. Otherwise, those who are looking will remember your ad and say to themselves, "That place must be a dog—they can't get it rented!"

What do you do if you haven't caught a tenant during the last two weeks of the month? If you want to continue running newspaper ads, run the minimum ad—usually two lines, just enough to give you exposure. And concentrate on the other methods detailed above.

What to Say

The hardest part of placing a classified ad for most people is figuring out what to say. The problem is usually one of perspective—the landlord's versus the tenants'. Most landlords tend to write things *they* like about the rental, not realizing that what should go into the ad are only things that tenants will find attractive. For example, a landlord may like a small yard because of its reduced maintenance, but tenants could be looking for a big yard for their kids to play in. Or the landlord may be thinking of the new double-pane insulated glass windows he recently installed to save on heating/cooling costs, whereas tenants want to know that the drapes and carpeting are clean.

Think benefits. When you're working to put together the words for your ad, think only about the benefits your rental offers a tenant. If you write down renter benefits, you really can't go far wrong. The next section lists some of the things tenants are looking for.

What Tenants Want to See in Your Ad

Tenant benefits include the following:

- **Location.** Mention a desirable neighborhood or school and note if the rental is close to shopping, buses, or freeways.
- **Size.** Note the number of bedrooms and if the house or lot is over-sized; also mention if there are extra rooms such as a family room.
- **Amenities.** Mention a fireplace, spa, pool, appliances, or other desired items that go with the rental.
- **Cleanliness.** Write if the rental is newly painted, has new carpeting or drapes, and/or is especially clean.

From the above list, one might think that an ad would have to be a dozen lines long to fit in all of the features. That's not really the case, partly because just a mention will do and partly because there are abbreviations that are commonly understood. For example, here's an ad that has benefits from each category:

Acacia Schools - 3 bdrm. 2 bath,
oversize fam. rm., spa, frplce,
just repainted. $975. 555-4321

Abbreviate. Here are some commonly understood abbreviations you can use to shorten (and thus reduce the cost of) your ad:

bedroom—bdrm
bath—ba
apartment—apt
included—incl
laundry—ldry
near—nr
room—rm
fireplace—frplc
dishwasher- dshwshr
townhouse—twnhs
washer/dryer—wshr/dryr

garage—gar
large—lg
small—sml

Don't be afraid to use abbreviations. Just be careful that the abbreviations you use are understandable. For example, I was recently reading the rental ads in the local paper and came across this strange one:

Fr. Rt. - 3b/2b, chc lct, $1,150. 555-8979

Does it mean "Free Rent" or "For Rent"? Are there three bedrooms or two? What is "chc lct"? Chocolate? (Actually, I think the ad meant to say "For Rent - 3 bedrooms, 2 baths, choice location . . .")

If there's any question about what you mean, always use the long form.

The hook. Every ad needs a hook—the word or words at the beginning that catch the reader's attention and force the reader to read the rest of what you have to say.

Generally speaking, your hook should be the best benefit your rental offers. In the above ad, it was the location. However, it could be almost anything. Here are some great advertising words you can use to hook potential tenants who are reading ads:

- oversized house
- close to schools (or close in)
- 5 bedrooms (emphasizing size)
- room to roam (oversized lot)
- just remodeled
- freshly painted
- new carpets and drapes
- garden living
- quiet cul-de-sac

You get the idea. Pick out the biggest benefit to your reader and stress it.

Don't be afraid of a short ad. It is possible to get away with a single-line ad. Remember that the ad is already appearing in a rental section of the paper, often under a specific area and type of property (such as "Condos"). For example:

New Paint - 3bdrm/2bath, $1,575, 555-4993

The problem is that in a competitive market, you won't be likely to draw many responses. Other landlords with bigger, more descriptive ads command tenants' attention. On the other hand, when the rental market is good (for landlords), almost any ad will do, even one as small as the example.

Don't sell the obvious. On the other hand, sometimes you have to go for the second-best benefit because the first is obvious. For example, your paper may list rentals by neighborhood or local area. Your biggest benefit may be your property's location in the choice Westwood area. Only you're already advertising in the section under "Westwood," so you don't have to repeat the area. List the next-biggest benefit. Maybe you have one of the largest homes in the area, or the house was just re-painted; go with that.

The price. Always mention the price when you don't give the address. (Don't give the address in an ad unless you or a manager is always there to receive lookers.) You not only want to get as many potentially acceptable tenants as possible to call, but you also want to eliminate as many potential tenants as possible who can't afford, or won't want, your property. Price is the great leveler.

Discounted newspaper ads. Don't overlook the possibility of getting discounted advertising. The most expensive ad you can place is the one for a single day, but newspapers will usually give discounts for longer placement. Sometimes it only costs a few dollars more to run an ad for a week than for a day; similarly, two weeks can be only a few dollars more on top of that. (I wouldn't run the same ad for more than one week as it gets stale and stops attracting calls.) Chances are you're going to have to run the ad for a week or two anyway, so why not sign up for it at the beginning and save money.

The same holds true for lines. A single line is typically the most expensive ad. Three lines can often be purchased for just a few dollars more than one line.

Also, consider special sections. Sometimes papers have deep classified advertising discounts for rentals that are below a certain price—for example, below $500 or below $800.

Beware Offering Move-in Discounts

Sometimes the rental market gets really bad with just too many properties chasing too few tenants. When that happens, landlords—particularly those who have a lot of rentals such as apartment building owners—cut their prices and then begin offering move-in discounts. For example, ads may start appearing that say "First Month's Rent Free!" or "Free TV to Move In!"

In these markets a kind of professional tenant evolves who chases after such discounts. These tenants stay a month or two—long enough to benefit from the promotion—and then move on to the next desperate landlord.

The point is that you don't want this kind of tenant. You want a tenant who is willing to rent for a long period (it's hoped for at least a year). If you are in an extremely tight market, it's better to lower the rent and get a good solid tenant than it is to try to "buy" a tenant with discounts.

In the final analysis, your advertising—whether a sign or a classified ad—is your entrée to the world of tenants out there. It's your first step in getting just the right kind of tenant you want.

If you're aggressive here, you'll rent your property faster and get a better-quality tenant who will stay longer.

10

SCREENING POTENTIAL TENANTS

Having no tenant is better than having a bad tenant.

Having an effective ad is only the first step. If your advertising works, prospective tenants will call. When they call, however, the next step is hooking them on your property and qualifying them to be sure you really want to rent to them.

Responding to a Prospective Tenant's Call

An entire art (if not science) is involved in responding to prospective tenants over the phone. If you master it, you'll have no trouble getting just the tenant you want. On the other hand, if you blow it here, you'll find yourself spinning your wheels, wasting time with unqualified tenants, and, worse, renting to tenants who end up not paying the rent. Get your phone response act together and you'll save yourself all kinds of problems down the road.

There are really only three steps in handling the phone when prospective tenants call. These are simple and easy to master, and

N *o t e*

Be sure to follow all antidiscrimination and fair housing guidelines, many noted in the previous chapter, when talking with prospective tenants.

they go a long way to ensuring that you get just the tenant you're looking for.

Step 1: Encourage the Hesitant Caller

H *i n t*

You may want to give out your cell phone number in your advertising so you can be reached immediately wherever you are.

When people call on the phone, they may be a little bit nervous and/or guarded. They usually want to get as much information as they can from you about your rental before giving you any information about themselves. The reason is that they are screening out rentals they aren't interested in and don't want to waste their time. They don't want to get into a discussion with some poor landlord who has a dog of a rental and tries to talk them into renting something they don't want.

This hesitant approach doesn't mean you're talking to a potential tenant you don't want. Quite the opposite; it probably means you're talking to someone who is sincerely interested in finding just the right property to rent. As with fishing, you're getting a nibble. Now, the art is to turn that nibble into a real bite.

I suggest you encourage the hesitant caller. The way you do this is to be polite and answer the prospect's questions as fully and carefully as possible. Your goal is to give the prospect enough information to be hooked and then to reel him or her in with questions of your own.

Step 2: Sell the Property

You need to promote your property to sell it to a prospect. After all, it's the only product you have. Tenants almost surely ask the following basic questions:

- How many and how big are the bedrooms?
- Does your rental have a large kitchen, family room, or yard?
- Is it clean?
- Does it have a big garage?
- Do you take pets?

They may, of course, also ask some rather specific questions geared to their specific needs. If your property has a pool, they may ask if it has a separate fence and gate surrounding it—a real concern for people with small children. They may ask if you have 220-volt electrical outlets in the utility room because they have an electric clothes dryer. They may ask if your house is near a particular bus route that they have to use.

The art here is to amplify your answers and then turn the conversation around to innocuous questions. After all, you're just as interested in qualifying the prospect as the prospect is in qualifying your property. For example, when answering how many bedrooms your property has or what their size is, you might say something such as, "It has three bedrooms, all good size. The master is 14 feet by 12 feet. Is that big enough for your needs?"

Or you might respond, "The house is located near the L-123 bus line, and there's also an I-405 freeway access nearby. Is that close enough to your work?" Or you might say, "It has a large three-car garage with three separate doors and openers. Were you planning to work on cars in the garage or do you have a lot of extra stuff to store?"

You get the idea. After you've established a rapport by answering a few questions directly, you can begin to turn each answer into a question of your own. Soon enough you'll be learning as much about the prospect as he or she will be about your property.

Eventually, if the potential tenant seems happy with your description of the property and you seem happy with the would-be tenant's responses, work the conversation around to meeting together at the premises. That way the potential tenant can see if he or she likes it, and you can qualify the person further.

H *i n t*

Remember, when a prospective tenant calls, the aim of your conversation should always be to get the person to the property. You can't sign a rental agreement over the phone.

Beware the professional tenant. Sometimes you'll get a call from someone who seems to know more about your property than you do. This person knows the area and the house and insists that you are charging too much but would consider renting from you for a lesser amount. In other words, the tenant wants a concession over the phone.

Beware of such prospects. They are nothing but trouble. You may indeed want to give rent or other concessions to get a particularly good tenant. But you can't do that after one phone conversation and before qualifying the tenant in writing.

Tenants who want small concessions early on often want bigger ones later on. They may be the very tenants who hopscotch from landlord to landlord—just the sort you don't want.

Step 3: Let Your Answering Machine Do the Work

Although I recommend the personal approach, sometimes you'll have a rental in a market where you are overwhelmed with phone calls; you simply don't have the time and energy to handle them all. In such cases, I suggest you leave a message on an answering machine directing the potential tenants to the property. Once they are there, you can better qualify them.

Your answering machine message should include the following:

- Address and cross street
- Clear directions to getting there (Don't assume prospective tenants know the area—they may not.)
- Brief property description (beds, baths, and main features)
- Rental rate
- Security deposit amount (You may want to omit this.)

Qualifying a Tenant

Next is the matter of deciding whether you're even interested in the person who calls from your ad. You need to have certain qualifying questions in mind ahead of time.

First, you want to know how many people will be occupying the property. You can usually determine the maximum occupancy of your property, but you can't discriminate by refusing to rent to people just because they have children. On the other hand, you usually *can* decide if your tenants will be smokers or nonsmokers, and you *can* require tenants to have minimum cash and financial qualifications. You can at least get an idea of how a prospect fits into these categories over the phone.

If the caller doesn't have enough money to move in, doesn't want to move in when your unit is ready, has too many family members for the size of the unit, or otherwise is disqualified, you would be wasting your time to show the property—you wouldn't want the caller as a tenant anyhow. (However, remember under antidiscrimination laws you may not be able to refuse to show the property.)

Minimum Tenant Qualifications

Here are minimum qualifications that you may want to consider when a prospective tenant calls about your property:

- Willingness to move in when your rental is ready
- Appropriate number of people in family
- Has the cash available to pay all rent and deposits
- Has no pets or only those you allow

Landlords' Dilemma

It's very important that you know something about a prospective tenant's financial condition—his or her ability to pay the rent and enough cash to move in. Yet you don't want to chase away somebody who's just phoning by appearing to be too nosy in a delicate area. One answer is to say right up front what's needed to move in. For example, after you've talked for a while and otherwise prequalified the prospective tenant, you might say, "The total cost of moving in is the first month's rent of $750 plus a $750 cleaning deposit, or $1,500. Is that going to be OK for you?" If the would-be tenant says it's no problem, you can proceed. On the other hand, if there's hemming and hawing and asking if part can be paid now and the rest in three weeks, you've probably eliminated this tenant.

Getting Prospects to the Property

As noted earlier, it's all for naught until a prospect actually sees the property and you see the rental application. So getting the prospect to the property is the next step.

I often say something such as this to get the conversation going where I want it to go: "You sound as though you'd like the property I have for rent. Why don't I meet you there in half an hour and show it to you? You can then look it over and see if it's really something that will meet your needs."

Ask if there's a problem. If the prospect seems hesitant to run out to the property, particularly after you've chatted for a while and he or she seems to like what you've said (and you like the responses), you should ask if there's a problem. You can be perfectly blunt. If there *is* a problem, it's best to get it out on the table before you spend any more time on this prospect. You can say something such as, "Is there some problem here that we haven't touched on? You seem hesitant . . . ?"

At this point the prospective tenant with a problem might blurt out any number of amazing things, such as, "Well, I didn't want to mention it, but I have a horse." Or "You see, I'm having a fight with my present landlord about the three months I'm behind on my rent." Or "I actually have seven kids, but I'm sure we'll all fit in your one-bedroom unit." Or "I plan to run an auto body repair shop out of the garage; is that OK?"

If you don't ask, you won't know.

Get Prospect's Name and Phone Number

If you're going to show the property, particularly if you're not on-site, the least you want to know is that there's a reasonably good chance a prospective tenant will show up. If the prospect is willing to give his or her name and number over the phone, it's a pretty good indication the prospect will meet you. Besides, if the prospect doesn't show, you want to be able to call and ask what happened. Or you could be delayed and may need to call and arrange a different time. It makes things easier if the prospect has a cell phone. (It's also a good reason why you should have one!)

Sometimes landlords are afraid to ask for a name and phone number from people who call about an ad for fear of scaring them away. My feeling is that if prospective tenants won't give you these basics, there's not really that much chance they'll even show up to see the property.

Give Prospects the Address

H *i n t*

The best way to avoid tenants who pay late, who ruin your property, and/or who need to be evicted is to not rent to them in the first place. Indeed, the cure for the bad tenant is the good tenant. Rent to the right person and you simply won't have any problems.

Sometimes prospective tenants say they are interested but want to drive by the property to decide if they like the location and the neighborhood. They'll ask for the address.

I have no problem with this. In fact, I find it saves me a lot of time. If a would-be tenant has already driven by, seen where the rental is located, and finds it acceptable, I'm way ahead when I go there to show it. I'm almost guaranteed the person will show up.

In fact, after talking to a would-be tenant on the phone and satisfying myself that this person is a likely candidate, I often suggest the person drive by and then, if interested, call me back. These call-backs are frequently from people who really want to rent.

But just because a prospect calls you back doesn't mean that you'll automatically sell that person on your rental. (You may want to call the prospect back, so it's important to get his or her number.)

When you call a prospect back, be sure the person understood what you have to offer. Again ask if he or she wants to see the property. Do the drill. Sometimes the call-back will net you a good tenant.

Meeting the Prospect

First impressions are important, both on the prospect's part and on yours. Therefore, when you meet the person, you should make an effort to look presentable and to be as personable as possible. After all, prospects are judging if they would want you as a landlord. If your appearance is poor, or you act as if you're hiring a lackey for a poor-paying job and otherwise demean a prospect, you'll do yourself great harm. Good tenants simply won't want to rent from you. And those who do won't be the type of tenant you want.

H *i n t*

Sign up for caller ID. Unless blocked, this will automatically give you a prospect's number.

Here are two stories, both true, about two very different types of landlords.

The Bad Landlord

Sarah met the prospective tenants dressed in her sweats. She had been on her way to the gym and their call interrupted her. She let them know she was inconvenienced.

She took them through the property and made sure they understood that she wouldn't tolerate any funny business. "I expect this place to be kept clean at all time. If you have a problem, I expect you to take care of it. It had better be a big emergency and you had better not have caused it before you call me. I don't want any parties and no more than one guest at a time. I live only three doors down, so I'll know.

"The rent is due on the first and you're 'outahere' if it's not paid by the third. You pay for all the utilities, including water and garbage; and you take care of the garden in front. I've been taken by tenants before and I know all the tricks and I'm not about to be taken again, got it?"

Tenants got it very quickly. If they rented from Sarah, they'd not only be on their own if there were problems with the rental, but she'd be micromanaging and in their face all the time. Sarah got a string of bad tenants who wouldn't pay and often messed up her property. She often swore that there just were no more good people in the world.

The Good Landlord

Erma was just the opposite. When she showed the property, she carefully explained that it had been cleaned, but anything not in proper condition would be taken care of before they moved in. Erma said she would take care of any repairs that were necessary, but it was the tenants' responsibility to call her promptly about them. If they damaged anything, of course, she would expect them to pay.

"I want you to consider this property as your home and treat it as if you owned it. I'll be available if problems arise, but I'm not going to be in your hair.

(continued)

I will come by occasionally to see if everything is OK, particularly in the first few months. After that, you just call me if there's a problem.

"The rent is due on the first, and I have an automatic deposit service that I would like you to use. I'll pay for water and garbage, and a gardener will take care of the frontyard. You'll be responsible for the other outside areas. I try to be extremely fair, and I've always had good luck with tenants. If at any time there's a problem, come talk to me and we'll try to work it out."

Erma wasn't lying when she said she had good luck with tenants. She always did. Tenants seemed to sense she was fair and reasonable and wouldn't seek to abuse or take advantage of them.

Avoiding Hubris

The moral to these stories can be found in the ancient Greek word, *hubris,* or false pride. The Greeks were concerned about not showing hubris, and you will be too if you're a wise landlord. Sarah's basic problem was her belief that because she was a landlord, she was a class above the tenants. She showed this attitude; good tenants recognized it and stayed away.

Erma, on the other hand, saw being a landlord as simply business. She was not a class above the tenants. Rather, she was a businessperson offering a product. She needed a good tenant as much as a tenant needed a good landlord. Her fairness showed through; good tenants recognized it and rented from her.

H *i n t*

It's better for the landlord to pay for water and a gardener to be sure that the yard is always in good shape. This makes it easier to rerent on a moment's notice. Paying for garbage ensures there are no problems with the health department.

What Should You Accomplish When You Show the Property?

Be sure that a prospect sees all of the property, including the closets, the garage, the basement (if one), and the yard. You want potential tenants to know up front what they are renting so that later on, after you've invested a lot of time in them, they don't suddenly realize your place is not for them.

Be sure to let prospects know about things that might not be obvious—schools, shopping, transportation, and the overall

H *i* **n** *t*

Don't try to oversell the rental.

neighborhood. Prospects with children are often concerned that other children are nearby as playmates. Potential tenants who don't have children are also often concerned about children nearby—but for the opposite reason.

Sometimes prospective tenants want to rent after the first look. But not always. Sometimes they want to think about it, to check out other rentals, to talk among themselves. Allow them time to do this. Remember, you'll never be able to force someone to rent your property who doesn't want to. So don't try. Besides, being too eager makes some people suspicious (afraid there's a hidden agenda—you're hiding something about the property) and scares them away.

On the other hand, you want to further qualify a potential tenant. As the situation allows, question prospective tenants about their ability to pay the rent, when they'll move in, if the property is appropriate for them (too many for the unit?), what kind of pets they have, if they have a water bed, and so forth.

Have Prospective Tenants Fill Out a Rental Application

You must offer every prospective tenant an opportunity to fill out a rental application. Besides the obvious need on your part to get information about him or her, you also don't want to be accused of discrimination. Remember, you cannot refuse to offer a rental application to any applicant, unless the applicant is underage—typically 18 but varying from state to state.

If there's more than one applicant (roommates or even married people), the safe approach is to have each fill out a separate application.

I'll have more to say about the application itself in the next chapter.

11

COMING UP WITH A GOOD RENTAL APPLICATION

The best way to avoid evicting a bad tenant is to not rent to that person in the first place.

No one rental application is the best nor will it fit every situation. What you want is a form that asks the right questions. With the help of modern computers and a word processor, you can create your own application in a short time. You should also have your attorney check it over. The application at the end of this book covers many of the essential areas you need to include.

Try to make the application form succinct. You want it to include all the information you need but not be so extensive as to take hours to fill out. A good application should require no more than 10 or 15 minutes to be filled out. And once it is filled out, be sure to read it over to see that the would-be tenant has filled it out completely and correctly and signed it.

There should be no legitimate reason a would-be tenant would refuse to fill out an application for you. Never rent to anyone who refuses to fill out an application. And never rent before checking out the application. Do a good job when you check out the tenant.

> **C** *a u t i o n*
>
> Don't refuse a rental application to anyone who asks for one. You don't want to be accused of discrimination by refusing to give out an application. I offer everyone who comes to see the property a rental application, even if they don't seem interested.

Make No Promises You Can't Keep

The application is not just a formality. Never, ever rent to people without first verifying the information on the form, no matter how perfect they seem. And never tell any prospects that the rental is theirs before you've finished checking them out. Later, if there's a problem and you don't want to rent to them, they can complain that you're discriminating because you first agreed to rent to them and now you are refusing.

Also, sometimes there will be two or maybe even three would-be tenants at the rental property at the same time, all asking for applications. Don't imply that the first person who returns the application gets the prize. You want to rent to the most qualified tenant, not the fastest writer.

Five Critical Tenant Tests

Getting a prospective tenant to fill out a rental application is only the first step. Now you must check out what the prospect puts down. I think there are five critical tests that can be derived from an application to determine if the applicant is a good prospect. If a would-be tenant fails any of these five, I wouldn't rent to him or her. These five tests are discussed in the following sections.

Test #1: Does the landlord before the current one recommend the applicants?

This is the most critical test of all. You're asking the person who is in the best position to know about the prospect. Note that I recommend checking out the landlord *before* the current one. I wouldn't waste my time checking out the current landlord. If your would-be tenants are a problem, the current landlord is going to tell you they are wonderful just so he or she can get rid of them! Only the landlord before the present one is likely to give you a true picture.

H *i n t*

Be certain that your application specifically and in writing allows you to check the prospective tenant's background (by calling previous landlords), finances (by checking with the bank), and credit (by securing a credit report). If the prospective tenant does not specifically give you the right to do this, you don't have the right.

Test #2: Will the applicants give up their pet? As landlords know, pets can take a high toll on a rental. They can scratch, tear, and urinate and defecate on the property, all of which can cause thousands of dollars of damage. (One cat urinating on a carpet can destroy that carpet, the padding, and even the flooring underneath!)

Ideally, most landlords would prefer to rent without pets. However, in the real world you must assume that most, if not all, tenants have pets. Therefore, the question is not will they have pets but how many and what kind. My suggestion is that you learn to live with the fact that tenants tend to have pets. Or be prepared to do a lot of shouting and evicting.

Once you come to accept pets, the real question is one of controlling their number, the kind, and their deportment. The first two are a function of the rental application, the last a function of the deposit. (A bigger deposit because of a pet often ensures that the owners take special care to make sure the pet is properly behaved.)

After filling out the application area about pets, many would-be tenants ask if you accept them. You can say something such as, "Yes, provided it's a small pet and only cats or goldfish (or whatever)." At this point the would-be tenant may say something such as, "But I have three Dobermans. They are wonderful dogs, so well behaved, so clean."

They certainly may be. But it's doubtful they would have room in a studio apartment with no yard. In fact, it might even be cruel to keep them in such close quarters.

L *a n d l o r d ' s* **T** *a l e*

Hal simply refused to rent to anyone who had a pet. He figured it was the easiest way to go. Consequently, as soon as would-be tenants learned of this, they would tell him they didn't have any pets. However, almost invariably, a few weeks or a month after they moved in, a pet (or two) would appear.

As soon as Hal found out, he would go over, shout at the tenants, and tell them to get rid of the pet or leave. Likely as not, the tenants would get angry and, after a few months, depart, often leaving the property a mess.

As a result, Hal lost a lot of rental time and spent a lot of money cleaning up his properties. No, he didn't have any pets, but he didn't have many tenants either.

When you explain this to a tenant, he or she may say, "It's a shame. But I want this place. OK, I'll get rid of them." I have a good friend, a property manager for more than 25 years, who says at this point, "I'm sorry, but I would never rent to anyone who would get rid of a pet!"

My point, of course, is that pets are like members of the family. Almost no one will give them up. If prospects say they will, they are probably fabricating. Rent to these people and chances are within a few weeks or months that pet(s) will be living there too.

Test #3: Can the applicants come up with the cash? These days it can take a fair amount of cash to move into a rental. Let's say you are renting for $950 a month. Of course, you want the first month's rent up front. But you will also want a security/cleaning deposit. It wouldn't be unusual to ask for a cleaning deposit equal to a month's rent or another $950. Now, the would-be tenant has to come up with $1,900. (If you're also looking for a lease with first and last month's rent, that's another $950, so the applicant now needs $2,850—sometimes an impossible amount.) That's a fair bit of change for an applicant interested in renting a place for under $1,000 a month.

Nevertheless, I always insist that this money must be paid (in cash or its equivalent) before an applicant can move in. Sometimes would-be tenants try to negotiate. They may say they'll pay the first month's rent right now, but they would like to pay the security/cleaning deposit in two or three installments over the next few weeks. They just can't come up with all of the necessary cash.

It's a believable explanation, and in a tight market you're tempted to accept it. But just ask yourself, what good's a security/cleaning deposit that you haven't collected? Further, my experience is that a tenant who can't come up with the money now will have trouble coming up with it later on as well.

The potential tenant should pay the first month's rent plus the security deposit (plus the last month's rent, if applicable) in the form of cash, a cashier's check, or a money order. I will accept a personal check with the understanding that the person won't move in until it clears my bank, usually at least two or three days.

Test #4: Do applicants have sufficient income to make the payments? This is like qualifying a person for a home mortgage. The rental application form asks for the prospective tenant's income. According to many property management authorities, you should be sure that the tenant's gross income is at least four times the monthly rent. That supposedly ensures he or she has enough money coming in to handle the rent. These authorities even have formulas for income, expenses, bank savings, and so on that you can apply to tenants to determine whether they will be able to make their monthly payments.

In my experience, however, that's a lot of bunk. I've rented to tenants who had no apparent income yet managed just fine with the rent. And I've rented to tenants who showed an income more than five times the monthly rent yet still couldn't make the rent payments.

In order to properly qualify tenants for their financial ability to pay, you would need to know not only their gross income but the taxes they pay, their monthly fixed expenses, any long-term debt (over six months, such as car payments), any personal debt such as alimony, and on and on. Quite frankly, you're not likely to get that kind of information on most rental application forms. (And even if you did, it still wouldn't prove anything—mortgage lenders use very fine pencils and highly sophisticated profiles, and a certain percentage of their loans still go bad.)

Therefore, what I do instead of using a sharp pencil and some arcane formula is sit down with the rental application form and a prospective tenant to whom I want to rent the property and ask something like, "Do you figure you'll be able to handle the monthly rent payments? Where will you get the money?"

Would-be tenants usually consider these reasonable questions from a prospective landlord. Those who have their act together often quickly outline their basic expenses (utilities, food, and the like), their fixed expenses, and their income in an attempt to prove to me that it will work.

I really don't pay much attention to the "proof." The fact that they have a plan is usually enough. I just want to be sure they know where the rent money is coming from and are confident they can find it. (I also check with their employer and bank to be sure they aren't making money up out of thin air.)

If potential tenants say they don't have much income but do have a lot of cash in the bank, don't hesitate to confirm that with a

C *a u t i o n*

To be in compliance with antidiscrimination laws, you need to ask the same questions and apply the same criteria to all tenants.

I once had a would-be tenant who said he was currently unemployed and, in fact, had been unemployed for the past 18 months. He had no regular income.

Naturally I was concerned and asked how he expected to make the rent payments. He proceeded to inform me that he was unemployed because he had been injured at work and had received a cash settlement of over $200,000, which he had banked. He was happy to have me confirm this with his bank. He said he planned on living on the money for a year or two before getting a new job. I rented to him and he stayed two years, paying right on the due date.

bank. Have them sign a standard Verification of Deposit request and send it to the bank. (See the back of the book for a typical form.)

If potential tenants say they are depending on income from their employment to make the rent payments, be sure the credit check you do (noted below) confirms their employment. If it doesn't, then use a Verification of Employment form yourself. (See the back of the book for a typical form.)

Test #5: Do applicants have a good credit and rental history? Although mentioned last, I consider this the second most important factor in qualifying prospective tenants. You must have some idea of how they handle bills, and about the only way you can find this out is through an independent credit and/or rental history check. (Note: As noted, your rental application should include space asking that would-be tenants give you permission to make such a check.)

Many landlords feel that getting a credit report is a hassle that requires too much time.

C *a u t i o n*

Be wary of prospective tenants who don't have regular employment or a good explanation for their income yet have plenty of cash with which to pay the rent and deposits. They may be selling drugs and intend using your property as a drug house. As a landlord, you can be held responsible for what goes on in your property and may be forced to evict them. What's worse: Under certain circumstances you could lose your property by confiscation to the federal government without trial and with little recourse!

L *a n d l o r d ' s* **T** *a l e*

Sally had never used a credit reporting agency to check on her would-be tenants yet had had fairly good luck with her rental. She would call the previous-to-current landlord, check with an applicant's employer and bank and let it go at that. But finally she decided to go with a credit report.

Imagine her surprise when the very first check she ran revealed that the prospective tenant had dozens of late payments and defaulted accounts. The would-be tenant's application *looked* perfect. Her employer verified her employment. The bank said she had enough money on deposit to move in. But the credit report revealed she was a true deadbeat.

Needless to say, Sally now uses credit checks for all her prospective tenants.

I don't. It may be confusing the first time, but after you've established a method for getting the report, it should be easy to do. Besides, the information it provides can be invaluable.

The question is how you, as a single landlord, can run a credit check and a rental history check.

How to Run a Credit Check

There are numerous credit checking agencies in every metropolitan area (listed under "Credit Reporting Agencies" in the yellow pages) in addition to the three national credit agencies:

- Equifax 800-997-2493 (http://www.equifax.com)
- Experian 888-397-3742 (http://www.experian.com)
- TransUnion 800-888-4213 (http://www.tuc.com)

A formal, written credit report from one of the major agencies, however, usually costs anywhere from $25 to $50 and may thus be prohibitively expensive for rental credit checks.

However, many local agencies have a special single-service option designed just for landlords whereby for a much smaller fee, often only

$10 or $20, they will do a minimal credit search. Sometimes the credit reporting bureau will only send you a minimal written credit report.

Finally, many areas have rental or landlord associations (see Chapter 1) that belong to a credit reporting agency and can run a check for you at a nominal cost.

Rental History Check

What can be even more revealing than a credit check is a rental history check. Today there are landlord associations in virtually all metropolitan areas. (Look under "Landlord Associations" or "Housing Associations" in the yellow pages.) These associations receive reports of late payments and evictions from their members and then make this information available to their members.

Sometimes you have to join an organization to get a rental history check (which could be quite expensive with annual dues), but other times the association will make it available to you for a nominal one-time fee, provided you agree to provide information on tenants to it. It's a kind of "I'll scratch your back if you'll scratch mine." Sometimes these associations are tied in to others across the state and even between states (see NAA in Chapter 1).

If a prospective tenant is shown to have a bad report from a rental history check, I would be very careful about renting to him or her. No matter what explanations are given, what tenants did to one landlord they are likely to do to another.

H *i n t*

You can ask a prospective tenant to pay all, or a portion, of the cost of a credit report. Some would-be tenants balk at this, whereas others feel it's perfectly natural, particularly if the cost is only around $10 or $15. I never ask an applicant to pay for the report. After all, I'm only going to get a credit report on a would-be tenant I'm pretty sure I want, and the report really benefits me.

W *a r n i n g*

Do not collect a fee for the credit report from a would-be tenant, pocket the fee, and then fail to run the report. The applicant could demand to see the credit report, particularly if it were adverse, and you could be in serious trouble if you can't produce it.

H *i n t*

Check with a local rental authority or apartment owner's association about language requirements. You may need to provide a rental agreement specifically in the language (other than English) in which the tenants speak.

If an applicant passes the five tests discussed earlier in this chapter, then I feel I've got a winner and will rent to that applicant.

Letting the Potential Tenant Know

Once you find an applicant you feel is qualified, you need to call back to say you're willing to rent to him or her, provided both of you can agree on a couple of issues. One of the most important is the *move-in date.*

Tenants always want to move in at a time that's most convenient for them. And, of course, they want the rent to start when they move in, not before. This, however, can cost you money.

For example, let's say that your property is available on the 1st of the month. However, you don't find a tenant until the 15th. Now you've qualified the tenant and are ready to have that person sign a rental agreement. The person is willing to sign and give you a check for all monies. However, the person can't move in until the 1st and wants the rent to start then.

If you allow the rent to start on the 1st, you will have lost another two weeks of income. I always tell the tenant that the property is now available and I can't lose two weeks' rent waiting. The tenant can move in on the 1st if he or she chooses, but the rent must start on the 15th.

What usually happens is a discussion ensues, and the would-be tenant comes back with an offer to compromise. What about splitting the difference? The rent can start one week before the 1st? I lose a week, and the tenant loses one as well. If it's a strong tenant in a weak market, I'm willing to compromise. After all, it could take me an additional two weeks to find another suitable applicant.

What I usually do is counteroffer in the following way. The rent will start one week before the 1st of the month. However, the following month, tenants will pay five weeks' rent instead of four. That moves their payment date to the 1st. As noted earlier, it's always to your advantage to have the payment date on the 1st day of the month. Most tenants agree to this compromise and are satisfied with it.

Result of Denying a Tenant the Rental because of a Bad Credit Report

The Fair Credit Reporting Act requires you to notify an applicant if you turn him or her down because of a credit report. You need to let the applicant know the following:

WHAT YOU MUST LET DENIED APPLICANT KNOW

- The credit reporting bureau you used (name, address, phone number, Web site).
- The applicant has the right to obtain a free copy of the credit report by contacting the agency directly. There's a 60-day time limit here.
- The applicant can dispute the credit report, demand an investigation, or request that additional information he or she provides be added to the report.
- If you received information from someone other than a credit-reporting agency, the applicant has the right, within 60 days, to make a request in writing for the nature of the information.
- Notice that the credit bureau provided only information about the applicant's credit history and did not participate in making the denial decision, nor cannot it provide information on the reason for the denial.

It's important that you give applicants a copy containing the above information and have them sign for a receipt of it to prove that you actually delivered it. (Technically, you need not give them the statement in writing, but if you don't, how will you later prove you did it?)

Other Important Tenant Checks

Even though you may think that if you've done all of the above, you've completed your tenant screening. There are other areas, however, that you should also check, if for no other reason than to protect yourself. These include the following:

Drug dealing. The applicant you rent to just might turn out to be a drug dealer. If so and if that person is apprehended, your property might be seized by the government as a drug house (even though you are innocent and had no knowledge of the dealing), and you could have a terrible time getting it back.

At the very minimum, you want to specify in your lease agreement that no drug dealing is allowed. And you may also want to be very cautious when the applicant wants to pay entirely in cash and shows no bank accounts.

Checking an applicant's criminal background can be done for a nominal fee (usually under $25) but is usually available only for the local county. As of this writing, most states do not require a criminal background check of a rental applicant.

Sex offenses. Under Megan's Law (adopted in almost all states), a list of sexual offenders is available. The FBI also keeps a database of anyone convicted of a sexual offense against a minor and/or a violent sexual offense against anyone. Local law enforcement agencies may also have their own database and are usually available to anyone.

A prospective tenant may ask you if any tenant in your property is a sexual offender. If so, I would refer them to the local law enforcement agency. I would also have them sign a note that you made such a referral.

Terrorism. Since 9/11, everyone in the country has been more keenly aware of the possibility of terrorist activities. As a landlord, you certainly do not want to rent your property to a terrorist. Yet how would you know?

Some landlords have attempted to restrict renting their properties to people based on their ethnic background or national origin, for example, refusing to rent to Muslims. This is illegal. However, you may verify an applicant's citizenship status.

According to HUD (the Department of Housing and Urban Development), it is unlawful to screen housing applicants on the basis of race, color, religion, sex, national origin, disability, or familial status. In the wake of the attacks of September 11, 2001, landlords and property managers have inquired about the legality of screening housing applicants on the basis of their citizenship status.

Current law does not prohibit discrimination based solely on a person's citizenship status. Accordingly, asking housing applicants to provide documentation of their citizenship or immigration status during the screening process would not violate the Fair Housing Act. In fact, such measures have been in place for a number of years in screening applicants for federally assisted housing. For these properties, HUD regulations define what kinds of documents are considered acceptable evidence of citizenship or eligible immigration status and outline the process for collecting and verifying such documents. (See HUD regulations 24 CFR 5.506-5.512.) These procedures are uniformly applied to every applicant. Landlords who are considering implementing similar measures must make sure they are carried out in a nondiscriminatory fashion.

For more information, check http://www.hud.gov.

12

DISCLOSURES

Disclosing can protect not only the tenant but the landlord too.

One of the biggest challenges facing landlords today is how to deal with environmental issues. Both the federal government and state governments are constantly issuing edicts and rules regarding environmental hazards, and keeping up with them can be a full-time job. For that reason, I strongly urge readers to check frequently Internet sites, such as http://www.epa.gov and http://www.hud.gov, that issue important notices in this area. It's also an excellent idea to join an organization that can provide up-to-date information on a timely basis—for example, the National Apartment Association at http://www.naa.com (also see Chapter 1 for more details about this organization).

It is important that every landlord provide not only a clean rental unit but a safe one as well. Although this includes correcting such obvious hazards as loose wiring or faulty plumbing, it also includes removing environmental hazards.

In this chapter we're going to look at some of the environmental concerns that face landlords. In some cases you have to submit a disclosure to your tenants. In others, you will want to investigate and correct any haz-

H *i n t*

It's a good idea to include a notation in your rental agreement that you've given tenants a copy of any disclosure. Also, get a signed and dated statement from tenants that they've received it.

ards to provide a safe environment for your tenants—and to reduce your liability!

Lead Contamination

Many first-time landlords, as well as many of those who have been in the business for years, are oblivious of the health and safety requirements affecting rentals in communities across the country. Today, you not only may be required to provide your tenants with a habitable home, but you may also be required to take precautions to ensure that the home is a safe and healthy environment.

Of course, this is nothing more than any of us would want in any event. I don't think any landlord wants to feel responsible for a tenant becoming sick or being injured, let alone facing the legal liabilities that would be involved.

One area of great concern involves *lead*. For many years, lead has been known to have serious health effects. That is the reason it has been banned from paint since 1978 and from gasoline and other products. In 1992, the secretary of the Department of Health and Human Services called lead the "number one environmental threat to the health of children in the United States."

In the home it is possible to be exposed to lead from dust in the air, from drinking water coming from lead-contaminated pipes, from ingesting food containing lead dust, and even from playing in contaminated soil around the yard. There are roughly 64 million housing units in this country that contain some lead paint. These are structures built before 1978, the date when lead-based paint was prohibited.

Lead is an insidious toxin because its effects, though sometimes deadly, may take many months or even years to produce visible effects. At high levels, lead can cause convulsions, comas, and death. At low levels, it can adversely affect the blood system, the kidneys, the central nervous system, and the brain. It can cause such problems as hyperactivity, muscle and joint pain, high blood pressure, and loss of hearing. Children and fetuses are particularly susceptible to lead poisoning because lead is more easily absorbed into growing bodies. Also, children are more likely to get lead in their systems because they tend to put their fingers in their mouths or lick or chew lead-coated areas such as door jambs or window sills covered with lead paint. A blood test can determine if a person has high levels of lead in the blood stream.

Lead in Paint

The principal source of lead in the home is lead-based paint, routinely used until it was banned in 1978. Today, when this paint weathers and dries out, it often turns into dust that can then be inhaled or ingested. In addition, lead paint on the outside of homes may chalk up and fall to the ground, where it contaminates the soil. Other sources of lead contamination are scraping, sanding, or open-flame burning lead paint in efforts to remove it.

Lead paint is most likely to be found in the following places in homes built prior to 1978:

- Windows sills and door jambs
- Doors and door frames, railings, and banisters
- Trim on the inside of the home
- Throughout the exterior of the home
- Any other painted surface

Lead in Water

In addition, there is also a potential threat from lead in the drinking water of some homes, particularly much older ones built before 1930. Even today, a short lead pipe may be used to connect a home's water system to the public utility, thus allowing the introduction of the metal into the water system.

In newer homes, copper pipes have mostly replaced galvanized steel, but until recently it was common practice to use lead solder to join the copper pipes together. It has only been within the past decade that lead solder has been banned from use in water pipes in many states. (It has been replaced by a silver solder that works just as well but costs more.) In addition, so-called brass faucets and fittings can also sometimes leach lead. Newer standards for these fittings have mandated that they be lead free, and many fittings advertise this fact on the boxes in which they are packed.

The Difficulty of Removing Lead

Lead-based paint, when in good condition, is not usually a hazard. (The exception is when small children chew on it.) When lead-based paint chips turn to chalk, crack, or peel, however, lead becomes a serious hazard. The reason is that dust or chips from the paint can well up in shifting air and be inhaled or settle on food and be ingested by tenants.

It stands to reason, therefore, that if you have a rental that was built prior to 1978, you would want to limit the lead exposure to tenants. However, doing so is not necessarily easy or inexpensive.

For one thing, it is not usually possible to tell just by looking if a paint contains lead. (Merely being glossy doesn't mean paint is lead based.) Only a special test can determine if lead is in paint; the test for a full single-family home costs over $300. (If you're interested, your state health department can usually suggest a private laboratory or a public agency that may be able to help you test for lead in paint. Also check http://www.epa.gov.)

Lead removal requires an expert, so you should never attempt to remove it from a rental yourself (unless you're fully qualified), or you may just make the problem worse. Remember, scraping, sanding, or using an open-flame torch releases lead dust into the air so that it can be inhaled or ingested. Also, do not use a home vacuum cleaner to capture lead dust. The bag that holds the debris may not be able to retain the tiny lead dust particles, and by vacuuming you may actually be spraying lead dust into the air.

Unfortunately, expert lead removal is very expensive, primarily because it requires qualified people, who must wear expensive protective gear during the removal. It is not uncommon for the cost to be from $10,000 upward to have lead paint removed from a whole house! For a 1,000-square-foot rental unit, the cost could be $5,000 or more.

Removing lead from the water system is equally difficult and expensive. Testing to find out if lead is in your water, however, is much simpler. Lead is colorless, odorless, and tasteless, but test kits are available for only about $20, and the cost for a professional is about $100. The only real way to remove lead from the water system is to replumb.

Federal Lead Disclosure Regulations

In 1992 Congress passed the Residential Lead-Based Paint Hazard Reduction Act (also known as Title X). As part of this act, section 1018 requires a landlord to disclose known information about lead-based paint and lead-based paint hazards before leasing most housing built prior to 1978. The statute, however, does not affect the following:

- Property leased for less than 100 days (such as a vacation house)
- Lofts, efficiencies, dormitories, and other units designated as zero-bedroom units
- Housing for the elderly or disabled unless children also live there

Lead Requirements for Landlords

Before ratification of a lease, as a landlord:

- You must disclose any known information concerning lead-based paint or lead-based paint hazards. This includes the location of the lead-based paint and/or lead-based paint hazards as well as the condition of the painted surfaces.
- You must provide any available reports (or records) of lead-based paint and/or lead-based paint hazards. (If you own a multiunit building, this would include common areas and other units when such information was obtained as a result of a buildingwide evaluation.)
- You must provide a *lead warning statement* (included in the lease or as an attachment), which confirms that you have complied with all notification requirements. It must be in the same language used in the rest of the contract. Landlords and agents, as well as tenants, must sign and date the attachment. (See statement example at the back of this book and check out http://www.epa.gov.)
- You must retain a copy of the disclosures for no less than three years from the date the leasing period begins.

- You must give tenants an EPA-approved pamphlet called *Protect Your Family from Lead in Your Home,* which was jointly developed by HUD (Department of Housing and Urban Development) and the EPA (Environmental Protection Agency). Booklets about lead are readily available from real estate agents and escrow and title companies. You can also secure them from the government by calling the National Lead Information Center at 800-424-lead, and you can obtain copies online at http://www.epa.gov. (Order bulk copies from the Government Printing Office (GPO) at 202-512-1800.)

Asbestos Contamination

Asbestos is a mineral fiber that in the past was added to a variety of products to strengthen them and to provide heat insulation and fire resistance. For years, potholders were commonly made out of asbestos, which has also been used in insulation, in certain types of vinyl tiles, and in the so-called popcorn ceilings blown onto some older homes. You can't really identify asbestos by looking at it; you need a microscope.

According to the American Lung Association, breathing high levels of asbestos fibers can lead to an increased risk of lung cancer; mesothelioma, a cancer of the lining of the chest and the abdominal cavity; and asbestosis, in which the lungs become scarred with fibrous tissue. However, the American Lung Association does point out that most people exposed to small amounts of asbestos, as we all are in our daily life, do not develop these health problems.

The real danger with asbestos in a rental is that it might be disturbed. When it is, asbestos material may release large amounts of asbestos fibers, which can be inhaled into the lungs. The fibers can remain there for a long time, increasing the risk of disease. Unfortunately, asbestos material often crumbles easily if handled or is released into the air if sawed, scraped, or sanded into a powder.

Determining If Your Rental Has Asbestos

Asbestos has in the past been used extensively in a wide variety of products, including roofing shingles, the insulation in walls and attics, sprayed-on ceilings, joint compounds (prior to 1977 when it was banned for this usage), artificial ashes and embers sometimes used in gas-fired fireplaces and heaters, some vinyl floor tiles, and heat protectors such as stove pads. It also has been extensively used in the form of blankets around ducts and heating systems (particularly in steam pipes) as a heat insulator.

As with lead, you can't easily tell if a product has asbestos in it. (Just because it's white and wrapped around a pipe doesn't necessarily mean it is asbestos.) The only way to know for sure is to hire a professional to conduct tests. (Don't try testing it yourself. The act of breaking open material to obtain test samples may actually release asbestos into the environment.)

What You Should Do If You Have Asbestos in a Rental

As of this time, I know of no federal disclosure rules regarding asbestos (although there may be some local or state rules). That means the federal government does not require you to find out if you have asbestos, to remove it, or to inform tenants.

Further, unlike lead, you may be better off simply not touching asbestos that is contained. According to the American Lung Association, if you think asbestos may be present, the best procedure may be to leave the asbestos material that is in good condition alone. Generally speaking, material in good condition will not release asbestos fibers. There is no danger unless fibers are released and inhaled into the lungs or ingested.

Of course, it is a good idea to check material regularly if you suspect it may contain asbestos. Don't touch it but look for signs of wear or damage such as tears, abrasions, or water damage. Damaged material may release asbestos fibers, particularly true if you often disturb it by hitting, rubbing, or handling it, or if it is exposed to extreme vibration or air flow. Sometimes the best way to deal with slightly damaged material is to limit access to the area and not touch or disturb it. Again, check with local health, environmental, or other appropriate officials to find out proper handling and disposal procedures.

If you discover asbestos material that requires removal or encapsulation, be sure to hire a professional. Don't attempt to handle it yourself. Also, during the removal period, you probably want to be sure there are no tenants in the property (certainly from a liability point of view).

In general, if you're aware of any asbestos that you think poses a health hazard, you probably want to have an inspection by a trained professional and then, if a hazard is demonstrated to exist, have such a person remove or encapsulate it. Unfortunately, as with lead, the cost is high and doing the work usually adds nothing to the value of the property.

What about asbestos ceilings? Between 1950 and the late 1970s, it was common practice in many parts of the country to spray an acoustical material on ceilings. This gave the ceiling a nice textured look, and the material also, supposedly, had acoustical properties. Unfortunately, often the spray contained asbestos.

Generally speaking, these asbestos-sprayed ceilings, which remain in many properties to this day, are typically considered to not pose much of a health hazard so long as they are not disturbed. Testing is required to determine if the ceilings contain asbestos, and removal is done by professionals, who usually wet the asbestos material and then scrape it. Other methods involve encapsulating by spraying with a shellac and then painting. Be sure to check with a professional for advice on how to handle your problem.

Government Regulations

As of this writing, I know of no federal regulations regarding asbestos in rentals, although there may be rules and regulations in your state or local district. Check with local and state officials.

For more information on asbestos, contact your local American Lung Association for copies of "Indoor Air Pollution Fact Sheet—Asbestos." The EPA also provides a booklet called *Guidance for Controlling Asbestos-Containing Materials in Buildings* (312-353-2211, http://www.epa.gov/epahome/publications.htm).

Black Mold

Black mold is probably the most recent environmental concern for landlords. Stories recently in the news have featured "bubble-suited" abatement engineers attacking "deadly black mold" in homes. Even though the imminent danger may have been overblown, there is reason to be concerned about black mold in the home environment.

Molds occur in almost all homes. They reproduce by means of spores that are so tiny that they can't be seen by the naked eye. Typically, they last in the environment for some time until they land on a wet surface and then begin growing. Virtually all mold requires some sort of moisture to grow.

For the majority of people, most molds are not a problem. However, they do produce irritants and allergens that can cause allergic reactions. They also can produce toxic substances called *mycotoxins,* which can be a potentially serious health hazard and are what are usually considered black mold.

Usually you can get a reaction to mold by either touching it or inhaling it; allergic attacks from mold are fairly common. Mold can also trigger an asthmatic attack in people who have asthma, and it can irritate the eyes, nose, throat, lungs, and skin of almost anyone. Some people claim that certain types of molds can produce deadly reactions.

Removing Mold

It's important to understand that mold spores are ubiquitous. Because you can't get rid of all of them, the best way to avoid mold growth is to avoid moisture or wet areas. And this means removing any mold that happens to be growing in bathrooms, kitchens, and laundry areas (the most likely sources of mold contamination). It also means eliminating moisture to prevent the formation of new mold growth.

Most of the common molds can be removed with a little bleach and a sponge or rag. In severe cases, sheetrock, wood, and other items on which mold is growing may have to be replaced. To be safe, you may want to hire a pest control company to assess and remove mold. Also, mold abatement companies have been springing up around the country.

As of this writing, I know of no federal regulations regarding black mold in rentals, although there may be rules and regulations in your state or local district. Check with local and state officials.

For more information about mold, check with the EPA (http://www.epa.gov) and the CDC (Centers for Disease Control, http://www.cdc.gov).

Black Mold Disclosures

To help reduce the chance of tenant litigation over black mold, some landlords have begun to include a black mold disclosure form in their rental agreement. This basically explains the nature of mold and states that it is commonly found in most homes and can be a source of allergic and other, sometimes potentially life-threatening, reactions.

These disclosures make tenants aware that the rental may now, or in the future, have black mold and ensure that tenants are aware of this but accept the rental with a potential black mold hazard.

It's not clear to me what effect such a disclosure will have other than alarming a potential tenant. However, you should check with your local apartment owners' association to see what, if any, kind of disclosure is being used in your area.

Other Toxic Substances in Rental Property

There is a long list of other toxic materials that may be in your rental property. Some of the more hazardous include:

- Carbon monoxide—in the air from faulty heaters
- Formaldehyde—in wall paneling and insulation
- Radon gas—in the air supply, particularly in basements and lower floors

As of this time, I know of no federal regulations requiring an investigation to determine if any of these problems exist or if they require removal or disclosure to tenants. However, it is not inconceivable that regulations may occur in the future. You should check with state and local officials to see if they have any regulations on these materials. Here is a brief summary of each substance and the hazard involved.

Carbon Monoxide

This is a colorless, odorless gas. Although it is not toxic itself, it impedes the flow of oxygen when inhaled and absorbed into the blood stream.

Often the person affected won't even be aware of the poisoning and may look for other reasons to explain the symptoms, which may include headache, dizziness, and nausea. Death can result from the poisoning.

Carbon monoxide is generated from burning many different types of fuels, particularly when there is inadequate oxygen during the burning process. The fuels include charcoal, heating oil, kerosene, natural gas, propane, and wood. The most common culprits are wood-burning stoves and certain space heaters that use propane and kerosene. Old fireplaces and gas stoves also can release carbon monoxide; and a furnace with a bad heat exchanger may release it into the air.

As a landlord, you may want to supply a carbon monoxide detector if you use such fuels to heat your rental unit(s). They cost about $50 and usually work well; some rural and mountain communities require their use.

Formaldehyde

Formaldehyde is a highly pungent-smelling, colorless gas. In sufficient concentrations (usually above .1 parts per million) it can cause burning sensations in the eyes and throat, difficulty in breathing, and nausea and even trigger attacks in people with asthma. According to the EPA, formaldehyde has also been shown to cause cancer in animals and represents a risk of cancer in humans.

Formaldehyde is widely used in the manufacture of building materials and household products; it can also be a by-product of combustion. Typical sources of formaldehyde in the home include building materials, gas stoves, glues and paints, kerosene space heaters, and preservatives. Perhaps the most common source of formaldehyde in the home is pressed-wood products, such as plywood, that use urea-formaldehyde resins as part of their adhesives. They also include particleboard (typically used as subflooring and shelving); plywood paneling, particularly when the wood is hardwood; and medium density fiberboard.

In 1985, HUD began restricting the use of plywood and particleboard in the construction of prefabricated and mobile homes to certain specified formaldehyde emission limits. In the past, some of these homes had formaldehyde problems, primarily because most were relatively small, well insulated, and sealed; and manufacturers had used large amounts of high-emitting pressed-wood products.

If you have a rental with a formaldehyde problem, you are probably aware of it because you can smell it yourself. Tenants may be more or less sensitive to it and may or may not complain about the odor.

If you have a formaldehyde problem, the easiest way to deal with it is removal; that usually means replacing the wood paneling or particleboards causing the problem. Increasing ventilation is also helpful as is maintaining constant heat and humidity levels. (Formaldehyde emissions can be increased by heat.)

For further information on formaldehyde, you can call the EPA Toxic Substance Control Act (TSCA) assistance line at 202-554-1404.

Radon Gas

Radon is a naturally occurring gas that is a known cancer-causing agent. According to the surgeon general, it is the second leading cause of lung cancer in the United States. However, its effects are not immediate but are instead long term. It may take many years of exposure to radon to produce health problems. However, because radon is colorless, tasteless, and odorless, it is difficult to detect exposure.

Radon occurs naturally in the earth when uranium in soil, rocks, and water breaks down. The radon that is in the earth can migrate into a building because air pressure inside is often lower than pressure in the soil. In effect, a house acts like a vacuum, drawing up gases from the earth. If radon is present, it can be "sucked up" into your home. Some parts of the country are much more prone to radon problems than are others.

Testing for radon can be done quite simply. Many different low-cost radon testing kits are available through the mail and from hardware stores and generally cost less than $50. (Be sure you buy a kit stating that it "Meets EPA Requirements" or the requirements that your state may impose.)

The testing itself is usually done at the lowest living levels of the house, typically the basement or the first floor.

If a test reveals radon, it is almost always possible to install equipment that will reduce it to acceptable levels. Equipment usually involves fans and ducts to supply greater amounts of air to the lower levels of the property. You can do the work yourself or hire it out. It has been estimated that properly installed radon-reduction systems can cut radon levels by up to 99 percent in a home. The cost of these systems varies from as little as $500 to $3,000 or more.

Should you, as a landlord, be concerned about radon? It is just one more hazard to watch out for. As noted, as of this time I know of no federal rules requiring inspection, correction, or disclosure of radon. However, in those areas of the country where there is a severe radon problem, local or state laws may be in effect. Again, check with a local agent or your local building and safety department.

For more information on reducing radon, check the EPA's *Consumer's Guide to Radon Reduction.*

13

HANDLING
THE DEPOSITS

*Always get the deposit in cash (or cash equivalent);
else you might end up holding an empty bag.*

No area of landlord-tenant relations is more contentious or burdened with more complaints than that of the deposit. I have yet to find a landlord who doesn't feel that he or she is entitled to at least a portion of the cleaning deposit when a tenant leaves. Similarly, tenants automatically seem to assume that they are entitled to get all of the cleaning deposit back.

Quite frankly, the truth lies somewhere in between. I see the reasoning of landlords quite clearly. On the other hand, I've been a tenant once or twice, just enough to know how it feels to not get a cleaning deposit back when I felt I was entitled to one.

A T e n a n t ' s T a l e

Many years ago, when I was right out of college, my wife and I rented a small house. We had a dog, which was OK with the landlord, and put up a $100 cleaning deposit, which in those days was a lot of money for us. We kept the house clean and did a thorough job of cleaning when we moved. We shampooed the

(continued)

carpets, waxed the floors, and cleaned everything. Then we asked for our cleaning deposit back.

To this day (decades later) I remember the landlord's walking through the house saying, "Yes, you've done a remarkable job of cleaning up the property. Only you had a dog in here so there's bound to be hidden damage, particularly to the carpeting. I'm keeping all of the deposit." And that was it. He kept it all. There was really nothing to be done back then.

I like to tell this story to landlords because, when you own and manage property, you see so much of the other side of things. These days I'm used to occasional tenants who leave carpets torn and badly stained, walls marked, stoves filthy with grease, toilets and sinks lined with grime . . . well, presumably you're a landlord too, and I don't have to say more. Frequently, those few tenants who leave a big mess are also the same ones who holler the loudest demanding their cleaning deposit back.

It's easy enough to become permanently inured to tenants' requests for the return of cleaning deposits. However, just keep in mind that there are good tenants out there, and even those who don't leave the property up to your standards may indeed have spent considerable time and effort trying to get the place back into shape and, from their perspective, may feel entitled to the return of a sizeable chunk, if not all, of the deposit.

Why Have a Deposit?

The purpose of a deposit is to guarantee, by requiring money, that a tenant will perform (or not perform) a certain act. With a deposit for a pet, for example, the landlord is hoping that having the tenant put up a sum of money guarantees the tenant will see to it the pet won't damage the property. With a cleaning deposit, the hope is that the deposit will ensure that the tenant will keep the property clean or at least clean it up thoroughly before leaving. Generally speaking, the bigger the deposit, the greater your security.

Collecting the deposit(s) is only the first step. Issues here involve how big a deposit to get (or that your state allows you to get) and when to get it. Real problems, however, usually occur later on, when it's time to return the deposit to the tenant. How much of the deposit can the landlord keep? What kind of accounting must be done? When can the landlord dip into deposits? Must the landlord pay interest on deposit money while holding it? We'll cover these and other deposit concerns in this chapter.

Collecting Deposits

Deposits are typically collected at the time a tenant signs the rental agreement and pays the first (and last) month's rent. Sometimes a ten-

---

L a n d l o r d ' s   T a l e

Sally had a small two-bedroom house she was renting out in a bad market with too many rentals chasing too few tenants. Her place had been empty for almost two months, and she was getting desperate. She was ready to accept the first person who wanted to rent her unit—and she did.

The new tenants seemed OK, a credit check showing a few problems but nothing catastrophic. She couldn't, however, verify their previous rental history because they were from out of the area and said they had always owned their own home.

The biggest problem was that the new tenants couldn't come up with all the rent money and deposits. But they wanted to move in immediately, on the 15th of the month, saying they would pay two weeks' rent in cash. Then on the 1st they promised to pay a full month's rent plus a large cleaning/security deposit. Sally accepted and they moved in.

But on the 1st they said that jobs they were expecting didn't pan out, and they didn't have any money. They were sorry and would move as soon as they could. The soonest they could move turned out to be six weeks later, just as Sally was halfway through eviction proceedings. She not only lost several months' rent (including cleanup time) plus costs, but she also had no deposit money to pay for the cleanup of the mess the tenants had left.

The moral here is that you shouldn't jump from the frying pan into the fire. Having no tenant is better than having a bad tenant.

ant may not have all the money to pay both the deposit(s) and the rent. There is nothing wrong with having the tenant pay the first month's rent on signing the rental agreement, with the written understanding that all deposits are to be paid in full when the tenant moves in (which could be several days or even weeks later). However, it is vitally important to *not* let a tenant move until all deposits are paid in full.

Any landlord who allows a tenant to move in, even begin moving belongings into the rental unit, without first having collected all monies up front is asking for trouble. The tenant may never pay you another cent, and then you'd have to go through the eviction process without the benefit of deposits to help ease the burden.

Always provide a receipt. Whenever you receive a deposit from a tenant, always give back a receipt. The receipt should not only state such obvious things as name, date, and amount of the deposit but also its purpose and under what conditions it will be kept or returned. Never accept a check as a deposit without giving a signed receipt. It's not good business practice.

How Big a Deposit Should I Get?

The obvious answer here: as big as you can. However, there are limitations. Tenants will balk at outrageously large deposits; they'll rent from someone else if you charge too much. Also, many states limit the size of the deposit you can take. (Check with your state department of real estate or housing.) For example, the cleaning/security deposit may be limited to a maximum of one and a half month's rent. (One way you may be able to get around this limitation is to accept several deposits for different purposes—for example, a cleaning/security deposit and then a separate deposit for a pet. Check with an experienced and knowledgeable property manager in your area.)

The Key to Getting a Large Deposit

The key to getting a large deposit is to make it very clear to tenants that you intend returning the money, providing the conditions of the deposit are met. If a pet does no damage, you will promptly return *all* of the deposit. If the property is left as clean as it was found—and you have a method for determining this (such as walk-through inspection sheets)—you will return all monies. If there is damage, you will subtract the cost, and tell tenants you have a reasonable method of determining fees.

Once tenants become convinced that their deposit is not your advance Christmas present, they are usually willing to comply.

As noted above, many states today limit the size of a cleaning deposit to one or two months' rent. Of course, whether the unit is furnished, how long the rental period is for, and other factors may influence the maximum you can get. Be sure to check with local officials in your state.

Where Do I Keep Deposits?

In the old days, many landlords simply put rental deposits in their own personal account and spent them immediately, as they would other

L *a n d l o r d ' s* **T** *a l e*

I have seen some rather amazing real estate transactions take place on the basis of cleaning/security deposits. In one instance, the owner of an overpriced 105-unit apartment building in a very bad market gave the building away (subject to its mortgages, of course) to a buyer, providing she (the original owner) could hang onto the cleaning deposits. Because the average rent in the building was $500 a month, and the original owner was holding about 100 deposits equal to one and a half months' rent, she came away with $75,000. Of course, the new owner had to answer to the tenants, who eventually wanted their deposits back.

In another instance a small group of investors took over an empty 500-unit apartment building after borrowing money for the down payment. They then quickly rented it up and used the security deposits they acquired—nearly a half million dollars' worth—to pay back the down payment loan. In essence, the deposits helped finance the purchase!

This is not to say you should practice such creative and potentially illegitimate financing. But it does point out the gray area into which deposits sometimes fall.

income. Depending on your state, this may or may not be legal. Many states feel that security deposits are monies that are held in trust for tenants. Legally, the tenants own the security deposits, though you're holding the money.

As a practical matter, putting a deposit in your account can create some serious problems. For one, as soon as you put the money in your own account, you should probably declare it as income for tax purposes. For another, when the tenant moves out, you need to come up with the deposit money, and what do you do if you've already spent it? Some landlords rob Peter to pay Paul. They quickly rerent the property and use the new tenant's deposit to pay the old—not a good practice.

Should I Use a Separate Bank Account?

Most good property owners I know keep their rental deposits in a separate bank account. (It's a must for a professional property manager.) They have a special record book for keeping track of the deposits, and when tenants move out, they have the money readily available to either pay for repairs or to pay back the tenants. (Deposit money kept in this fashion may not be considered taxable income—talk to your tax advisor.)

There are two hidden problems here that new landlords don't usually appreciate. The first is mundane—namely, how do you create the separate bank account?

The answer is that you can simply open an account in your name and then refer to it as the "John Smith Rental Deposit Account." Most banks won't bat an eye at setting it up that way, and checks can be easily deposited to your *deposit account.* Another, but more complex, method is to set up a *trust account.* This is more complex because you must keep very accurate records, including for whom you're holding the money in trust. You may need an attorney to set up a trust account. Most real estate agents have these, although some banks may balk at setting them up for individuals.

A trust account may get into difficulty with regard to the second hidden problem with deposits: *interest.* If you accept a $1,000 deposit and then stick it into a non-interest-bearing account, most people would say you're a fool. On the other hand, if you stick it into an interest-bearing account, who gets the interest? You or the tenant whose money you're holding? Currently in many states, you can claim the interest for yourself unless you stick the money in an account that is in trust for someone else.

Legislation in some states now requires that landlords pay tenants at least a minimal amount of interest on deposit money. These statutes often require, for example, that landlords pay tenants 1 or 2 percent per year on their money or something similar. Today, however, many savings accounts are paying less than 1 percent! And these low interest rates have thrown the whole issue up in the air.

Must You Really Return Deposits?

Some landlords want to think of a deposit as nonrefundable. If you think about this for a moment, that is a contradiction in terms. How can you have a nonrefundable deposit? Some states nevertheless do allow nonrefundable deposits, but this acts as a disincentive to tenants to keep the premises clean.

The next question becomes, How much of the deposit can you keep when tenants move? The basic rules here have not changed much, although the actual practice has shifted enormously. As landlords know, tenants must leave the property in about the same condition as they found it, normal wear and tear excepted. It's this last part that often trips up a landlord.

L a n d l o r d ' s **T** a l e

Hal rented out a two-bedroom, two-bath apartment to a couple who had children. When the couple moved out, Hal discovered marks from colored pencils, crayons, and other materials on the bathroom walls. He hired a cleaning crew to wash down the bathroom walls, but it turned out that when Hal had painted the apartment a year earlier, he hadn't used high-gloss paint in the bathrooms but instead had used standard flat wall paint. As a consequence, when a cleaning person tried washing the paint, she only smeared the marks. The paint couldn't be washed, so Hal hired a painter to repaint both bathrooms. Then Hal charged

(continued)

the cost of both the failed cleaning and the repainting to the tenant by with-holding the amount, now up to around $300, from the cleaning deposit.

The tenant protested and eventually took Hal to small claims court. There the tenant agreed that Hal was indeed entitled to the cost of cleaning the bath-rooms, about $100. But he was not entitled to the cost of repainting, about $200, as he hadn't originally painted the rooms with the right kind of paint nor-mally used for bathrooms—the kind that could be washed. The judge agreed, and Hal had to return $200 of the deposit to the tenants.

The above story illustrates two points. The first is that you have to be very careful about how you characterize money you withhold from the cleaning deposit. If tenants can say the damage is caused by normal wear and tear, or in the above case by the landlord's own actions, then they may be entitled to the return of all, or a portion of, the deposit. What constitutes damage and what normal wear and tear are gray areas.

Second, if you aren't careful, tenants can take you to court to sue you for the return of the cleaning deposit and may possibly win. In the above case, the tenant only got a portion of the cleaning deposit back. However, if you violate state laws regarding the return of a cleaning de-posit, you could also be liable for fines.

When to Return the Deposit

Most states have passed regulations determining how long a land-lord can hang on to a deposit after a tenant moves out. For example, the landlord must pay back the deposit in full or give a complete account-ing of how the money was spent within 21 days after a tenant moves out. The time limit varies, so be sure to check in your area.

Most tenants, understandably, don't want to wait 21 or however many days. They may need the money as a deposit on the next place into which they're moving. And they are probably afraid that any delay at all means that you may not return all or most of the money. As a consequence, there is a tug-of-war over the deposit at the time tenants move out; some tenants resort to rather clever tactics to get their deposit back quickly.

But a new landlord may ask, If a tenant leaves the property clean, why shouldn't I immediately return all of the deposit? Aha, I can hear experienced landlords saying wait and see!

The reason has to do with hidden damage that may occur sometime after the tenant moves out. What's hidden damage? In one case of a property I was renting out, the tenant's children had flushed several toys down the drain and plugged it up. But this didn't show up until several days after they moved out, when a cleaning crew was at work in the house. In another case the tenant's pet had left the carpeting infested with fleas, but the tenant had set off a flea bomb that killed all the mature fleas. It wasn't until two weeks later that flea eggs hatched, producing a house full of new biting insects and the need to call a pest control company to get rid of them.

It's to a landlord's advantage to hang on to that cleaning deposit as long as possible to ensure you have money to pay for any hidden damage that occurs after a tenant moves out. As noted, however, tenants want that money right away, and some resort to creative methods to get it.

L a n d l o r d ' s T a l e

Sally owned a three-bedroom house that she rented out to a minister. The man didn't have a great deal of money, but he had excellent credit, and his past history of renting was impeccable. He managed to raise the first month's rent and a cleaning deposit almost as large and moved in on a month-to-month tenancy.

After about seven months, the minister called to say things just hadn't worked out with his new church. He was giving three weeks' notice (almost a month) and would be out on the 1st. He would leave the place clean and wanted—and expected—his cleaning deposit returned on the day he moved out. Sally explained it would be mailed to him within 21 days. He replied, "We'll see."

On the appointed day, Sally was at the property to receive the key. She had decided to forget the fact that she had received only three weeks' notice instead of a full month and went through the property with the minister, conducting the "move-out walk-through inspection" (described in Chapter 16). The property was generally clean, although a few things needed attention; and either

(continued)

the minister said he would fix them immediately or Sally said she would get it done. They agreed to her keeping $35 from a $1,000 deposit. The minister then insisted on getting the remaining $965 at once. Sally balked, saying that she would send the money to him within 21 days, provided no other damage appeared. He said he would pay for any damage but she would have to report it to him, and then he would send her a check. He wanted his cleaning deposit—now. She politely refused.

At that point the minister led Sally outside to the large mobile home he had parked in the driveway that was filled with his belongings. He informed Sally that, God willing, the mobile home with him and his family living in it would move on the day she paid him his cleaning deposit . . . and not a moment sooner.

Sally considered. She could, of course, have taken the matter to court. The minister couldn't live in a mobile home in her driveway, and they both knew it. But suing would take time, probably more than three weeks; court would be costly and suing a minister was no slam dunk. In the meantime, it would be hard for Sally to rerent the property with the minister and his family living in the driveway.

She finally said she would give him half the deposit back now and half after two weeks. He was adamant. He wanted it all. Finally, Sally gave the minister a check and waved goodbye as he drove off. As it turned out, she rerented within a few days and there were no hidden problems.

We've just seen how a tenant creatively handled the matter of getting the cleaning deposit back when he wanted it. There is another technique that tenants use much more frequently, however, and that's using the deposit as the last month's rent.

When the Tenant Uses the Deposit as the Last Month's Rent

Today, many landlords don't use a lease demanding first and last month's rent but instead use a month-to-month rental agreement, getting the first month's rent up front plus a security deposit equal to one month's rent. The idea here, of course, is that you don't have to automatically pay back the deposit and can instead use it to pay for damages. The last month's rent can be applied only to rent.

Many, dare I say most, tenants, however, would be very pleased to consider that security deposit as the last month's rent. In fact, they may take steps to ensure that it is the last month's rent.

L *a n d l o r d ' s* **T** *a l e*

Hal rented a flat (one story of a three-story apartment building) to college students for a nine-month period, collecting the first month's rent plus a security deposit equal to one month's rent.

The last month was June, the end of the school year, and when Hal went to receive the rent, he was told by the precocious students that they wouldn't pay the last month's rent. Instead, he was free to use the security deposit for the rent. Of course, they said they would leave the flat spotless.

Hal didn't like this one bit as it meant that when they moved, he would have no deposit left to cover any lack of cleaning or damage they might have done. He told them he would have them evicted. But the students said that would take a month at the least and be expensive. Besides, they would be out in 30 days, so why bother? They said that any judge would probably feel the same way.

Hal said he would report them to a landlords association and a credit-reporting agency. They seemed surprised at his reaction and said he was being mean. But after talking it over, they said they were students anyhow, had no assets, and didn't care about their credit!

Hal reluctantly gave in. However, after the students moved, the place was a mess; Hal paid nearly $500 in out-of-pocket expenses to get the place in shape for the next tenants. What could Hal have done to have avoided this problem?

One way to avoid Hal's problem is to not charge a month's rent as the security deposit. If you charge exactly one month's rent, it's too convenient for the tenant to use it as the last month's payment. On the other hand, if you charge slightly less, it makes it harder for the tenant.

For example, let's say the rent is $1,000. Instead of charging $1,000 for the security deposit, why not charge $965? The $35 isn't going to make much difference to you. Yet the different amount makes a big psychological difference when it comes to trading the security deposit for the rent.

Another thing to do is stress big and bold in the rental agreement: "THIS DEPOSIT MAY NOT BE USED FOR THE LAST MONTH'S RENT." It gets the message across more clearly.

Yet another technique is to meet with tenants *two* months before their planned move and carefully explain to them the consequences of trying to use deposit as the last month's rent. One experienced property manager I know does this, carefully saying that if they tried to use the security deposit as the last month's rent, he would feel duty bound to report them to a credit-reporting agency, which could affect their future ability to rent or buy another property and even their ability to get future credit, including a credit card. When thus explained beforehand (instead of after the fact, as Hal did in our example), most tenants are less inclined to take rash action.

Finally, it's important to make it perfectly clear to tenants that you have their security deposit safely in hand and that you fully intend and want to return it to them, provided they meet their obligations. If they see you are honest and well intentioned, they are going to be less inclined to try to use pressure against you. Note: a *security* deposit can usually be applied to either back rent or cleaning. A *cleaning* deposit can only be used for cleaning and not for back rent.

Special Problems with Pets

Finally, there's the matter of the deposit for pets. My feeling, after having been burned many times, is that the deposit for pets should be very high indeed. As noted earlier, a single cat urinating on a carpet can destroy it, costing you thousands in replacement costs.

It's important to make clear to the tenant that you expect the pet to use the great outdoors for its bathroom or a special litter box for use inside. Any damage to the carpet or the house will come out of the cleaning deposit. As you add hundreds of dollars to the pet deposit, you can almost see the deportment of the animal improve.

Note: It's probably a good idea to separate the pet deposit from the cleaning/security deposit. That emphasizes your special concern.

L *a n d l o r d ' s* **T** *a l e*

Hal had a nice house that he rented to a family with two dogs. He got a big $1,000 pet deposit and felt quite secure.

Several months into the rental, the toilet backed up, flooding the apartment. The reason for the backup was a mystery. The tenant said the toilet had stuck and had kept on flushing, which was apparently true. The plumber said that he thought tree roots had gotten into the line, plugging it, and the additional water had then backed up. It was hard to blame the tenant for this. And in any event, Hal immediately had the carpets and padding taken out and sterilized—something that had to be done to avoid a health problem and potential landlord liability.

After the carpets were returned, the tenants complained the rugs smelled bad. Hal ignored them. At the end of their year, they moved out. When Hal inspected the property, he found that the dogs had urinated on the carpets, ruining them. He was furious and refused to return the deposit.

The tenants countered that the dogs had not urinated. Instead, Hal was smelling the remains of the sewer backup, about which they had complained. Eventually the tenants prevailed and Hal had to return their deposit. Moral? Even a big deposit is no guarantee!

Most states today require a landlord to do two things with regard to returning a cleaning deposit:

1. If you don't return the entire deposit, you must give the tenant a complete accounting of where the money was spent. *Note:* If you do the cleanup work yourself, you cannot pay yourself a salary or fee from the deposit (see below).
2. You must return the deposit or a portion of it along with the accounting within a maximum period, frequently 14 to 21 days.

Just following the guidelines, of course, doesn't mean that you're home free. If tenants disagree with your accounting, particularly the amount you have withheld, they can take you to court, usually small

L *a n d l o r d ' s*
H *i n t*

If a tenant leaves the place a mess and you hire someone to clean it up, generally speaking you can deduct the cost of the cleanup from the cleaning deposit. On the other hand, if you clean up the place yourself, you can deduct your cost of materials, but you probably cannot deduct a figure for the time you spent. Thus, it often pays to hire someone else to do the work.

claims court, and sue to recover all or part of their cleaning deposit. Because many courts these days tend to look with favor on tenants' complaints in these matters, it's now up to you to substantiate your claims for damage.

14

RENTAL AGREEMENTS THAT WORK

Get it in writing—never trust your memory; no one else will.

Most people would concede that the most important document in landlord-tenant relations is the rental agreement. After all, it spells out in writing just what that relationship actually is (subject, of course, to local, state, and federal laws). Armed with a strong rental agreement, you will have a much easier time dealing with your tenants. For one thing, they will know exactly what you expect. For another, if push comes to shove and you end up in small claims court, a good agreement will help you prevail.

Rental agreements are abundantly available. Call up almost any real estate agent, and he or she can provide you with one, often on a complimentary basis. It's part of the goodwill agents offer in the hope that eventually you will sell your property through them. A wide variety of companies publish rental agreements and sell them in stationery stores, in book stores that have real estate sections, and sometimes even through realty boards; some state departments of real estate also have suggested forms. Of course, you could always go to a lawyer and have one drawn up from scratch specifically for your own needs.

After you've looked at a lot of different rental agreements, you'll begin to see that they all contain about the same boilerplate as well as referring to the same sort of potential problems. Most property managers

The rental agreement discussed in this chapter and found at the back of the book works for me. But it may not work for you. Keep in mind that real estate rules and laws are different from state to state and even within local areas within states. As a result, just because a form works in one area doesn't mean it is appropriate everywhere. It may not be suitable for your area and may even contain clauses that are illegal or unenforceable in your state or locale. And the wording may not be acceptable to a court in your area.

Therefore, my suggestion is that you do *not* use any prepared forms, unless you first take them to your own attorney to have them adapted to your specific locale and usage. Yes, that might cost you a few bucks, but it could save you a lot of money down the road. And the cost will be spread out over the years that you're a landlord.

I know start with a published form and then add to it, adapting it to their own needs. This usually works very well for them.

Should You Rent Month-to-Month or Get a Lease?

The first thing you are going to discover is that there are two basic types of rental agreements. One involves month-to-month tenancy; the other is a lease. (Actually the two types technically used are oral and written, but these days a landlord would be a fool, in my opinion, to use anything but a written agreement.) There are proponents of both month-to-month rentals and leases. Keep in mind that the type you choose has important ramifications for your relationship with your tenants.

The basic difference between the two types of rental agreements is that month-to-month is for an indeterminate period. Once begun, the agreement typically continues in force until canceled, usually by a 30-day notice from either party. A lease, on the other hand, is for a very specific period, most commonly one year, although it could be for a longer or shorter period.

Most new landlords immediately seize on the lease as the best document to use. They reason that it ties up the tenant for a specific period, often a year as noted, so that the landlords presumably don't have to worry about rerenting the property. They anticipate signing the lease and then forgetting about it.

Unfortunately, that's not always the way it works out. With leases there can often be a big difference between the way things are supposed to work and the way they actually do work out.

What Are the Concerns with Leases?

A number of concerns about leases are often expressed by experienced property managers. These concerns usually lead them back to the month-to-month tenancy as preferable even if not wonderful. Let's look at some of these concerns.

Inability to Raise Rents

Not only does a lease lock in tenants for a specific period, but it also locks in the landlord. For example, if the market tightens during the lease period and you discover that rates of rentals similar to yours have increased $50 to $100, you can't increase your rates short of breaking the lease. The lease specifies not only the amount to be paid each month but the total amount to be paid over the life of the lease. You're locked in. This is of particular concern with longer-term leases—those of a year or more. (It is possible to include automatic bumps in the rent based on such things as the price index or the housing index in your area, but these are mainly devices used in commercial leases and usually impractical for a residential landlord.)

Further, if during the term of the lease you decide to sell the property, you can't kick the tenants out so the new owner can move in. The tenants have the rights to the property until at least the last day of the lease. In order to get them to agree to move out, you might have to offer some inducement, such as giving them an amount equal to six months' rent. You're the one locked in!

But, of course, new landlords point out that the tenants are locked in as well. Technically that's true, but for practical purposes, tenants are locked in only to the degree that they want to be.

Tenants Aren't Really Locked In

For example, let's say you have a two-year lease with a tenant for a house; after three months the tenant loses his job and can't find work. He may very well be able to break the lease on grounds that he no longer has access to the money he was anticipating having when the lease was made. He may be able to get out of the lease and, essentially, owe you nothing for the remainder.

Maybe the tenant entered the military service during the course of the lease. According to the Service Members Civil Relief Act passed in 2003, that tenant might be able to terminate the lease if it's covered by the act. (See Chapter 25 for details.)

Further, what if tenants don't have a good reason for breaking the lease but simply up and move out? What are you going to do then? Usually your only recourse is to sue for the rent, usually as it comes due. The problem is that the tenants may be hard to find. They may leave the city or even the state, and tracking them down can be costly. Moreover, even if you find them, they may be "judgment proof"—that is, they have no assets that you can easily attach.

Finally, you have a duty to mitigate damages, meaning you have a responsibility to try to rerent the property while you're out there trying to track down the tenants. This is not only a legal but a logical thing to do. After all, why leave the property vacant when it can be producing rent? The problem is that the money you receive in rent must normally be subtracted from the amount you can claim from the tenants who moved out.

In short, what usually happens with tenants who skip out on a lease is that the landlord quickly rerents the property and then turns the matter over to a collection agency with the hope that sometime in the future he or she may get some money back. As often as not, nothing comes in.

On the other hand, let's say that you want to break the lease and get the tenant out, but the tenant is unwilling. Your recourse may be to go to court. In a situation like that, you had better have an ironclad reason for wanting the tenant out and an attorney as good as Perry Mason.

By the way, you can sell your property even if you have a lease on it. If you sell a property with a lease on it, however, the new owner normally takes over subject to the lease—that is, the new owner inherits the old tenant and the old lease. The biggest problem here usually involves the cleaning/security deposit. The new owner is probably responsible for paying back the deposit when the tenant moves out (assuming the property is left clean). But the old owner may keep the money unless provision for it to be transferred over is specified as part of the sale. In fact, as noted in Chapter 13, handling the cleaning/security deposit money is one of the more important elements in the sale of a property with a lease on it.

A Lease May Preclude a Cleaning/Security Deposit

Finally, the practical reason that property managers cite the most for not wanting to use a lease is that it may preclude your ability to get a substantial cleaning/security deposit. The reasoning here is really quite simple.

In a lease the landlord typically asks for the first and last month's rent. Let's say you're renting a property for $1,000 a month. Double that (first and last month's rent), and the tenant now must come up with $2,000 in rent money before moving in. True, what you're asking is nothing more than paying the last month's rent first; when that last month rolls around, the tenant won't have to pay anything. But many tenants don't have lots of cash sitting around unused.

Add on top of this rent money a security deposit, which might be another $1,000 dollars or so, and move-in costs now rise to $3,000. In a tight rental market where loads of tenants are chasing a few properties, you might indeed have this situation. In a more normal market, however, where landlords are competing for a limited supply of tenants, you probably won't. Before coming up with all that money for you, a tenant is more likely to go to your competition who charges less.

As a result, many landlords who insist on a lease end up receiving a smaller security deposit or perhaps none at all. They may, for example, accept only a couple of hundred dollars as the deposit. The mistake that these landlords are making, in my opinion, is to think that the last month's rent is better than the security deposit. Remember, you can't apply the last month's rent to cleaning. You can apply it only to rent. But a security deposit usually can be applied either to rent or to cleaning. (See below for leases without the last month's rent and a larger deposit.)

L a n d l o r d ' s   T a l e

Sally purchased a mountain rental home and found tenants who were willing to rent it for $750 a month. The tenants, however, were quite savvy and insisted on a lease offering Sally first and last month's rent plus a $100 cleaning deposit. Sally was eager to rent as the property was located several hours by car from where she lived, and showing it was a real hassle. So she accepted the offer.

The tenants stayed for the entire lease period, 15 months, and never called once to complain about anything. Their rent was also paid promptly, and Sally thanked her lucky stars that she had been so fortunate, particularly because the rental was so far away from her home.

When she came to get the key from the tenants on the day they were to move out, she found they had already left and had trashed her mountain home. Apparently, they had used the property for a long series of orgies, during which the walls had suffered stains and holes, one toilet had been ripped from the floor and broken, a small fire had taken out part of the kitchen and roof, and the grounds had gone totally to weed.

Yes, Sally had the $100 deposit, which the tenants didn't even bother to claim, but they had done thousands of dollars of damage, most of which her insurance wouldn't cover. She lost another month and a half in rent getting the property habitable again.

There are three lessons here. The first is always get as big a cleaning/security deposit as possible. The second is to always check regularly on your rentals, even if you don't hear complaints from your tenants. And the third is never buy a rental far from home.

When a Lease Expires

One point that many landlords fail to realize is that in most states, when a lease expires—the time period runs out—the tenants don't automatically have to move. Rather, the tenancy converts to month-to-month and can stay that way indefinitely. To get the tenant out you must now give notice, usually 30 to 60 days. The same applies to the tenants when they want to leave.

Note: Most state laws governing notice in month-to-month tenancy specify 30 days as a minimum. But there is no actual maximum. Sometimes, if there's a need, I have agreed to 60 or even 90 days' notice. Tenants might insist on this, for example, if you're planning to sell the property. They want to be sure they have time to find a new property if you sell and ask them to leave.

Unnecessary to Collect the Last Month's Rent on a Lease

You don't have to insist on the last month's rent in a lease. It can be a lease in every way, including a start and end date and a listing of all money to be paid. It just doesn't have to specify a last month's rent paid up front. You still get the first month's rent and, usually, a larger cleaning deposit (which answers the problem noted earlier of a small deposit with a lease).

The advantage of a lease is that it is for a specific period. At least for its psychological advantage, tenants are made aware that they are expected to stick around for the lease's term, perhaps a year or more.

The downside is that in forgoing the last month's rent, you lose the only real leverage you have with the lease. If the tenant walks, there's no cushion of a month's rent to ease the blow.

The Problem with Asking for Attorney Fees

Historically, at least going back about 40 years, rental agreements tended to include a section mandating that if landlord and tenant went to court over enforcement or other provisions of the agreement, the loser would pay the winner's attorney fees. (Note: If the issue goes to small claims court, usually no attorneys are involved.)

I suspect the reason behind this clause was twofold. First, it put tenants on notice that filing frivolous lawsuits against their landlord was going to be costly. And second, it gave landlords at least the possibility of collecting the costs of their attorney fees after they won the suit.

But What If the Landlord Loses? Years ago it used to be a foregone conclusion that unless there were unusual circumstances, by the time a suit involving a tenancy got to court, the landlord would win. Not any longer. Today, as noted elsewhere, courts may actually favor tenants. Even if you feel you are 100 percent right, you have no guarantee that you are going to win. (Check out the movie *Pacific Heights,* on video tape, to get some idea of how bad things can go.)

Consider the consequences of losing:

- You're out your rent.
- You're out your attorney fees.
- You're probably out cleaning costs.
- And now you're going to have to pay the tenant's attorney fees!

As a result, many landlords today think twice before including a clause that the winner pays the loser's attorney fees. It's one of those apparently great ideas that could come back to haunt you.

Arbitration Clauses

Some landlords now insert binding arbitration clauses in their leases. If there is a dispute, both parties agree to take it before an arbitrator and agree to abide by the decision.

The trouble is that arbitrators who are specialists and belong to a national arbitration association often charge high fees. Thus, the cost of an arbitrator could be more than the amount in dispute. And getting both landlord and tenant to agree to some other third party as an arbitrator can be difficult.

Avoid Unenforceable Clauses

A rental agreement is a contract presumably binding on both parties. But even so, you cannot give up rights that you have under law by signing a contract. For example, you might want to have a clause in your rental agreement that precludes tenants from suing you for injuries they sustained while renting your property. The problem is that it's very hard to preclude tenants from suing you. They usually have the right to sue just as they have the right to free speech and the "quiet enjoyment" of your property during the rental period.

Including unenforceable clauses only confuses and clutters up your rental agreement. Besides, such clauses may give the other side more ammunition if push comes to shove and you end up in court.

Also, avoid a lot of legalese in your rental forms, even if you're a lawyer. Make it plain so it can be understood. You don't want your tenants to say they couldn't understand what they were signing.

Creating Your Own Rental Agreement

I have included my rental agreement at the end of this book. As I noted in the beginning, it's mine, not yours. Before you make it yours, have your attorney determine if it will work for you and adapt it to the laws in your area and your specific needs.

Also, keep in mind that your rental agreement should be considered a "work in progress." Existing laws and regulations are constantly changing with new ones always coming on the books. And the specific needs of your property are evolving and being discovered by you. What works today may not work tomorrow. You need to be prepared to alter this agreement to meet your needs in the future.

Hanging Your Hat on a Month-to-Month Tenancy

As already indicated, the most popular alternative to a lease is the month-to-month tenancy, which leaves both the landlord and the tenant free to pull the plug on proper notification. If you want tenants out, you simply give notice. On the other hand, if the tenants want out, they just give you notice and move. It's usually 30 to 60 days for either party.

The Revolving Door Tenancy

The biggest problem with a month-to-month tenancy is its very indeterminacy. Most landlords don't want tenants moving in and out as though through a revolving door. No matter how big a deposit or how clean the tenants leave the property, there's always going to be some cleanup work after each tenant that you will have to do yourself or pay for yourself.

Plus there's the time it takes to rerent—anywhere from a few days to a few weeks or a month or more when you lose rent.

A landlord who has one tenant who stays for a year is usually doing far better than a landlord who has three tenants who each stays for four months. Unless you're running a motel/hotel, the last thing you want are itinerant tenants.

Incentives to Stay

Hoping to persuade tenants to stay longer, several landlords I know build incentives into their month-to-month agreements. They ask for a somewhat lower cleaning/security deposit and, in addition, ask for a nonrefundable, one-time cleaning fee (where allowed by local and state statute); typically, this fee is about $125. Tenants pay it up front and realize it is not going to come back.

However, the landlord then tells tenants that for each month a tenant stays in the property, a portion of the fee will be refunded, perhaps $15 for each month. If a tenant stays for nine months, the tenant gets back the full $125.

No, it's not a huge amount of money. But it is something that sticks in tenants' minds. When they think about moving, they are reminded of the refund, and it might be just enough to keep them staying put.

15

MOVING TENANTS IN

The Walk-Through

You set the tone of the tenancy the day the tenant moves in.

You've found a tenant, checked out his or her qualifications, signed a rental agreement, and now the tenant is ready to move in. How are you going to deal with the tenant? What will your relationship be?

To do it right, you'll strive for a successful landlord-tenant relationship. To do it wrong, you'll set yourself up for more trouble than you can imagine.

Set the Date

Get an agreement between yourself and the tenants for the date of the move-in. For your convenience, it's usually best at the first of the month, but it can be any other day.

Once the date is agreed on, meet the tenants at the property. There has to be a time when you "officially" turn the property over to the tenants and it is usually set up as a combination event. You'll collect any money still owed, conduct a walk-through (described shortly), review the rules you have, go over any special concerns, and hand them an instruction sheet explaining when and where to pay the rent and how to handle moving out. You then hand them the keys, and when you turn over the keys, it's their rental.

This is a very important meeting because it sets the tone for the tenancy. Plan on setting aside an hour or more for this meeting, as you have many things to accomplish.

Get the Money First

As noted in Chapter 13, before a tenant moves in, you need to get the money for both the first (and last) month's rent plus all deposits. Preferably this will be in cash or some form of cash equivalent such as a cashier's check. Practically speaking, however, most tenants hand over a personal check. If you accept a personal check, run it over to their bank (at least this first time) to get it certified. This means that their bank certifies the funds are available and puts a hold on them—it pretty much guarantees the funds to you. This may take you a few minutes, but it's well worth the time.

Once you're satisfied that the money is in hand, you're ready to help the tenants move in. Keep in mind that how you handle the move-in sets the tone for the tenancy and will have repercussions later on when the tenants move out.

If tenants move anything onto the property (particularly if you loan them a key to do this), you have, for practical purposes, given them possession. And if for any reason you don't go through with renting to them (they don't come up with all the money; there is a problem with the walk-through; they decide to back out), you face the problem of getting their possessions out of the property. In the old days (again, a long time ago), you might have just taken their stuff and dumped it outside. Not anymore. Now, you might actually have to evict them to get it out!

I'm very firm when it comes to moving anything in early. The answer is *no*. In most cases, tenants can find a friend or relative

> **H** *i n t*
>
> Never let tenants move in until you have the cash. After all, what if you take their personal check to their bank and find they don't have sufficient funds to cover the check and they're already in your property?

who can store their things. In the worst case, they can use a public storage facility.

About Locks and Keys

After you've finished the walk-through and you've both signed off on the inspection sheets, you need to give the tenants the keys to the property. It's a good idea to get a receipt for the keys, and it's also possible to incorporate this on the walk-through sheet. You can include a statement that the tenants have received X number of keys and have them sign (initial this).

A word of caution should be made here regarding door locks. As the landlord, you have the responsibility for providing a property that can be properly secured. That means a reasonably safe door lock; and most such locks that you buy will fit this need. (*Note:* For added safety you may also want to include both a boltlock, particularly in rental units located in high-crime areas, and a peephole in the door to see who's on the other side without opening it.)

One problem, however, arises if you indeed have a good lock system but then hand over the keys to a new tenant without changing the locks. It's conceivable that the previous tenant could have made additional keys and retained them unknown to you. He or she could now use it to easily get back into the property during the occupancy by the new tenants, perhaps to rob them or do something worse.

Because it costs a fair amount of money to put all new locks in a property, one solution is to remove all of the locks and take them to a locksmith, who, for a relatively small amount of money, can not only rekey them but make sure one key fits both front and back. This only works, however, if you have good-quality locks to begin with. Cheap locks often can't be easily rekeyed.

I know one property manager who tries to save money by having tenants sign a statement that they will not make additional keys. In addition, on each key he gives them he has stamped "Do not duplicate." He claims

L *a n d l o r d ' s* T *a l e*

This story is so bizarre that it's almost unbelievable. But I swear it's true.

When I first started in real estate (too long ago to think about), I had a property manager friend whose job was overseeing a large apartment development with hundreds of units. She received rents, took in deposits, and, in the course of business, handed out keys to tenants. The owner had provided her with an elaborate set of keys, several for each unit, and she took great pains to be sure that each renter received the correct key.

One day when I had brought in a couple who wanted to rent a unit, a tenant came in to complain that his neighbor had gotten into his apartment and, he said, stolen some items. Naturally, my property manager friend was quite upset and went to investigate. I went along too.

It turned out that the owner of the building had not bothered to have each lock separately keyed. Instead, there was only one master key, which opened all of the units. My friend had unknowingly handed out the master to each tenant! There had been no problem until one unscrupulous tenant had discovered the fact and taken advantage of it.

My friend immediately confronted the owner and demanded an explanation. The owner laughed and said it had worked fine until someone had discovered what he had done. "As long as nobody knows," he said, "what's the difference?!"

Needless to say, all the locks were rekeyed and the owner had to make good on the items taken. But that such a thing could happen is almost unbelievable. (Think of the landlord's liability if one tenant had accosted another as a result of this!) The moral, of course, is don't let your tenants find out the hard way that you haven't rekeyed the locks. Do it automatically every time you get a new tenant. (In some locales, rekeying is now a legally mandatory requirement.)

that he's never had a problem with this system. To me, however, it seems chancy. The safer way is to change the locks.

Inform tenants about the rekeying. When I hand over the keys, I always make it a point to note that the locks have all been rekeyed. I then hand the tenants a copy of my receipt from the locksmith to show that the work was done. The tenants frequently say that it's OK and don't need the receipt, but I insist they look at it. It establishes my credibility and demonstrates my concern for their security. I also have them sign a receipt for the keys.

What to Give and Tell New Tenants

When new tenants move in, I always give them a welcoming tour that includes a couple of "presents" and saves me a lot of headaches down the road.

Renters Insurance

During the move-in tour, I explain a few things, one being renter's (or tenant's) insurance. I tell the tenants that although I carry fire and liability insurance, my insurance would not cover their furniture if the building were to burn down or otherwise be destroyed. Therefore, I advise them to purchase their own renters insurance. I even keep a couple of insurance agents' cards handy that I pass out to them.

Plumber's Helper

Usually under the sink in one of the bathrooms, I indicate that I've given them a "plumber's helper"—a plunger that can be used to unplug a toilet. I then proceed to show them how to use it.

A plumber's helper is almost a necessity in any home because toilets become plugged for a variety of reasons. To use the plunger, you just fill the toilet with water and plunge away, being careful not to slosh water out of the bowl. A tenant who has, and uses, a plumber's helper can save you the cost of a trip to the property by a plumber. (I also point out that the cost of unplugging clogged plumbing is borne by me if the problem is damaged pipes or roots in the drain system but by the tenants if it's caused by something—toys, sanitary napkins, hair brushes, or whatever—they've dropped down the drain.)

W *arning*

There could be some liability in providing the wrench and plumber's helper. Tenants could conceivably injure themselves when attempting to fix the problem. If you're worried about this, then don't provide the tools. Instead, bite the bullet and pay to have repair work done (or do it yourself).

Allen Wrench

I also provide them with an Allen wrench that fits the garbage disposer, assuming the rental unit has one. The Allen wrench goes underneath and allows you to manually turn the garbage disposer, thus clearing it when it's clogged. I show the tenant how to put the wrench in and turn. A tenant who's good with an Allen wrench can save me lots of trips to the property.

Don't worry about the cost of the plumber's helper and the Allen wrench. Between them they are far less than $5 and well worth the expense.

How to Work the Appliances

I also go through and carefully explain how to use the various appliances. If the stove has a timer oven (many do), I explain how to use it. I show them how to work the dishwasher and how to set the temperature if the unit has a refrigerator. Don't assume that tenants automatically know how to work all the appliances. Even if they know how to operate one brand of dishwasher, for example, they may not know how to work the brand in your unit.

How to Operate the Sprinklers

If the rental unit has lawn sprinklers that are electrically controlled, I show them where the box is and explain that the sprinklers are set to water on certain days and hours. I ask them what hours they would prefer to have the sprinklers come on and then set them. I then ask the tenants not to change the watering settings without calling me first. There are two reasons for this: First, it's often difficult to set the timers for electric sprinklers, and tenants may inadvertently set them too often, too sel-

Sally rented a 15-year-old home to a couple without explaining the use of the appliances. Later that year, during Thanksgiving, she got an emergency call from them saying that the electric oven was broken; their Thanksgiving turkey was inside the oven, and it had no heat.

Sally sympathized with them and let them cook their bird in her own oven. The next day she sent an electrician to fix the problem. The electrician reported back, however, that there was no problem. The tenants had inadvertently set the timer on the oven; and with it activated, the oven wouldn't go on until the designated hour, which happened to be at two in the morning. The only correction needed was to turn the timer off. The electrician showed the tenants how to do that; they were mortified but pleased. He also sent Sally a bill for $85.

This true story was one of those situations in which Sally was at fault. She hadn't shown the tenants how to use the equipment. If she had, she would have saved herself a lot of trouble and money.

dom, or for the wrong times; second, if the tenants are paying for the water, there's a tendency for them to set the timers back so the lawns don't get enough water.

Where Are the "Turn-offs"?

It's also a good idea to walk around the property and show the tenants how to turn off the water, gas, and electricity. This is particularly important if your property is on the West Coast in earthquake country. After a severe earthquake, quickly turning off the gas, in particular, can save your property from being burned down. However, it's important to inform tenants that once the gas has been turned off, it must not be turned on again until the gas company comes by to do it. Turning off the gas turns off pilot flames in appliances that must be individually lit once the gas is turned back on.

Where Are the Smoke Alarms?

I also show tenants exactly where the smoke alarms are located and test each one to demonstrate it's working. I point out the location of the fire extinguisher(s) and any other special feature the unit may have, such as sprinklers in case of fire or a security alarm system. I also have tenants sign a statement that they've inspected the smoke alarms/fire extinguisher and they are in operating condition.

How to Turn On the Utilities and Locate Other Services

It's a good idea to walk tenants to the area where garbage is kept (if it's an apartment building) and explain about not overfilling dumpsters. For a single-family unit, explain what day garbage is collected and where the tenants are expected to place their cans. Also, tell them how many cans are allowed and if recyclables are to be separated.

I also provide a list I've drawn up that shows the phone number of all the utility companies. (These days it's often found in the front of the local phone book.) That makes it a lot easier for the tenants to get the utilities turned on. The list also provides other service information, most of which is readily available in the phone book, but presenting it to the tenant on a sheet they can keep handy is useful to them and makes a good impression.

Wishing the New Tenants Well

Finally, I wish the new tenants well and leave. But that's not the end of it.

Over the next few days the tenants are usually going to be working hard moving in. I try to stop back to see how they're doing and bring them a basket of fruit as a housewarming present. No, it's hardly necessary. But I once read that when you do more than people expect, you get results beyond those you anticipate—this is the extra bit that makes the difference.

A good landlord continues to maintain a business relationship with tenants, which doesn't mean letting the tenants become your best friends.

Rather, I mean such things as sending a card at the holidays, calling or stopping by every month or two to see how things are going, and asking if there's anything the landlord can do to make the place better. Most landlords never come by as long as tenants don't call to complain. That's usually a mistake on two counts. The first is that the only time tenants see such landlords is when they're complaining, and that sours the relationship. Second, by stopping by early, you can many times nip problems in the bud and avoid bigger costs down the road.

The Walk-Through Inspection

What can you do to protect the deposit and ensure that you will be able to deduct appropriate expenses when a tenant later moves out?

Probably the best thing you can do to avoid big arguments and possible lawsuits when the tenant moves out is to document *before* and *after*. You need to show how the property looked *before* the tenant moved in and then how it looked *after* the tenant moved out.

Arguments can grow over the cost of certain repairs, but the most common area of disagreement is what the property looked like before. Usually the landlord says the unit was in perfect shape, whereas the tenant claims it was a mess to begin with. Who's right? Keep in mind that today many courts tend to favor tenants' claims over those of landlords.

Film and Video Documentation

Some landlords, burned by tenants who argued successfully that the rental unit was in bad shape when they moved in, have taken to recording the initial condition of the property with a camera and/or a camcorder. The idea is that before renting, you walk through the property while visually preparing a record of the condition of the floors, walls, appliances, and so on. Thus, when a tenant moves out and claims the property wasn't clean or newly painted or whatever, you have a visual record to prove otherwise.

Certain problems, however, are inherent in a visual record. First, there's the cost. To document every room using a film camera would require many rolls as well as careful photography, including a special close-up lens. Second, as those who are sophisticated in the field know, you can make any wall, for example, look either clean or full of scratches just by how you illuminate it. Thus, you need to have good, neutral lighting and expensive equipment. And third, through the use of sophisticated computer enhancements, any digital photograph can be changed (using programs such as Adobe Photoshop); a broken countertop, in short, can be made whole again—on film.

Taking "before" pictures therefore can be a hassle and unreliable. Further, because you don't know where damage may occur, you would have to photograph everything in detail to be sure that you have a clean "before" picture—a daunting task. (This is not to say that taking "after" pictures of damage is not worthwhile. Pictures clearly showing damage can help your case immensely after a tenant moves out, and there's a dispute.)

Camcorders do a better job than stills because they are more realistic. You can easily pan across a floor and wall and in a few moments capture almost everything. Video can be manipulated just as film can, but it's more difficult and more expensive to do because there are 30 frames per second to be manipulated.

The only real trouble with video is the inconvenience of playback. You need a playback VCR (the camcorder itself will do) and a TV set. Setting these up in a small claims courtroom can be a hassle. (I do know landlords who shoot VHS video and then bring a small VCR/TV combo right with them to court to show a small claims judge just what damage a tenant did.) Of course, you have to "index" the tape so you can move to just the images you want to show. Most judges aren't pleased to wait while you search through an hour of video for the right scene.

With any kind of visual record, tenants can always dispute the time when you shot the original, saying the condition wasn't that way when they moved in. They can claim your "before" video was shot years ago when the rental was new, but it was already damaged and dirty when they moved in.

One landlord I know attempts to solve this problem by having an independent person, such as a neighbor, walk through the video while saying the date and time. (I've heard it said that you can tape or photograph the tenants themselves, capturing them in the picture to definitely prove when the film or tape was taken. I find that impossible as a practical matter. You certainly can't get them in every shot and having them walk around backing up to walls, carpets, and the like is not just a *little* demeaning—no good tenant would put up with it for a minute!)

In short, visual records can be helpful, but in my experience their aid is more as secondary support for what you've otherwise demonstrated to be the case, particularly with damage after the move-out.

If a visual record doesn't work, how then do you demonstrate the condition of the rental before the tenants moved in? What's worked for me and a lot of property managers over the years is a *walk-through inspection sheet*, which goes a long way toward substantiating the true condition of the rental. (Check out the inspection sheet at the end of the book.)

What Are Walk-Through Inspection Sheets?

I have a friend, a property manager for more than 20 years, who swears by walk-through sheets. She says that she has been called to court by tenants on a number of occasions, and these sheets have always resulted in her winning.

What's so impressive about walk-through sheets? It's the fact that they are written documentation signed by both you as the landlord and the tenants. It's very hard for tenants to say later that a wall was marked or a stove was filthy when they have certified that both were clean and in good condition when they moved in.

The idea is that after you've approved the tenants and received the rent, but before handing over the keys and as a condition of renting, they must go with you through the property and at the same time fill out the sheets.

The tenants are made aware that the purpose of the walk-through inspection sheet is to document the condition of the property before taking possession, and it's to their advantage to note any problems. You'll almost never find a tenant unwilling, even uneager, to go through this process.

Go Room by Room

The walk-through sheets are for each room—one for each bedroom, bathroom, dining room, living room, hallway, kitchen, and other area.

There should be no area of the house left out, including closets. Further, the sheets note the condition of the walls, ceilings, floors, windows, screens, fixtures, appliances—in short, everything in the house.

And the sheets specifically state that each item is without damage and clean with no marks except as noted. There is a place to write where any dirt, marks, scratches, or damage can, and should be, noted. My property manager friend insists that tenants not only sign at the end of the list but initial each sheet as well and also initial such important items as the stove (a big area of contention over cleanliness), the sink, the refrigerator, and so on.

Conducting the Walk-Through

A whole psychology is involved in the walk-through. Remember, it's done *before* tenants move anything into the property, before taking possession. As a result, there isn't any pressure (as there is at move-out time) for the tenants to worry you're going to say they did anything. Rather, they are looking for faults, and you, as the landlord, often have to defend the condition of the property! (That's another reason to be sure that each time you rent a property, it's in tip-top shape.)

Further, there's usually an upbeat feeling of good cheer during the walk-through. After all, the tenants have nothing to worry about—they haven't moved in yet and can't be blamed for anything wrong. Further, because the tenancy is just starting, they naturally want to be on a good footing with you. Hence, at this time, before they move in, they are least likely to exaggerate a problem. After all, if they insist there's a big hole in the carpet and there's no hole there, you aren't going to be too likely to give them the key to move in.

On the other hand, most tenants will be scrupulously careful going over these sheets with you. They will carefully point out every mark, scratch, tear, and other dirty or damaged part of the rental unit. After all, they understand full well that anything that goes on this sheet will come back to haunt them when they move out.

Getting an Accurate Description

It is absolutely necessary that you use very *precise* language to describe any exceptions to "clean and undamaged" that you write down. For example, there may be a mark in a wall caused by the previous tenant having hit it with a dresser while moving out. If you write down "Back wall of bedroom is marked," you could be in for real trouble. When this tenant moves out, that wall could be covered from floor to ceiling with marks; when you protest, the tenant will point to the walk-through and say, "See, you wrote down that the wall was marked!"

My property manager friend always puts down something specific, such as, "Small single mark on back wall approximately two inches long by half an inch wide." That pretty much limits the claim that the whole wall was marked.

Don't Forget Safety Features

Almost every area of the country today requires that a rental be equipped with smoke detectors and other safety features, such as fire extinguishers and carbon monoxide detectors. A move-in walk-through sheet is an excellent place to note not only that your rental unit has a smoke detector, but that it is in working condition. Have tenants sign (or initial) that they've seen the smoke detector and tested it themselves.

Some locations also require fire extinguishers. Be sure tenants sign that they have noted the location of the extinguisher and that it is full and in working condition.

Special Attention Items

Watch out for any black mold or pest infestation, including spiders and cockroaches. If any are found, be sure you take care of them immediately. These are health issues, and you don't want to be liable for your tenants getting ill.

Working with the Tenant

There are, of course, bound to be areas of dispute, one of the most common being carpeting. Tenants will say that the carpeting looks old and worn. You may reply that it's nearly new and fresh. How do you come up with a description that you can both live with?

One answer that my property manager friend has is to list the age of the carpet, as evidenced by her bill of sale, and the last time it was cleaned, as evidenced by her invoice from the carpet cleaning company. It's hard for tenants to argue with these two items. Then any specific damage or wear, such as cigarette burns or stains, can be noted as to size and location.

Try using the walk-through inspection sheet. It takes a little extra time, but it can be well worth it later on.

16

MOVING TENANTS OUT

Returning Deposits

*Planning early is the best guarantee of a fair
and friendly move-out.*

You should never think of tenants
as permanent. All tenants leave, sooner or later. Therefore, the goal of
a good landlord is to make that eventual move-out as painless and as cost
free (to you) as possible. And that means taking active steps to ensure
that things go smoothly.

Good property managers know that the time to get started preparing
for the time when the tenant moves out is on the day the tenant moves
in. Many good managers on move-in day hand the new tenants a printed
sheet explaining just what's expected of them, including the procedure
for moving out. It includes such things as giving notice and leaving the
place clean. Don't think that all tenants automatically know how they are
supposed to conduct themselves when they move out. Many are completely in the dark unless you tell them. (See the end of this book for a
tenant move-out instruction sheet.)

A move-out instruction sheet covers a number of areas that are important to tenants and vital to you. Let's consider each in turn:

Giving Proper Notice

Assuming you're renting out on a month-to-month basis, you're going to expect to give or receive 30 days' notice (or whatever you've agreed on) from tenants before they move out. (In some states, such as California, landlords may be required to give 60 days' notice if a tenant has rented for a year or more.) But just what constitutes notice? I once had tenants who included a note with a rent payment saying "We will be moving soon." A month later, they came by to drop off the key. When I asked what was up, they said they had given me written notice of their intention to move.

Inform tenants that you expect them to let you know the exact date when they intend to move out. For practical purposes, in most cases this will be in the form of a phone call. Ideally, however, they will send you a written note. And presumably their notice will be sent at least 30 days (or whatever you've agreed on) before they move.

You should also indicate that you want the notice given within 30 days of the next rent payment so that the tenants understand they are going to need to move on the first (presumably when the rent is due), not sometime in the middle of the following month. (Some states do allow notice to be given at any time—check in your area.)

H *i n t*

Notice by tenants is normally given 30 or 60 days from the day the rent is due.

L *a n d l o r d ' s* **H** *i n t*

If a tenant must move other than on the rental date, you can, of course, agree. However, I would insist on the rent's being paid until the first. If this is a tenant who's given you trouble, of course you may be happy to see him or her go and may be willing to compromise by splitting the difference.

When they let you know they're going to move. As soon as you get wind of the fact that your tenants are going to move, it's a good idea to send them another one of the move-out instruction sheets noted above. They may have lost the original, so another sheet acts as a reminder.

A good idea is to include a tear-off at the bottom of the move-out instruction sheet that specifies when they will move out and that they can send back to you. If you are asking the tenants to move, be sure you get a signed statement from them indicating the move-out date agreed on. (Some landlords have an actual Notice of Intent to Vacate form they use in which tenants are required to specify the exact date as well as any other conditions of the move-out.)

What Moving Out Really Means

It means that tenants will have *all* of their possessions out of the house and the garage. Everything will be gone. There won't be clothes left hanging in a closet, boxes in the bedroom, cooking utensils in the kitchen. Everything out means just that. Emphasize that you can't consider them out until they are fully out and have returned their possession of everything in the rental back to you. (Anything they leave after that is presumably garbage, which you will dispose of and bill them for the actual costs.) Letting them know that you will require them to pay rent until everything is out helps ensure compliance.

How and When Deposits Will Be Returned

Having a procedure and letting the tenants know what it is up front avoids confusion and unhappiness at the end. Let tenants know you expect the property to be left in the same condition in which it was found, except for normal wear and tear, and explain exactly what you mean.

Let them know that you will deduct from their deposits your costs for repairing damage that they did. If you have a pet deposit, indicate that you'll deduct from this any damage the pet may have done. Indicate that any repair work will be done at the current market rate by professionals in the field, not by you. (If you do repair work yourself, many tenants assume your time is free and won't expect to be charged for it. Indeed, it may be illegal in your state or area for you to charge for your time spent on repair work on your own property.)

Also let tenants know that they will receive the deposit money back within 21 days (or as specified by the laws in your state) along with a complete accounting. This is a good place to put a notice in big type that the cleaning/security deposit may not be used as the last month's rent.

Keys Are to Be Returned

At some point tenants return possession of the property to you. This is normally done after they have removed all of their personal property. Returning possession of the property to you is evidenced by their returning the keys.

Be sure you let them know that you want *all* the keys returned. Even though you change the locks, you don't want someone out there who even thinks he or she can still get back in.

They Must Disconnect Utilities and Phone

Normally, the landlord has the utilities turned on for "cleanup and showing" on the same date as the tenants move out. Point out that if they move later than the appointed date, they'll also be charged a prorated cost for any utilities they use.

Letter of Recommendation

If your tenants were good ones who always paid on time and never caused a problem, I also usually call and ask them if they would like a letter of recommendation for their next landlord? Most tenants are astounded at this offer and, of course, happily accept.

I have no problem recommending a good tenant to someone else. Further, giving a letter of recommendation often puts tenants in such a friendly state of mind that they do an extra good job of cleaning up the property just to live up to what I've said about them! (Check the back of this book for a typical recommendation letter.)

Note that if tenants move out in order to purchase a property, their new mortgage lender will almost certainly request a formal letter (sent to you by the mortgage company) asking for specifics about the tenants. Giving a copy to the tenants showing how you recommended them accomplishes the same thing as the separate letter noted above.

Confirm Moving Dates

A good landlord quickly learns not to leave anything to guesswork or chance. The tenants have said they would be out by August 1. Great, it's the middle of July, so call them to confirm the date. Also confirm that they received the move-out instructions. And reconfirm that they understand what's required to get the cleaning/security deposit back.

No, it shouldn't be necessary for you to go this extra step. But if you don't, there will come a time when you think they're moving out on one day and they'll be moving out on another. Think of it as another case of whatever can go wrong, will. Think of it anyway you like. Only reconfirm by phone.

When it gets closer to the actual move-out date, say a few days before, call again. Arrange a time for the tenants to meet you in the rental to go through the move-out walk-through described earlier. Also, emphasize that at that time they will need to have all of their personal property out of the house and will need to return the keys.

L *a n d l o r d ' s* **T** *a l e*

Hal had a rental on the other side of town. It was a good property that rented easily, but he had to take the busy cross-town expressway to get to it; that was inconvenient, so he went there as rarely as possible.

One day his tenants called to let him know they'd be moving the next month, and he made a mental note of it. They called again a week before they were to move to let him know their move would be on a Sunday, and they'd be out by noon. He could come by at that time and check out the property and get the keys back. Hal again made a mental note of it, which he promptly forgot.

It was a week and a half later on a Wednesday that Hal thought about the rental, mainly because he hadn't received the rent. He then remembered the tenants had said they were moving on the previous Sunday. He called them but learned the phone was disconnected, so he drove there, much to his irritation, on the busy cross-town expressway.

(continued)

Hal found the front door open and the tenants gone. The flooring and carpeting were a mess because neighborhood kids had apparently wandered in with muddy shoes and tracked up. Other than that, however, the rental was clean and in good shape. The keys were on the counter along with a note saying the tenants had cleaned the apartment and waited for him that Sunday until two. They had called but had been unable to get through. When they had to leave, they locked the doors, left the keys on the counter, and a forwarding address for their deposit to be returned.

Hal promptly had the apartment cleaned and deducted the cost along with the three days until he picked up the keys. The tenants protested. They said they had made every effort to contact Hal and return the keys on the day they left. They claimed to have left the apartment spotless and the doors locked and had no idea how the neighborhood kids had gotten in. And they produced a copy of their letter to Hal that they had left on the counter.

Hal wanted to stonewall them but, on the advice of a property manager friend, decided to avoid a hassle when told he couldn't win. He returned all of their deposit. After all, the loss of three days and the extra cleaning were entirely due to his own lack of attention.

Meet with the Tenants at Move-Out Time

When you meet with the tenants on the appointed day for their departure, you should immediately check to see that they are completely out of the rental unit. Furniture, boxes, clothing, and the like left anywhere indicate that they are not out. You should point this out to them and indicate that you can't proceed until they have *all* of their possessions removed. If necessary, tell them you'll come by later, although you can emphasize that this will be an inconvenience to you. If it takes them another day to get their goods out, you can point out that you will have to deduct a day's rent from their deposit.

Assuming that they are completely out, you should ask them for the keys to the unit, making sure they return all sets. Once they have moved their personal property out and given you the keys, they have returned possession to you.

Now it's time to go over the walk-through inspection sheet with them. (You can do this before you receive the keys, of course, but I like to get the keys first as an indication they are finished with the cleaning.)

The Move-Out Walk-Through Inspection Sheet

This sheet is the same as the one you used for these tenants when they moved in—exactly the same one. Presumably you've kept it safely stored awaiting the day they move out.

The idea is that you bring it or a photocopy of it out, and then you go over it, room by room, with the tenants. Along the way you discover any damage that's more than normal wear and tear, and you and they account for it, indicating what damage will be deducted from their cleaning deposit.

When you're finished, you've agreed on damages, even if not exact amounts; everyone shakes hands, and you've successfully concluded the tenancy.

Not likely. That's the ideal scenario. In actual practice it's rarely simple. Let's consider what's more likely to happen.

Scenario 1: The Tenants Don't Show for the Move-Out Walk-Through Inspection

But it's to their advantage to show up, you point out. They can be right on hand to dispute any damage that you feel may have been done. They point to the inspection record and note that the damage was right there before they moved in.

True. In most cases tenants show up for the move-out walk-through inspection. But in some cases they won't. Maybe their schedule makes it impossible for them to be there. Maybe they left the place in such a mess that they're too embarrassed to show up. Or maybe they just can't handle the apparent confrontation involved in walking through with you.

In any event, it isn't necessary for the tenants to be there for the move-out walk-through inspection. Their not being there doesn't prevent you from conducting the inspection yourself; it only weakens the tenants' position should they dispute anything you say later on.

My own feeling is that if the tenants aren't there for the move-out walk-through inspection, I want to document anything I find. This can mean having a neutral third party, such as a neighbor, walk through with me and sign that what we found is indeed the way it was. Or it could also include taking photos or videos of damage. (Remember that in Chapter 15 I noted the problems with taking these beforehand, because it was difficult to photograph clean areas, as you wouldn't know where the damage would occur. Now, there's no problem. You can zero right in on the damage.)

Scenario 2: The Tenants Show Up and Walk Through with You, but Deny They Did Any of the Damage

This is what can happen: You walk into a bedroom and see crayon marks all over the walls. You point them out to the tenants and say they can't be washed off without ruining the paint. Instead, the walls will have to be thoroughly washed, then painted twice—once with a sealer to keep any remaining crayon marks from bleeding through and a second time for the actual painting.

The tenants look aghast and say that their kids couldn't possibly have done the damage. Maybe a little bit of it, but the walls were definitely marked before hand. Now you both turn to the sheet on this bedroom that the tenants initialed when they first moved in and look to see what's written there.

You hope it will say, "All walls clean and freshly painted—no marks or scratches of any kind." You point to this and what can the tenant argue about?

Instead, however, the sheet says, "Walls generally clean with a few marks and scratches."

"Aha!" The tenants say, "See, we told you. It was marked up before we moved in."

Once again this points out the importance of being extremely careful and precise when you fill out these walk-through sheets. Remember my telling you to list each mark by size, shape, and location?

You are going to be hard-pressed to keep any of the tenants' cleaning/ security deposit if your own sheets note there were marks and scratches on the walls before they moved in. On the other hand, you're going to be in an excellent position to use the deposit to clean up the damage if your sheets indicate no marks or scratches were there beforehand.

Scenario 3: The Tenants Agree They Did the Damage but Now Want to Correct It Themselves

If you did your move-in walk-through sheet correctly, there really won't be much to dispute about who did the damage to your rental. There will be the tenants' own signatures and initials on a written document saying there were no marks, scratches, and so on when they moved in. And now here's the damage. Yes, they can still always deny it, but anyone based in reality is going to see that theirs is a losing cause.

> **H** *i n t*
>
> Always paint and clean your rental thoroughly before tenants move in. That way you'll be able to give the rental a clean bill of health on the move-in walk-through inspection sheet, which will provide you with the evidence you need to collect for damages when you conduct the move-out walk-through inspection.

So now the tenants may say something such as, "Yes, we didn't realize how marked up those walls really were. We're surprised but would like the opportunity to correct it ourselves."

Letting tenants who did the damage correct it after they move out is like giving an award to the people who help put out the fire in your barn after they set it. Here we have a trap that is very difficult to avoid. The tenants have already moved out and, presumably, given you the keys. Now, the tenants want the opportunity to go back and clean up or repair damage that you both agree they did.

You may argue that they should have corrected the damage before they moved. However, if the tenants now get angry and eventually sue you, they can argue they offered to fix the damage once it was revealed to them, but you didn't give them the opportunity to do so. Not giving them the opportunity to correct a problem, once it's revealed, could mean you'd lose.

You're in a sort of lose-lose situation. If you don't give them the opportunity to repair/clean up, it could come back to haunt you. But if you do give them the opportunity, it could be even worse.

When the tenant "corrects" the problem. In our example, there were crayon marks on the walls; the problem is that the grease in crayons bleeds through most paints. The easiest way to handle this, as noted earlier, is to wash, seal, and repaint.

However, a tenant who's already vacated the premises isn't likely to want to take the time to go through the various steps, which can take a couple of days. When this situation once happened to me and I let the tenant attempt the cleanup, she used a heavy industrial cleaner on the walls and rubbed hard to remove the crayon marks. Not the easiest way to go but very thorough. Too thorough.

She did remove the marks, but she also removed the paint and some of the plaster where she had rubbed. Now, instead of crayon marks, there were paintless areas and gouges in the plaster that stood out distinctly from the other areas of the wall. It would require not only painting but replastering and retexturing to correct. The price was going up. The tenant, however, proudly pointed to the area on reinspection and dared me to find any crayon marks on the wall!

In a situation where tenants want time to correct a problem, I try to point out the obvious: Attempting to correct a problem may only make it worse. Further, I need to get in quickly to clean up so that the rental can be shown and rerented. If the tenants want time to do further cleanup, then I'll just have to assume that they have possession during that time and deduct daily rent while they're cleaning.

When I point out the problems involved and the timing concerns, frequently the tenants back off from their desire to repair the damages themselves. I've found that most tenants who do damage aren't really that anxious to spend a lot of physical effort correcting the problem.

Disputes over Price

Matters may now evolve to a question of how much it will cost to have the work done. As I mentioned, I no longer do the work myself, so we're talking in this example about having someone come in, wash the wall, seal it, and then repaint. How much for that?

I have a handyman who can do that for around $75 per wall plus the cost of the materials. I give that figure to the tenants, who may acquiesce, figuring it's worth it just to avoid any hassle.

This, however, brings up a point that's in dispute among property managers. Some managers prepare a pricing chart, an actual list of prices for various services they may perform on a rental. There's a price for cleaning a clogged drain and one for repainting a wall with crayon marks on it. There's a price for fixing a broken window and one for removing a stain from the carpet. In short, there's a price listed for almost everything.

When there's a dispute over the cost of a repair, the landlord brings out the list, points down to price for repainting a wall with crayon marks and says, "That's $95 including materials." There it is in black and white— so clear cut and easy. Many managers even make their pricing list available to tenants when they first move in and again when they give notice they are moving out so that there won't be any confusion over costs.

A list is indeed neat and clean, and I have no argument with those who use it. But I don't like it myself for two reasons. First, prices change— and change often—which means I would have to be constantly updating my list. I'm simply not sufficiently well organized to be doing that all the time for a variety of costs. Besides, I find that much of the work is done by handypeople, and they change frequently, and each tends to charge differently.

Second, lists tend to be overly restricting. By that I mean that the problem may not fit the list's description or the price given. For example, a drain's clogged; how much does your list show is the charge for that? It all depends, of course, on exactly what the problem is. It could cost only $55 to have the rooter service person come out and run a "snake" through the lines. Or it could cost $700 to dig up a blockage caused by having a steel rod flushed down the line until it wedged at an elbow joint. (This latter happened to me when I rented to a mechanic who worked in a body and fender shop; his child somehow got one of his tools into the drain system.)

After a while, you get a pretty good idea of what services cost so you can give an estimate to tenants right on the spot. If, on the other hand, the tenants don't like your price or you're not sure of the cost, you can say, "I'll have someone come in to look at it immediately, and he'll tell me the cost. I'll get back to you on that."

Admittedly, this latter isn't the best of all possible solutions as it takes time. But it does have the advantage of your ending up with a truly accurate price. And, quite frankly, by the next day the tenant is even less inclined to dispute the pricing.

The Value of Having the Tenant Walk Through with You

As difficult as it can be at times, having the tenant go through the move-out walk-through inspection with you has one enormous benefit: you usually end up with an agreement at the end.

The tenant's being there forces you to be fair in your estimates (not that you wouldn't anyhow, of course). Your being there forces the tenant to see things from your perspective and to acknowledge that some damage may have actually been done.

In short, the tenant is more likely to accept deductions from the cleaning/security deposit after the walk-through. And, in my opinion, the tenant is far less likely to feel angry and get into a dispute with you that ends up in court. In other words, even though at times it can be hard on the blood pressure, walking through with the tenant can end up being the most amicable way of ending a tenancy, especially one in which there are going to be deductions from the tenant's deposit.

When to Return the Deposit

As noted earlier, give the deposit money back promptly in accordance with the laws of your state. But hang on to it long enough to uncover any hidden damage that may have occurred.

I have, on occasion, given back a portion (as much as half) of the deposit right on the spot at the time the tenant moved out if, after going through the move-out walk-through inspection, nothing obvious appeared. Yes, I realize this is not a good property management practice because a large hidden cost could crop up later. But I do sympathize with tenants who worry about somebody else holding their money when they need it right away to move into another property. I also think I have a pretty good feeling for problems that are likely to occur. I haven't been burned yet by doing this, but there's no doubt I could get into trouble in the future. It's just what makes me feel comfortable being a landlord.

You, of course, have to make your own decisions.

17

KEEPING GOOD TENANTS

There's no downside to being fair.

Ask any landlord what makes for good tenants and you'll be told, "They pay their rent promptly!"

True enough. But what if that "good" tenant moves out after six months or complains all the time? The other elements that landlords often forget to mention is that the good tenant stays in the rental for year after year and doesn't complain a lot. Longevity and tolerance are likewise important.

A good tenant—one who pays on time, doesn't complain, and stays a long while—is like the goose who lays the golden eggs. You want to keep both the tenant and the goose happy. How to do that is the subject of this chapter.

Keep a Maintenance and Replacement Schedule

One of the biggest criticisms of landlords that good tenants have is that even though they pay their rents regularly, their landlord doesn't maintain their rental on a regular basis. After all, carpets wear out (particularly the inexpensive kind found in many rentals). Kitchen and bath floors become scratched and worn. Appliances not only break but simply become obsolete or worn out. "Why," the good tenant reasonably

Jimmy had an older apartment building with 24 units. He maintained a regular schedule of replacing carpeting and linoleum as well as repainting. Every five years he would go through a unit, replacing and repainting as needed. Of course, the new carpeting and flooring wasn't expensive, but it looked good. And the painting made the units look terrific. Jimmy did this regardless whether the tenants were new or existing ones.

As a result, he had one of the lowest turnover rates in the area. Indeed, some of his tenants had been in the building since it was new, nearly 20 years earlier!

Yes, he had the regular expense of maintenance. But he saved himself the much more costly expense of repeated tenant turnover.

asks, "will the landlord put new carpeting in for a brand-new tenant, when he won't do it for me, when I've been living here and paying rent regularly for years?!"

As a landlord, it's your responsibility to maintain and replace items that wear out, especially for good tenants. Just because a tenant doesn't complain, doesn't mean he or she isn't concerned or won't take action and move.

The only time many landlords replace or maintain such items as flooring and painting is when there's a tenant turnover. And, as a consequence, existing tenants become dissatisfied and move out, resulting in a lot of turnover. Indeed, by not taking care of the good tenants, you could increase both your turnover and your maintenance and replacement costs.

Maintain a Positive Environment

Another reason that good tenants want to stay a long time is that they like the environment. This usually means three things:

1. The common areas, such as walks, gardens, and parking spaces, are attractive. This requires employing a good gardener as well as paving necessary surfaces with blacktop on a regular basis.

2. There are no loud parties or noisy tenants. In some areas, this is unavoidable. But in others, it's something that landlords work hard to achieve. I know of one apartment complex with 360 units where strict noise restrictions are applied. In spite of the density, the landlord won't tolerate loud music or noisy parties, certainly after ten in the evening. As a result, this complex has a far lower vacancy rate than do competing units.

3. The property is maintained in a neat and clean manner. The landlord or a manager is around to sweep leaves, pick up and clean up debris, and to see that everything is always in order.

Keep the environment appealing, and the tenants will want to stay.

Deal with Problems Promptly

Then there's the matter of legitimate complaint calls. A good tenant calls up and says that the faucet in the bathroom is dripping and keeping him awake at night. What do you do?

Simple; get out there yourself (or hire a handyperson) the next day and fix it. You've got a good tenant. You don't want to lose him because of a leaking faucet.

Or a tenant calls up and says the garbage disposal is broken; only it's Saturday, and you can't get anyone out until Monday. What do you do?

You sympathize, say you're sorry, and explain that you can't have someone come out until after the weekend. Most tenants will be understanding. But suppose a good tenant, who rarely complains, says she's having dinner guests that night and can't use her sink! What now?

Get it fixed right away. Do it yourself or pay extra to have the handyperson do it. No,

H *i n t*

Many old-time landlords may take issue with the preceding recommendations. Their philosophy is the only things that tenants remember are what you do wrong, so why go out of your way for them? Having been in the business many years, I think that's too jaded a perspective. I've had far, far more good tenants than bad ones, and I firmly believe that a large part of that has to do with treating them as I would want to be treated.

I'm not recommending this on a regular basis. But tenants have crises too. And if it's not their fault and occurs very rarely, take care of it. They'll remember what you did (or didn't do) for them.

Be Friendly with Your Tenants but Not Too Friendly

On the other hand, it's possible to get too friendly with tenants. Although it's important to get to know your tenants so that if something goes awry, you'll know with whom you're dealing (it's a bit late to strike up a relationship when a tenant is fuming mad about something), you don't want to become their friend. A friendly tenant can turn into a pest.

Just as the tenants want to have the "quiet enjoyment" of your property, you as a landlord normally want to be isolated from the tenants' life and small problems. Except in unusual circumstances (such as when you rent to relatives—an act of pure self-punishment), you want to be friendly but not a friend of your tenants. You want to be able to drop by or call them up on the phone and hear a hearty "How're you doing!" on their end. But you don't want to see them every other day. The idea is that you want your tenants to respect you, not love you, and even more important, not bring you into their life.

L *a n d l o r d ' s* **T** *a l e*

Sally is a landlady who owns several houses. (She's also a real estate agent and should know better when it comes to dealing with tenants.) Not long ago Sally had a problem tenant. No, this tenant wasn't paying late or messing up the property—the tenant paid promptly and was extremely neat and clean.

Rather, this tenant was overly friendly. Sally had at first made a point of getting to know the tenant to the point where they exchanged recipes and occasionally chatted on the phone.

However, the tenant began calling Sally at all hours with trivial concerns. For example, the tenant called Sally at ten thirty one night to report a dripping faucet in the kitchen. That's certainly something that needs to get fixed, but it's not an emergency requiring fixing at night. Sally sent a handyman over the next day, and he took care of it.

Another night at eleven thirty, the tenant called Sally to say that a doorstop had fallen off, and the door handle was in danger of making a hole in the wall (a fairly common problem with rental property). Sally had the handyman go out a few days later. In the meantime, the tenant called twice more about the "problem."

In fact, hardly a week went by that the tenant didn't call once or twice with minor problems—from a broken screen to a sprinkler head aimed the wrong direction.

Needless to say, Sally was ready to kick the tenant out because of the intrusions into her life. Only the tenant always paid well, often in advance of the time the rent was due. And the tenant was always so friendly when she called, treating Sally like an old acquaintance asking for a small favor.

Eventually, the only way Sally could solve the problem was, at an additional cost, have a management firm take over the property. Then she changed her phone number!

The problem, of course, that Sally had stems from the fact that Sally initially struck up the wrong relationship with the tenant, a single woman apparently lonely and looking for friends. Sally, being gregarious (a requirement for real estate agents), naturally took the tenant under her wing; by the time the woman moved in, she considered Sally a kindred spirit. Sally, on the other hand, simply thought she was being friendly in an agent's sort of way.

At first, Sally responded to the frequent calls with her normal friendly demeanor, never realizing this was being misinterpreted by the tenant. Soon the one-way relationship was established that was driving Sally crazy. The costly way out for Sally was to get someone else to take over management of the property.

A Business Proposition

From the first, you must establish that although you may be a friendly person, the landlord-tenant relationship is basically a busi-

H *i n t*

Always be friendly with your tenants; never be their friend.

ness one. Yes, as a landlord you are available for handling problems that occur with the property—at normal business hours of eight to five or in the early evening if you work during the day. If a tenant calls late in the evening, it has to be a real emergency threatening the inhabitability of the property.

One landlord I know has cards printed with his name and address on them as well as his business hours. Because he works during the day, his business hours are from 6:00 PM to 9:00 PM. The phone line is just for rental calls, and he has an answering machine on it to take calls at other times. As he frequently checks in on the answering machine during the day and can monitor calls after 9:00 PM, he is able to keep up-to-date on any tenant requests or emergencies without having them intrude on his regular work or his personal life.

The Unreasonable Tenant

Sometimes, it's more than just keeping a good tenant happy. Sometimes, it's dealing with a tenant who pays on time but is simply unreasonable.

Unreasonable tenants may call at all hours of the day or night with problems that may or may not be legitimate complaints. For example, tenants may call complaining about the color of paint in the living room—it doesn't go with their furniture, and they want you to repaint.

Or the sliding screen door leading to the patio doesn't slide easily enough on its track. Yes, it works fine and doesn't come off the track, but it doesn't function as smoothly as the tenant would like. Or a closet door creaks when it is opened. Or the dishwasher isn't getting the dishes clean enough.

The list can go on and on, but you get the idea. The demands are in a gray area. They certainly aren't threatening the inhabitability of the property. They don't qualify as true problems requiring immediate repairs; they don't exactly require alterations—they require—sort of but not quite—improvements. In short, they are unreasonable.

Drawing a Line in the Sand

If you allow a good, but unreasonable, tenant to have his or her way, you'll spend the entire period of the tenancy (and probably a great deal of money) making changes to the property—changes that aren't really necessary from your perspective as a landlord.

What you need to do is make clear to such a tenant what you are willing to do . . . and what you're not willing to take on. You need to draw a line in the sand and indicate you won't step over it.

When I get the first such request from tenants who are paying rent on time—assuming the request isn't too costly—I usually go along and make the change or have the work done. However, while it is being done, I tell the tenants that this is not something I feel obligated to do but am just doing it because they're such good tenants. In the future, however, I won't do any more such work.

I might say something like this: "I'm greasing all of the door hinges (actually adding white graphite powder—grease or oil drips and stains) so they won't squeak. I'm doing this only once because you're such good tenants. However, door hinges in any house always tend to squeak. In the future you'll have to take care of this yourself. I'll always fix anything that breaks, such as a furnace or a leaking faucet. But squeaky door hinges or a sliding screen door that works OK but doesn't move quite as smoothly as you want or a dishwasher that operates properly but doesn't get dishes quite as clean as you'd like are not broken items. And I won't fix them. If you want a new screen door or a new dishwasher, I can arrange to have them put in, but you'll have to pay for them yourselves."

That usually ends the discussion. It also indicates what I'm willing to do and what I won't do. I've given the tenants my parameters. Even though some tenants may continue to "push the envelope" to see what more they can wring out of me, most quickly understand the situation and stop being demanding. For persistent complainers, doing one small job and sending them a bill for it, even if it's only $10 or so, quickly ends the demands.

Remember that if you lie down in the street, someone will walk on you. It's far better to be erect and let others know where you stand. Yes, once in a great while it might cost you a "good" tenant. But the rest of the time you'll sleep peacefully at night without pesty phone calls. Keeping good tenants happy doesn't mean acceding to their every wish.

REMOVING TENANTS

18

DEALING WITH TENANT DAMAGE

Never insist that a tenant follow your lifestyle or family standards.

There are two ingredients involved in getting tenants to take good care of your property. The first is *clarity*—you have to make absolutely sure that tenants are clear about what they are supposed to do. The second ingredient is *having reasonable expectations*—you must make absolutely sure that tenants can reasonably accomplish what you and they agree on.

When a Tenant Doesn't Maintain the Property

When a tenant doesn't keep the premises clean, mow the lawn, trim the trees, water the grounds, keep up the pool, and, in general, maintain the property the way you feel it should be maintained, your first job is to determine whether it's an unreasonable expectation on your part or an impossible task for the tenant. Making those two determinations often helps far more than do ranting and raving at the tenant for not doing the work.

At the time you sign the rental agreement with a tenant, it's not enough that you both agree who is to be responsible for which maintenance. It's also important that the agreement be reasonable and that the tenant be able to handle what you've both agreed to.

L a n d l o r d ' s   T a l e

Hal wrote into his leases that his tenants were to pay for all utilities including water. (Why should he pay for utilities that the tenants used?) In addition, on one enormous property in particular, he also emphasized that the tenants were to maintain the lawn and shrubs in the front and rear yards in good condition.

Hal rented the property during the early summer; he drove by a couple of months after the tenants moved in, only to see that the lawn was brown and thinning and the leaves falling off the shrubs. He stopped his car, jumped out, and ran to the door, startling the tenants by demanding to know why they were killing his lawn and shrubs.

They shrugged and said they had watered heavily the first month until they got a $145 water bill. Since then, they were watering only minimally. If Hal wanted to pay the water bill, they'd water as much as he wanted; otherwise, they couldn't afford more.

Hal ranted and raved and threatened to throw them out for violating their lease. A month and a half later they moved on their own, leaving a dead lawn and dying shrubs that made rerenting much more difficult.

Never ask tenants to take on more maintenance than they can handle—obvious in the case of lawn watering. Many landlords automatically pay for water to be sure that lawns and shrubs are adequately maintained, unfortunately sometimes leading to excessive use of water by tenants. Having a nice green front yard, however, can be essential to rerenting the property—and you can't grow a lawn overnight. (Yes, you can plant sod and new shrubs, but that really isn't cost effective.) Most landlords feel it's cheaper in the long run to pay the water bills than it is to run the risk of tenants allowing the greenery to die.

One exception is in drought areas, where there's a hefty monetary penalty for using too much water. There you may want to give the tenants a "water allowance." You might pay $30 or whatever of the water bill for each month that you come by and see that the yard is green.

When the Tenant's Messy

I've had tenants who kept the inside of the house or apartment so clean that the old expression "You could eat off the floor" was almost no exaggeration. And I've had a few tenants who made such a mess of the premises that you had trouble walking between rooms as you stepped over piles of debris.

Naturally, I, like you, would prefer the former tenant. But if you rent out long enough (and it won't take that long), you'll get the latter. What do you do about the messy tenant? Stop by your rental periodically and walk through. It doesn't have to be a formal appointment (although technically you do need to make an appointment to get in). Just drop by and ask how things are. Mention that there was an old leak in one of the sinks and you want to check to be sure it's fixed. Or you want to change the furnace filter. If you're on good terms with the tenant, you'll most certainly be asked in—and be able to look around.

Mess versus Damage

Some people are just not neat, and there's nothing you can do about that; for example, they may allow clothes to fall everywhere. (I once had a tenant who had a "clothes room," meaning all her clothes were dumped on the floor of one room, some clean, some dirty, some needing ironing—you get the idea. I swear that at times the clothes in that room were three-feet deep!)

That's not the way our family is run, and I don't think any family should be run that way. But I know it's also none of my business how other families are run. As long as there was no damage to the property (and there wasn't), I couldn't say anything, except weakly point out a possible fire hazard. It's important that you don't insist your tenants follow your lifestyle or your family's rules. You will only become ineffectual and frustrated.

Damage is quite different from mess. When property has been damaged, you must make it perfectly clear to tenants that they must correct the problem themselves, or you will correct it and charge them for it. In other words, the property must be returned to its original state.

L *a n d l o r d ' s*   T *a l e*

Sally was called by her tenants one day to say that their son had driven a baseball through one of two large plate glass windows in the back of the residence. They wanted it fixed immediately, as jagged pieces of glass were all over.

Sally immediately sent over a glazier, who took care of the window for $350, which she paid from the tenants' security deposit. She sent a bill for that amount, requesting the tenants to bring their security deposit back up to its full level. They were outraged at the price (it was safety glass) but agreed to pay.

The real story started a month later when Sally dropped by for a surprise visit. The tenants invited her in, and she immediately noticed that the *other* plate glass window was also broken. (Apparently their son was a strong, but not highly talented, baseball player.) However, they hadn't reported it. Instead, they had used several sheets of transparent tape to tape up the broken shards and thus hold the broken window together. They casually mentioned that it was a lot cheaper than replacing it.

Sally said it was a tremendous safety hazard and told them it had to be fixed. She also immediately sent them a note repeating what she had said. She gave them one week to correct the problem on their own, or she would hire someone to come in to fix the window and charge it to them.

They took care of the window. But they no longer invited her inside when she casually dropped by. So now she makes an appointment to stop by once every month or so. (Your rental agreement should contain a clause allowing you to enter and examine the property on giving tenants adequate notice, usually 24 hours.) In any event, there are no more broken windows.

The difference between damage that must be corrected immediately and damage that may be corrected over time has to do with safety and liability. Damage that poses a safety hazard must be corrected immediately.

Typical damages requiring immediate correction include:

- Broken glass
- Broken sinks, stoves, faucets, heaters, floor tiles
- Large holes in walls
- Broken walkways
- Any damage affecting the safety or security of the dwelling

Typical damages requiring correction but not immediately include:

- Paint or heavy crayon marks on walls, often caused by allowing children to run free with crayons or paints (Crayon marks, in particular, can be hard to remove as they often stain through wall paint. If you don't catch these marks quickly, they may occur on many more walls during the tenancy.)
- Animal urine or feces anywhere inside the property except in a special animal litter box and unless there is a health hazard
- Torn carpets (unless they present a hazard to walking), drapes, broken cabinet doors, and the like
- Normal wear and tear, including small holes to walls (particularly behind door knobs), dirty drapes, window coverings, sinks, or stoves, and the like

Maintenance Tasks You May Let Tenants Do

Several maintenance tasks that tenants usually expect to do and that landlords assign to them are discussed in the following sections.

Yard maintenance. When you are renting out a single-family house, a duplex (two units), or a triplex (three units), it is quite common to have the tenants take care of the yard, at least the sides and back. If a tenant balks at this, a good way of handling it is to offer to hire a gardener but add the cost to the monthly rent. (Some landlords ask a higher rent and then offer to negotiate lower if the tenant will agree to take care of the yard work. In this case, it is better to send the tenant a separate check each month than it is to simply settle on a lower rent payment.)

When you are renting smaller multiple units (small apartment buildings or, in some cases, duplexes, triplexes, or even fourplexes, where there are common areas), you may want to give one tenant an allowance for sweeping, cleaning, and, if the total areas are small, mowing and gardening. This avoids the problem of who is supposed to take care of what area. For bigger buildings, it is almost always advisable to hire a gardener.

Simple plumbing work. This is also sometimes taken care of by tenants who express willingness and have the ability. This work includes using a "plumber's helper" to unstop plugged toilets or drains, changing washers in faucets, cleaning heating filters, and so on. I have one tenant who is more than happy to do all of these things just so I won't bother to come around. This tenant loves his privacy.

Cleaning kitchens, baths, and floors. Tenants should maintain the property in a condition at least clean enough to avoid health hazards. Also, tenants who keep a place filthy aren't likely to leave it clean when they move out, and it may cost more than their cleaning deposit to put it back into shape.

Maintenance Tasks You Should Never Let Tenants Do

The list here is far longer and includes the following tasks.

Cleaning out plugged drain lines. This is the opposite of just "plunging" the sink or toilet when either is plugged. A long mechanical rooter device is required, and it's most easily handled by professionals.

Painting. What do you do when tenants call up to say they've been living in the property for three years now, and the bedrooms, living room, and dining room need to be repainted. The paint wasn't in wonderful condition (as you agree) when they moved in, and it's time to repaint.

They know that repainting is costly, so they have a plan. If you will pay for the paint, they will do the work. Of course, you'll have control over the colors they choose. The response to this seemingly fair request varies according to landlords and their experiences. Many landlords will acquiesce. I personally will not. The problem I have found is that most people are lousy painters. I include one of my sons and most of my relatives in this category.

The average person, in my experience, doesn't do a good job of covering the whole wall or ceiling evenly with paint. Most people leave streaks, drips, and bare spots on the trim. And they often accidentally get spray, drips, and puddles on the floor and carpeting. In short, to have the average person paint my property usually means not only will I have to have it repainted to get a good job, but I may also need to repair damage (such as paint on the carpet) along the way. Further, once I agree to let tenants do it, any repainting and repair costs are probably going to be out of my pocket.

At this point, I can hear other experienced landlords pooh-poohing what I've said. "Explain what you want. Show them how to paint. Tell the tenants that any damage to floors or carpets will come out of their deposit."

I've talked to many other landlords who have had perfectly good luck letting tenants do the painting. I have, too, on occasion. But I've rented out enough units to see tenant painting go bad and when it does, it's a mess. Besides, as noted, once you give your permission to let tenants paint, you'll get a big argument from them when you later try to charge them for clean-up.

If a property needs repainting, either I paint it myself or I hire a competent person (often a handyperson to do it). It usually doesn't take me long or cost me much, and I'm assured of the result.

If, however, you feel that you want to try saving money and decide to allow a tenant to paint, here's a suggestion: Buy the paint, rollers, and brushes yourself; and always buy the very best quality. The best goes on easier and covers better, improving your odds of getting a good job.

Washing walls. Walls get dirty over time. Washing them only makes the dirt stand out more. The reason is that you can't really wash a wall very effectively. Because you can wash only a portion of it—usually the lower half and then only sections—there will be visible dirt lines where the washed and unwashed areas meet. I always discourage tenants from washing walls. When they're dirty, they need to be repainted.

Major fixups. Even though tenants may have good intentions, they may not be competent to do a good job when fixing anything major that goes wrong—for example, a water heater, furnace, air conditioner, compactor, or garbage disposal. And if a tenant gets hurt doing work you authorize, your liability could be enormous.

Taking care of pools and spas. Tenants are often willing, but their expertise and stick-to-itiveness are weak. Pools and spas require at least weekly cleaning and chemical correction. Let them go even an extra week or two (particularly during the hot summer months), and damaging algae can grow quickly. Besides, necessary regular cleaning of filters can be hard, dirty work, something most tenants won't want to do. Either you or a pool service should take care of this.

Anything involving health or safety. Your liability here is simply too great to let anyone but a professional handle the task.

L *a n d l o r d ' s* **T** *a l e*

Our poor friend Hal owned a property with a large pool and was paying $75 a month to a pool service company to maintain the pool. One day his tenant suggested that Hal turn over the pool maintenance to the tenant. "It only costs $5 or $10 worth of chemicals each month, and I'm here anyway. Just cut the rent by $40 a month. We'll both save money that way." Hal jumped at the opportunity.

When Hal next came back to the property several months later, he was aghast at the pool's condition. It had been bright blue; now it was green with yellow and black algae growing profusely on the sides. He demanded to know what had happened.

The tenant sheepishly confessed he had tried to save money on chlorine and probably hadn't added enough. But, he told Hal, he'd cure it.

Hal came back a month later and the condition of the pool was even worse. The tenant admitted he couldn't handle the pool and said Hal had better take back its maintenance.

The real problem: When Hal called his pool service company, the people there told him they would have to drain the pool, acid wash, and even replace some of the filtration equipment. It was going to cost him big bucks—close to $1,000.

As I noted earlier, taking care of a pool or a spa is not the simple task that most people think it is. It requires constant attention and the right kind of care. If you let it go, you can ruin it. I know of one landlord who let a pool in a rental go for six months. When he finally tried to have it cleaned up, he was told the algae had eaten into the plaster walls. The plaster had to be sandblasted off and then new plaster put on. It cost him over $6,000 to have the pool reconditioned!

Yes, some tenants may be capable of maintaining your pool. But are you willing to risk the potential damage if they aren't? Besides, we haven't even gone into the health hazards that exist. What if a tenant or his or her child is burned by the harsh chemicals used, including chlorine and acid?

The Tenant Who Wants to Improve the Property

Occasionally a tenant will come to you with a request that sounds very reasonable. One of the most common I've run into has to do with lawn sprinklers in single-family homes.

The tenant is usually responsible for watering the lawn (unless you have a gardener). However, it's a time-consuming burden to run a hose out and turn on a portable sprinkler head. The tenant says that what's needed is underground sprinklers. If you will pay for the materials and perhaps a minimum hourly wage, he'll do the work.

As a landlord, you should know that sprinklers are an absolute necessity as is an electric timer that turns them on automatically. That's the only way you have any assurance your lawn will be watered regularly. You need sprinklers, and the tenant's offer may seem like a request from heaven.

My advice is not to give into the temptation of having tenants do the work. Although installing a sprinkler system requires only rudimentary plumbing skills, it does require *some* skill . . . and a great deal of hard work. Besides, in most locales these days it also requires a building department permit. (You will, after all, be tapping into the potable water supply.)

Few tenants have the determination to dig the long holes (sometimes a foot deep) required for the pipes. Or really want to spend the several weekends the work requires. You may have tenants who get started and give it a good try but then end up leaving you with an unfinished and half dug yard. They won't complain (although they may think about moving), but it will be up to you to get someone (yourself or a professional) to complete the work. And finishing a botched job, quite frankly, is tougher than doing it correctly right from the start. Yes, it does cost money to do it right, but do you really want it done wrong?

The same holds true for other "projects" that your tenants may come up with, such as building a deck or a patio cover, adding a greenhouse window, or converting a bedroom to a family room (or vice versa). My advice is to risk offending the tenants by just saying no.

Beware Deducting Payments for Work from Rent

I never give rent deductions. For example, I don't reduce the rent by $30 if a tenant waters the yard properly. If I did, almost immediately the tenant might think of the rental rate as $30 less and forget about what has to be done to earn that money. On the other hand, if I send the tenant a check made payable to the water company for $30 each month (for watering the lawns and shrubs), I have a continuing incentive tied directly to the maintenance task I want accomplished.

Also, if you reduce the rent, forgo the acceptance of rent, or pay a tenant directly for performing work such as maintaining a pool, you could actually be setting up an employee-employer relationship as defined by federal, and perhaps even state, law. If such a relationship exists, you could be responsible for withholding tax, workers compensation, and other employer responsibilities.

When a Tenant Makes Changes without Permission

Probably one of the most shocking rental experiences I have ever had occurred many years ago when I stopped by a rental (actually one unit of a triplex) to collect the rent and was asked in by a friendly tenant, who proudly displayed her new color scheme. I gasped in surprise and horror to see the walls and ceilings painted a very shiny (and probably very permanent) deep purple.

The tenant saw my distress and immediately pointed out how well her black leather couch went with the new color scheme as did her very dark green throw rug. I had to agree that, indeed, the colors did seem in harmony.

What I was seeing, however, but the tenant wasn't, was my inability to rerent when she eventually moved out. Normally, light colors make a place seem airy and roomy and are attractive to most people. Not many prospective tenants are willing to move into a dark, cavelike dwelling.

And painting over a dark color with a light color can be next to impossible, short of putting on three or four coats—an expensive proposition.

I dutifully informed the proud tenant that the rental agreement specifically forbade painting without the approval of the landlord, and, in any event, the landlord had to agree to the colors. The tenant just scoffed at that and said something to the effect of "Who wouldn't like their place repainted; and, by the way, what's wrong with the color?"

What was I to do? After all, it was already painted!

I duly noted that when the tenant moved out, the unit would have to be repainted back to the original color and the cost would come out of the security/cleaning deposit, if there was enough money. Then I left, hoping this tenant would stay there a very, very long time . . .

Avoiding Unapproved Repairs or Improvements

In the above example, the tenant disregarded a written part of the rental agreement and altered the property without the landlord's consent. Unfortunately, I (the landlord) didn't find out until the deed was done, and by then it was too late to do anything except corrective work.

The idea is to nip this sort of thing in the bud. You want to head off unapproved work before it starts. You do this by emphasizing your expectations from the very beginning, when the tenant first moves in.

Today, when a tenant moves in, among other things discussed, I emphasize there are to be no alterations, improvements, or repairs to the property without the specific written approval of the landlord. I even highlight this part of the rental agreement and have tenants initial it, indicating they have indeed seen it.

An area of landlord-tenant relations that can prove to be a minefield for the investor occurs when you refuse to make needed repairs, which we'll explore in Chapter 23.

19

WHEN TENANTS ARE LATE WITH THE RENT

There are no acceptable excuses for late rent.

Every landlord sooner or later experiences late rent payments. If you're reading this chapter now, perhaps you're currently having this problem and are looking for a solution. If so, let's clearly define what you are worried about.

What Late Rent Really Means to the Landlord

There are three worries that most landlords have when the rent is late (and the tenant has not called to explain):

1. Will it cause me to miss my own payments for mortgage, insurance, and utilities?
2. Does the late rent portend more serious trouble to come in the future? (Will this rent be late again next month and the month after? Is the tenant going to refuse to pay altogether and cause me real grief?)
3. Assuming it's the first late rent payment from a good payer, how do I handle this without offending and potentially losing a good tenant?

It's important to understand that when the rent is late, most landlords, particularly those new to the game, experience two emotions: fear and anger. You're afraid because the late rent threatens your ownership of the property. In most cases, landlords have a very thin margin. You are probably counting on that rent to make a hefty mortgage payment. Without the rent, you'll have to come up with the money elsewhere, and that can cause you serious difficulty. And you're angry at the tenant for putting you in this position.

What's important to remember is that the tenant is also probably experiencing fear and anger. The tenant is probably afraid of what will happen because of the late rent. In the case of most tenants (we'll talk about "professional tenant" problems later), they don't know what you can or will do. They're worried about their credit standing and the roof over their heads. And they are often angry at themselves (though this can quickly be redirected at you) for letting this situation occur.

> **H** *i n t*
>
> Rent must be paid at a specific location, and you should spell this out in your lease/rental agreement. In some states it must be paid at the premises; in others it can be a mutually acceptable location. If the tenant doesn't know where to pay, and you haven't spelled it out, you could be in trouble when it comes time to collect.

If you allow your emotions to rule and respond in a fearful or angry way, chances are you will provoke a similar response from the tenant. You could actually turn a harmless situation of a lost payment in the mail into a serious problem that could mean really late rent, a lost tenant, or worse.

How Do I Proceed?

It's important at the onset to control your emotions. If the rent is late, it's a business problem and needs to be dealt with accordingly.

Before taking any action, you must determine *why* the rent is late. There are many, many reasons, from the simple and innocuous to the difficult and underhanded. You can't know what to do until you figure out what the problem really is. In case you're scratching your head and trying to figure it out, here's a list of possible causes for late rent:

- The check was lost in the mail. Yes, once in a great while a rent check really does get lost in the mail!
- The tenant forgot. Incredible, isn't it? How can anyone forget to pay the rent? But it happens.
- There's a problem with the house. The tenant is purposely holding back the rent until you fix it. You should know about this already from earlier conversations with the tenant.
- The tenants don't have the money. A check they are expecting is late. That's their problem, right? Except now they're making it yours.
- The tenant lost his or her job. And just doesn't have the money.
- The tenant is sick. He or she can't work, can't even get out of bed to call you. It helps if you're a doctor; if not, you could have a problem.
- The tenant won't give a reason. You could have a serious problem.

How do you know if the problem is easy to solve or more difficult? The answer: Talk to the tenant. You can never define the problem yourself. You can only figure it out through communication.

When the rent is late, I always make it a point to drop by to see the tenant. If it's a tenant who has previously paid well and who pays through the mail, I might wait as long as three days before dropping by. For a really good tenant, I might just call up and say, "By the way, the rent payment hasn't arrived. Is there a problem?" Chances are this tenant will be

---

L *a n d l o r d ' s* **T** *a l e*

Sometimes you just have to accept late rent. I once had a tenant who depended on her Social Security check to pay the rent. She was always five days late. The reason? Her Social Security check arrived on the fifth day of the month.

I had a choice. I could rant and rave and demand that payment be made on the 1st, in which case it would still arrive on the 5th. Or I could accept the fact that she would always be "punctually" five days late. She was a good tenant, always paid late but "promptly," and I never said a word. She stayed for nearly seven years and never complained about anything, even once. One of the best tenants I ever had.

surprised, say she mailed it a week ago and will be happy to cancel the check and give me a cashier's check or even cash if I want it. I then drop by and pick up the rent. There are no hard feelings. I haven't lost a good tenant. And my worries are assuaged.

L *a n d l o r d ' s*
Q *u i z*

What's a landlord in if he or she never goes out to talk to tenants?

Answer: Foreclosure!

Locating the Tenant

When the rent is late, therefore, your first task is to find the tenant and determine why. Why is the rent late and what does the tenant intend to do about it?

Finding the tenant is usually easy. When I'm looking, I just come by at dinner time when most tenants are at home. Sometimes, however, tenants *aren't* home. They aren't home when you come by at dinner time, in the morning, or in the afternoon. You come back several times and tenants still aren't around. It's easy to become aggravated, frustrated, even hostile, and lose your perspective. Even if it's innocent, you can begin to see a plot and overreact.

Who knows? There could have been a family emergency—perhaps a son or daughter was injured in an auto accident or a distant parent took desperately ill. In times like those, most of us forget mundane things like rent and just react to the immediate need.

What to do? A good rental agreement and application will list a couple of phone numbers of relatives. Give them a call. After all, you have a legitimate concern—your rent. Find out if something happened to the family. If there's an emergency and the tenant is a good one, be especially nice. Let the person you call know you're concerned. Ask to have the tenant call you and let the person on the phone know that if the tenant needs time, you'll work something out. Chances are you'll get a call back within a few hours and a rent check the next day.

If the relative phone calls don't work out, then it's time to become a snoop. Go around and talk to the neighbors—it's positively amazing what neighbors know. Tell the neighbors you own the property, you can't find the tenant, and you're worried that something might be amiss. Chances are if the neighbors know anything, they'll dump it right on

> ## L *a n d l o r d ' s* T *a l e*
>
> I had a very good tenant who stayed in my property for over two years. Then one day, the rent was late. I called but there was no answer. I came by and the front door was locked and nobody was home. I talked to the neighbors, and they said that the night before my tenants had packed up their belongings in a rental truck and left.
>
> I rechecked the property and found the back door unlocked and the house dirty but empty. They had abandoned it.
>
> I was perfectly happy. They hadn't cost me any lost rent. I still had the security deposit to take care of cleaning, and I could reclaim my house. Yes, I would have preferred a more orderly termination, but given the alternative of what they could have done (stayed, not paid, and ruined the house), I was thrilled.

you. Maybe instead of an emergency, there are marital troubles. There was a terrible fight and they split—husband in one direction, wife in the other. Or the tenant was laid off at work and just packed up and took off to someplace else.

In a worst-case scenario where you can't find the tenants and the relatives and neighbors aren't helpful, leave a card on the front door saying you were there—and keep coming back. You hope that sooner or later they'll turn up. If they don't, you may have to start an unlawful detainer action (see Chapter 21), but that's particularly hard if the tenants simply aren't there.

Take heart; in 30 years of being a landlord, only once did tenants leave all their furniture and bug out on me, and that was a long time ago. Usually, tenants who don't pay the rent are there, even if just hiding out and pretending not to be home.

Listening to Tenants

Remember: Your first goal is to find out why the rent is late. Only after you've discovered the problem can you take appropriate action. You're there first and foremost to listen.

OK, the rent's late, you've found the tenant, and you've listened. Now what? Assuming the problem isn't something simple such as the rent's simply been lost in the mail, you now have to decide on a course of action. What do you do?

We'll discuss what action you should take in the next chapter. First, however, here are a couple of side issues to help you make sure the rent isn't late in the future.

Mailing versus Picking Up the Rent

Should you have the tenant mail the check to you or should you go out and pick it up personally? The answer, of course, depends entirely on the tenant. In my experience I have found that tenants in low-rent properties most often expect the landlord to come by on rent day and collect payment. If you don't come by, they don't pay.

Middle-rent to upper-rent properties, on the other hand, often attract tenants who would think you absurd, if not a little paranoid, if you came by to collect the rent monthly. They assume they will send it in along with the utility, phone, and other bills.

I have done it both ways and can assure you that getting the rent check in the mail is by far the easier method—when it arrives. In either case, however, you must make a personal appearance and do it quickly if the rent is late.

If you are having the rent sent to you, one technique that some landlords use successfully is to mail the tenant a postage paid envelope around the middle of the month. All the tenant has to do then is put the check in and drop it in a mailbox. This simple device is inexpensive and can avoid a lot of late payments.

If the Check Bounces

Sometimes a rent check bounces—either the regular rent check sent in the mail or the check you get when you show up in person. What do you do?

The answer is that from then on you avoid personal checks from that tenant and get cash, cashier's checks, or money orders instead. You sim-

H *i n t*

You may be able to establish a direct deposit system with a tenant, which must be set up by the tenant with his or her bank. On the 1st of the month (or whatever date), the rent money will automatically be deducted from the tenant's checking account and electronically deposited to your account. The system can be set up with an alert given to you if there are insufficient funds in the tenant's account to make the deposit.

ply have to say you can't be bothered with the delays and inconvenience of bounced checks. If the tenant wants to continue on, he or she must pay in cash or a cash equivalent.

As an aside, any rent check that I get in the mail I deposit immediately—the same day if possible. I also have an arrangement with my bank (and you can have a similar one with yours) whereby any check that doesn't clear results in an immediate phone call to notify me. I don't wait the three to five days it takes for the bank to send a letter.

Thus, I usually know within two days when a rent check doesn't clear the tenant's bank. What do I do then?

I go to my bank and pick up the check, which usually has a stamp saying it wasn't paid because of "insufficient funds" stamped on the back. I take the check and go to see the tenant. I inform the tenant that now, not only is the rent late, but I've been given a bad check. The criminal penalties for issuing a bad check vary from one area of the country to another but are becoming increasingly more severe. I know what the penalties are in my area, and I mention these to the tenant.

I'm willing to accept payment in cash in exchange for the bad check (plus my bank costs). I will also accept a money order and, if they are legitimate, traveler's checks. I will *not* accept another personal check, although I will accept a cashier's check. (Note: Within the past few years, banks have sometimes weaseled out of honoring cashier's checks, sometimes even their own, depending on the circumstances.)

If the tenant can't or won't give me cash or a cash equivalent for the bad check, I serve the first eviction notice. (I also hang onto the bad check—it can prove helpful if the matter ever gets to a court hearing.)

Beware Partial Rent Payments

Many times tenants say they can't pay the entire month's rent, but because they *can* pay a week's worth or two weeks' worth, they'll promise to give you the one week or two weeks and pay the remainder in a few more weeks. Most landlords feel that a bird in the hand is worth 12 in the bush when it comes to rent. Better to take the two weeks and worry about the rest later.

Yes and no. If you have a good tenant in a bad spot who needs just a little help, you're probably OK in taking the partial rent. However, an unscrupulous tenant can now say that by accepting part payment, you've changed the terms of the rental arrangement, and now it's a weekly rental instead of a monthly one. (Many areas have very different laws regulating weekly rentals.)

Further, if you serve an eviction notice (the first one) and then accept a partial rent payment, you have, in effect, called off the eviction proceedings. If the tenant subsequently fails to pay any further, in most locales you must start all over with that first eviction notice. You could have lost many weeks of your most precious asset: time.

Late Fees

Some landlords build late fees into their rental agreements. This can be a flat fee ($25 or $100 or whatever) or a percentage of the monthly rent (typically 5 percent). Some landlords also use a daily rate, say $10 a day.

My own feeling is that these fees rarely accomplish their goal—getting the rent on time. The conscientious tenant is the one who responds best to late fees, yet this tenant is almost never late. The tenant who really doesn't care about payments being late isn't likely to care much about late fees either.

Sometimes, however, an incentive for getting the rent in on time will help. Getting the rent in promptly for six continuous months might result in an award—maybe a dinner at a local pizza restaurant. It doesn't have to be much to be an encouragement.

The Bottom Line

Don't ever let late rent slip by. The rent is your due for providing housing to tenants. Every day that it goes unpaid means that you are providing free housing. Further, unpaid rent means that your financial security and even ownership of your property are being threatened.

20

WHEN TENANTS REFUSE TO PAY OR LEAVE

*The only thing worse than a tenant who doesn't pay and moves is
a tenant who doesn't pay and stays!*

The rent is late; you've gone to see the tenants. You still don't have the money. Now what do you do?

In the last chapter we talked about the easy solution. The rent was lost in the mail, so you simply ask for and receive cash or a cash equivalent. Now the problem is more difficult.

An Argument Ender

If the tenant continues to insist the check was lost in the mail, don't argue. Just agree and say you want another check—a cashier's check this time or cash—immediately. The lost check can be cancelled, or you'll return it whenever it shows up. That should end that line of argument by the tenant.

When the Tenant "Can't" Pay

The most common reason I've found that tenants give for not paying the rent (after you've cleared up the business about its being lost in the mail) is that they don't have the money right now. There's been an unfortunate delay; the tenant's boss didn't get the paychecks out that week, or the money expected from Aunt Bertha simply hasn't shown up, or whatever. The tenant wants to pay but explains he or she simply can't right now. If you're just willing to wait a while, a few days, perhaps a week or two, the tenant will get the money to you.

Should you wait?

No one wants to be unkind, but it's important to remember that renting property is a business just like any other. How long do you think a gas station owner, for example, would stay in business if he gave free gas to all the people who said their tank was empty, but they didn't have any money now but could pay next week?

Your tenants obviously have a problem, but it's important to see just what they want to do with it. It seems they want to make their problem yours. Their problem is their inability to pay the rent right now, but it's their responsibility to find a solution. And that solution has to be either getting the money from somewhere or moving out.

If, however, you agree to allow them not to pay even for a short while, such as a week or two, now it's your problem. You have a nonpaying tenant. What are you going to do about it?

Demanding Rent

Don't let tenants put you off. Experienced landlords know that in most cases tenants can come up with the money if they feel they have to. People usually have money in a savings account, or they can borrow it from relatives. But they hesitate to get it from such a source unless it's an emergency. And often they don't define late rent as an emergency.

It's important that rent be defined as a high-priority item. The rent must be paid first, or it can be put off to the end of a long list of other bills.

You can be sympathetic, but you must make it clear that the rent must be paid and paid on time. Perhaps you might say, "I'm sorry to hear that . . . (fill in the blank with the tenant's problem), but as you must know, the rent comes first. You have to have a roof over your head. I've made a special trip to collect it. I'm here for the rent."

Once you make it clear that you are there for the rent and will not be moved until it's paid, tenants often come up with it. They also learn that you are someone who stands up for himself or herself and will think twice next month about putting you at the end of their list of people to be paid.

Demand the rent you are entitled to, and you will get it most of the time.

On the other hand, even though it's important to be a no-nonsense landlord, *never* be abusive, mean, vindictive, loud, insulting, overbearing, or threatening. You don't want to give the tenants a reason to call the police (or initiate a lawsuit) because of your behavior. Always speak quietly and calmly but firmly. The rent is due. You're here to pick it up. There are no excuses.

The Tenant Won't Pay

On the other hand, a tenant simply may not be able or willing to pay. You must dig deeper to find out why, as I advised in Chapter 19, when rent is late. Is the breadwinner out of work? Was there an emergency (a car accident)? Was the money spent elsewhere? Is the rent simply too high?

It may be time to reason with the tenant. If the rent is simply too high or the tenant is in an impossible financial situation, you may want to suggest that the tenant consider moving to a lower-cost rental, or even to a relative's home, until things get better. You can point out that this will save the tenant's credit reputation and will convert the tenant from being in an impossible rental situation to one that the tenant can handle. You may even want to use some of the security deposit to facilitate a move. Remember, quickly removing a tenant who can't pay is far better than having the tenant stay while you try to collect rent in court.

I have even chipped in to help pay for movers to get out a tenant who couldn't pay. Remember, you can't squeeze blood from a turnip or get water out of a stone. If tenants just don't have the money, then your best solution is to find an amicable way for them to move somewhere else.

L *a n d l o r d ' s* **D** *i l e m m a*

You want to keep the tenants, so you're afraid to begin eviction for fear of offending them. It's true that you could lose a tenant by serving the first eviction notice. On the other hand, you may lose the tenant anyway; and the sooner you begin eviction, the sooner a nonpaying tenant will get out, so you'll be able to rerent to someone who'll pay.

On the other hand, if their excuse is implausible, or they are adamant about staying, or they refuse to work with you, you're probably in a situation that's only going to get worse. You will probably be best off then to serve such tenants with a first eviction notice right on the spot. (See Chapter 21 on evictions.)

Sometimes serving an eviction notice results in your getting your rent within a day or two—if not immediately. If a specific tenant does pay up, however, I would make it perfectly clear that in the future you expect the rent to continue to be paid on time, or else that eviction notice will be back.

The One-Time Problem

In a few cases, you may find that a tenant is late in paying the rent, but you're sure that he or she will eventually pay and this is only a one-time problem. If tenants are responsible (they call you before you call them) and explain a one-time extenuating circumstance, you may want to allow them time to get the rent together. But be careful. If in the end they still don't pay up, each day's delay is another day's rent lost, probably forever. Be absolutely sure you and your tenants agree on the final date when the rent is due and that there's a *penalty* for the late payment. The penalty rams home the fact that a late payment is not without consequences.

I once had an excellent tenant who lived with her son, an airline pilot. She depended on her son's paycheck for the rent. One month he was in Saudi Arabia, and his company sent his check to him there instead of to the house. The pilot's mother had to wait until he got back nearly three weeks later before the late rent payment could be straightened out. However, she didn't simply let things hang. She called me the day the rent was due and explained the situation. I agreed to wait, and three weeks later I received full payment.

The "Softy" Landlord

A word needs to be said about a landlord who feels overly sorry for his or her tenants' difficulties (usually a freshman landlord). A tenant may be out of work or sick or may have lost his or her wallet. You are human and feel sorry for such troubles. You want to help out and, unfortunately for you, the means to help is oh so obvious and easy: You can just allow the tenant to pay late. Just a few days late at first, then a week, then two, then maybe a month. . . . It will help out the tenant so much.

If you decide to operate your property as a charitable venture, that's fine. Just be sure that you know what you're doing up front and that you're prepared for the consequences (such as not being able to make your own mortgage, tax, and insurance payments).

If you don't want to end up a pauper yourself, however, you'll very quickly realize that not only your profits, but your financial survival, require that you see yourself strictly as a businessperson.

If you simply can't overlook the plight of the helpless and the poor (who just happen to be occupying your house), then I suggest you get out of the rental business at once. You don't belong being a landlord. You will lose money, become frustrated, and probably earn yourself an early grave. Further, you may even end up doing a disservice to those who come to you for help by inadvertently conspiring to lead them further into debt.

Tenants Can Be Tough

As a landlord, always remember that tenants are constantly sizing you up. If you look like a soft touch, you'll find that even the ones who pay regularly begin appealing to your sympathies. It may not be late rent; it could be repainting the premises in colors they prefer . . . or adding new carpeting . . . or even reducing the rent.

Further, problem tenants, particularly those who have survived the threats and feeble actions of less adroit landlords, can become quite skilled at taking advantage. They probe with late rent payments, with unreasonable demands, and even with threats to sue you if you don't comply with their wishes. They are looking for softness, and if they find it in you, you can be sure they will take full advantage of it.

If you let them, some tenants put the rent payment last, after the car payment, clothing, bowling, eating out, or whatever. They may stop keeping up the property. They may leave it a mess. Certainly not every tenant—not even the vast majority of tenants—will do this. But the few who will, will change your hair from whatever color it now is to gray.

The Landlord's Guidelines for Rent Collection

Here are effective guidelines for collecting rent that you should post next to the phone you use for determining and receiving rents:

- The rent must always be paid—first.
- Whatever you give away in rent to a tenant, you probably will never get back.
- There are no acceptable excuses for late rent.

One person to whom I showed these guidelines suggested that someone who followed them would be a Simon Legree. I disagree.

Good tenants expect a landlord to act like one: businesslike, professional. I've been both a landlord and a tenant. When I was a tenant, I paid my rent on time. If I didn't, I fully expected the landlord to come around asking for it and acknowledging that he had every right to demand it from me. If I couldn't pay or refused or simply spent the money elsewhere, I wouldn't have blamed the landlord a bit for giving me an eviction notice. I would deserve it! In fact, if the landlord overlooked my lateness or refusal to pay, I would have had every right to think him a fool.

Next time you feel you're being too strict, reread the guidelines and the above paragraph. Imagine how it was when you were a tenant (if you ever were). You'll find that suddenly you feel a lot stronger in your position as a landlord.

A Word about Receipts

When tenants pay up, give them a receipt. They're entitled to one both morally and legally. Be sure, however, that the receipt specifies the period for which the rent was paid and is dated and that your copy is signed by the tenant as having received a copy. Putting in the exact period—for example, June 1 through June 30—avoids later confusion and argument over for which period the rent was paid.

If you receive partial payment—for example, two weeks' worth—indicate the dates those weeks cover. Otherwise, if you later are forced to proceed with eviction, the tenant may claim that the partial payment was to cover the whole month. (Note: Partial payment almost always delays eviction proceedings; see Chapter 21.)

You're a Landlord—Be Proud of It

Once you become a landlord, for whatever reason, it becomes your job to collect rent, even when it's late. If you do it fairly both to yourself and to your tenants, you will find not only do you prosper, but your tenants respect you and in most cases pay promptly.

21

EVICTING TENANTS

Eviction should be your last resort, not your first.

Because it is fairly common and because time is of the essence, the eviction process is fairly straightforward and quick in almost all areas of the country. When you seek an eviction, you usually have priority in terms of court time, and you can usually get a judgment and the eviction in a matter of a few weeks to a month. (But not always, as we'll soon see.)

Experienced landlords know the eviction process quite well but may pick up a few ideas in this chapter they hadn't considered before. For those who have not yet gone, or are just now going, through your first eviction, read on.

Do You Need an Attorney?

The answer is absolutely yes, at least the first time. After that, you'll see how it's done and may want to try it yourself. Some experienced landlords do handle their own court evictions and, as long as everything goes according to plan, have little trouble doing this.

The biggest question for the new landlord is often how to find a good eviction attorney. I suggest that you check with local property managers and real estate agents who handle rentals. Usually, one or two attorneys in a county do nothing but handle evictions—that's their bread and butter. They know all the nuances of the local laws, they know the judges, they know from vast experience what's going to happen, and they know how long it's likely to take. And they also usually have set fees.

Sometimes their fees may seem excessive, particularly when you learn how little work is actually involved. However, it's best to learn from an expert, and I feel their fees are usually worth it. You may learn enough to be able to handle it yourself in the future.

The Eviction Process

The actual eviction process is usually straightforward. Keep in mind, however, that each state has its own laws for eviction, which means that time limits, required document filings, and overall procedures differ. The following eight steps constitute a typical eviction procedure:

1. Serve the initial pay or quit notice (three-day, five-day, or whatever notice).
2. File the unlawful detainer action papers.
3. Serve the eviction papers.
4. Show up in county, municipal, or whichever court is appropriate in your area.
5. Tell it to the judge and, if the tenants don't show, get a judgment to collect the monies owed you and an eviction.
6. Have final eviction papers with the date of eviction served on the tenants.
7. Have the sheriff or other local law enforcement agency evict the tenants on the date. If it gets this far, you will probably have to pay for a local moving company to take the tenants' belongings and put them in storage for later disposition.
8. Have the sheriff give possession of the property back to you.

The total time of an uncontested eviction shouldn't be much more than four to eight weeks with five to six weeks about average. Of course, if the eviction is contested, then all bets are off. We'll discuss this later, but first let's consider what many landlords would really like to do with tenants who won't pay and won't quit the premises (i.e., leave).

Don't Try Self-Help Evictions

What should be obvious from the eviction procedure outlined above is that it takes time and involves court. You may lose about six weeks' worth of rent in a simple eviction. And there are other costs. You have to pay certain court costs; you have to pay an attorney (at least the first time out); and you conceivably could have to pay a moving company to collect and store the tenants' furniture. Wouldn't it simply be much easier to just get a bunch of your burly friends, show up one night, and throw the tenants out?

This sort of self-help eviction would indeed be simpler—trouble is, it wouldn't be legal today. (Around the turn of the century, it was legal almost everywhere in the country!)

L *a n d l o r d ' s* T *a l e*

A number of years ago, Hal was having a lot of trouble with some tenants in a house he owned. First they were late with the rent. Then they stopped paying altogether. Finally, they wouldn't answer their phone when he called.

Hal was getting frustrated and decided to kick the tenants out. However, when he heard that a local attorney wanted $1,000 to handle the eviction for him, he scoffed and said he'd do it himself.

It was the dead of winter and nights typically dropped well below freezing. Hal showed up one morning at the house and banged on the door until the tenants finally answered. He told them he wanted them out by that afternoon. If they weren't out, he was going to come around with a hammer and break all the windows. (He figured he could get the windows replaced for a lot less than paying an attorney.)

The tenants said that was against the law. If he did that, they would call the sheriff. Hal said they could indeed call the sheriff if they wanted, but by then the windows would be all gone and they'd be sleeping in the cold.

Needless to say, Hal impressed the tenants as being something of a madman, and, sure enough, they were out by that evening. Hal congratulated himself on a job well done.

Of course, Hal was just very lucky. If the tenants had been savvy, they might have sued him for threatening them. If they were really savvy, they might have simply stayed and waited. If he carried out his threat, they could have claimed (indeed, it might have been true) that one of them had been injured on broken glass and perhaps that their furniture had been damaged by rain coming in the broken windows. Perhaps someone had come in and robbed them while the windows were gone. Before the tenants were done, they might have ended up owning the property, and Hal could have been a tenant himself somewhere else.

I mention the above tale, first, because it's absolutely true, and, second, because it illustrates the stupidest thing a landlord can do. The last thing you want is to put yourself in a position where a tenant has good grounds for suing you. In today's litigious society, you can be fairly sure that if you try any sort of self-help eviction, you will get caught and it will *cost, cost, cost!*

Here's a partial list of some self-help actions that you *do not* want to do:

- Do *not* break the windows of the house, remove the doors, or do anything else that makes the premises uninhabitable.
- Do *not* turn off the utilities (water, gas, electric, etc.) or plug up the sewer or septic system.
- Do *not* padlock the tenants out of the property.
- Do *not* kill their pets or leave gates open so the pets will run loose.
- Do *not* threaten the tenants.
- Do *not* disturb their right to "quiet enjoyment" of the property.
- Do *not* do anything else that would give the tenants cause to sue you.

Although it might still be condoned in some backwoods area some-where, I personally know of no part of the country that allows self-help evictions. If you want the tenants out, you go to court.

Serving Notices

Earlier in this chapter I went through a typical procedure for the legal eviction of tenants. Let's go back now and dwell a bit longer on one aspect of that: serving notices.

The Pay or Quit Notice

In almost all areas, you must begin the eviction process by serving a pay or quit notice. The purpose of this notice is to give tenants written notice that either they must pay the full amount of rent then owed or they must quit the premises within a specified time period, which varies according to state. In Illinois, for example, it's five days and a five-day notice is used; in California it's a three-day notice, and tenants have three days to get out or pay.

Only after you have served this notice and tenants have neither paid nor quit can you commence the actual eviction proceeding, usually called an "unlawful detainer" action.

The pay or quit notice is usually presented by a landlord directly to a tenant. Most landlords use it sparingly, as it's sure to alienate a tenant. Some use it to get faltering tenants back on track, to let them know you really do mean business. A few landlords hand out these notices as though they were neighborhood flyers. A tenant is one day late with the rent and out goes the three-day notice.

Used sparingly and only when absolutely necessary, pay or quit notices can be very effective in spurring a delinquent tenant into performing. Used indiscriminately, they can anger perfectly good tenants and result in excessive move-outs. (See the end of this book for a sample notice.)

The notice itself does not usually have to be in any special form, al-though it typically should have the following items on it:

TYPICAL ELEMENTS OF A "PAY OR QUIT" NOTICE

- Address of the rental
- Correct names of the tenants
- The total amount due and the period this covers
- The time to pay it (You can give them more time if you want—the state only sets the minimum time you can give.)
- The date
- Your signature

The notice to quit. A variation of the pay or quit notice is a similar document that doesn't specify a monetary amount. This is used when tenants have paid the rent but refuse to "quit" (leave) after you have given proper notice asking them to move out. Everything else is essentially the same except there is no dollar figure on the notice.

Having the Sheriff Serve Notices

After you've served initial notice but the tenants haven't quit the premises or paid up the rent, there are now other notices to be served. The number and purpose vary according to your area, but there usually will be at least two: the initial notice of eviction and the later court order notice that the tenants must move. There may be intermediate steps as well.

You can serve these notices yourself. However, a better way is to have the local police department or sheriff's office serve the notices. They will do this for what is usually a small fee.

The importance of this, of course, is that when tenants see cops coming to the door, they are likely to be far more impressed than when they see you coming to the door. A few dollars spent here might be just enough to get the tenants to move on their own and thus allow you to avoid the need to follow through on the entire eviction.

Keep Your Eye on the Goal

This brings us back to your primary goal: getting the tenants out. If you're a typical landlord, you're usually not all that interested in going through the entire eviction process. If you can just get the tenants out before the problem gets to the judge, you can save yourself considerable money in filing fees, attorney costs, and additional lost rent.

An exception here is the situation of tenants with assets. If they have assets, you may want to get a judgment against them in hopes of collecting back rent and costs later on down the road. In most cases, however, tenants who fail to pay rent are "judgment proof." That simply means they have no assets you can attach. In that case, just getting them out quickly, as noted above, is usually your best bet.

Most Tenants Will Move First

Most tenants know they are in the wrong when you threaten eviction. They know they haven't paid the rent. They feel guilty. Perhaps they are just trying to stall and gain some time.

I can recall only fewer than a handful of situations—in my decades of being a landlord and being involved with other landlords—in which tenants actually stayed right to the bitter end, and the sheriff had to move them out "to the street." Most sane tenants will move before the date this happens.

Sometimes, however, particularly if there's a nasty divorce involved, tenants will be unable to act. They will be arguing between themselves even as they are physically evicted.

H *i n t*

In my experience, most judges won't grant you an unlawful detainer until all the money you hold, meaning the security deposit, has been applied to the rent. That means that if you hold a month's security deposit, it will be at least 30 days after the tenant stopped paying rent before the judge is likely to act.

Tenants Who Contest the Eviction

Thus far I've been discussing an eviction that the tenants don't contest. In some cases, however, savvy tenants appear in court before the judge and contest the eviction.

If you're a new landlord, you may ask on what grounds the tenants can possibly contest eviction if they haven't paid their rent. (We're assuming here the eviction is strictly for nonpayment of rent, not because you want tenants out for other reasons after serving proper notice, which often results in tenants' contesting the eviction.) The answer is that, at the least, tenants can claim they did pay the rent and that your bookkeeping is in error. If they produce a canceled check, you're in trouble. At the worst, they can claim that you've not maintained the property, and they withheld rent pending maintenance and repair work.

L a n d l o r d ' s T a l e

Sally rented an apartment to a family with two small children. After staying there nearly six months, they stopped paying rent and refused to move. Nothing she could say or do would change their actions. So she tried eviction.

At the court proceeding, the tenants showed up with their small children, claiming they had both lost their jobs and were looking for work. They just needed more time. They were particularly worried about their children's missing school if they were evicted. Besides, they said they had nowhere to go. The judge gave them a month to come up with the money they owed.

A month later they were back in court. The children were crying, the mother was crying, the father was choked with emotion. They had tried, but they needed more time. The judge gave them another month.

It happened three times for three months. At the end of the third month, they just didn't show, and the judge finally ordered the eviction to take place in three weeks.

Sally served all the papers, of course, but the tenants didn't move . . . until the day before the sheriff showed up along with the moving van Sally had paid for. They were suddenly gone, leaving the property a mess.

They had been able to stay in the property altogether for four and a half months without paying rent. Because they were essentially judgment proof, Sally had no real chance of recovering any of her lost costs.

If you want to learn what could happen in a worst-case scenario, then I suggest you rent the video *Pacific Heights*. I found the movie, though not aesthetically pleasing, absolutely mesmerizing in terms of its portrayal of a "tenant from hell." In the movie, an unscrupulous tenant rents an apartment with the specific goal of ruining the owners-landlords so that he can take over the building after they can no longer afford the mortgage payments and consequently lose the property through foreclosure.

A Caution Regarding Partial Payments

After you begin the eviction process, a tenant may come to you with a partial payment. For example, the tenant may owe five weeks' rent and say she doesn't have the full amount but has one week's rent. She wants to give it to you as evidence of her good intentions to pay the rest.

Most beginning landlords will take the money on the assumption that "one in the hand is worth five in the bush." At least you've got some cash.

The problem is that accepting any money at all in partial payment from a tenant may corrupt the eviction process. In other words, once you've accepted partial payment, you may have to start all over again with all of the notices if you want to evict the tenant. Accepting one week's payment, in this example, could have the effect of setting you back a month or more in the eviction process. Be sure to check with an attorney in your state to see what local policy is regarding the acceptance of partial rental payment during an eviction.

If the tenant pays up. It's now up to you to dismiss the court action. This helps preserve the tenant's reputation and credit standing. It also helps you in the eyes of the court—you appear to be an upstanding individual who has done the right thing.

Keep things timely. Everything you do once you start the eviction process has time limits. You need to file within certain periods and to give notices to your tenant along specific timelines. Be sure you follow these. Failure to meet deadlines can throw your eviction off track.

The tenant has similar time constraints, and the tenant's failure to meet them can move the eviction process along much faster.

After the Eviction

Along with the eviction, you normally also get a judgment from the court for your costs. You can now attempt to trace the former tenant, garnish wages, attach bank accounts, and so forth. It's actually an intriguing process if you have the time and the gumption for it.

A simpler method, and one that often nets better results, is to turn the whole mess over to a collection agency. The agency usually has far more resources than you can muster and probably has both a better chance of tracking down the former tenant as well as of getting the cash.

Be aware, however, that most collection agencies work on a percentage basis. Thus, they may recover the funds, but they may keep one-third to one-half or more for their efforts, depending on the difficulty of getting the money and their policy. Nevertheless, a part of the otherwise lost funds is better than none at all. Collection agencies can be found under that heading in the yellow pages of the phone book.

After You Get the Property Back

As soon as a tenant is legally evicted, secure the premises. That means new door locks throughout as well as locks on all windows. Immediately begin refurbishing work, particularly on the exterior, to make it quite apparent that someone is taking care of the property. Also, if it's a single-family house, get someone to frequently check the premises, at least for the first few days. A rental, particularly a separate property, left vacant after an eviction is a prime target for vandalism. A rare danger is that the former tenant, angered by the eviction, might come back and attempt to damage the property; this is probably far less likely, however, because such tenants are usually long gone.

Eviction should be a last resort. But when you use it, move quickly and forcefully.

22

WHEN A TENANT ABANDONS THE PROPERTY

*A tenant who clears out often means
you don't have to pay for eviction.*

The tenant who abandons the rental may, at the time, seem like a real headache to you; in actuality, however, it's probably a gift. After all, with the property abandoned, you may be able to get in there more quickly, clean it up, and rerent it. What's far worse is the tenant who won't pay and won't leave (see Chapters 20 and 21).

There are several different scenarios with abandonment, each with its own problems and solutions. I'll consider several here.

When the Tenant Who Is Behind in Rent Abandons the Property

If you've been a landlord for any time at all, you've run into this situation. Your tenant, for whatever reason, isn't paying rent. A week or two goes by and you're getting increasingly frustrated. You've stopped by many times, but the tenant just won't, or can't, pay. You're calculating how much of the security deposit is left after you've applied it toward the unpaid rent, and it's quickly working its way down to zero. You're angry and frustrated and wondering if you'll have to go to a formal eviction.

Suddenly, one day when you show up to argue with the tenant, you find the door is wide open. You peek in and discover that the tenant and all the furniture are gone. The tenant has abandoned the property. What do you do?

If it were me, I'd whoop with joy! I've just saved the cost and hassle of an eviction.

I'd get someone else to go in with me (to be able to later say that I didn't take any of the tenant's possessions that might still have been there) and check out the premises. If the rental is truly empty (no food-stuffs, clothing, bedding, furniture, etc.), I'd serve my state's legal notice regarding abandonment. (Check with a local attorney or landlord association for the correct form and how to serve it.) Once this is done, change the locks, get a crew in to clean it up, and rerent. I'd do it as quickly as possible to save rental time.

The only real problem with this course of action is that the tenant never gave me back the key or gave formal notice of leaving. And until that happens, the tenant, technically, might have rights to the property. However, I suspect it would be difficult in the situation described above for anyone to contend that the tenant intended to continue living there.

It's a different situation when part of the furniture is gone and part remains. I've known landlords who stayed in front of a property at night waiting for tenants who were clandestinely moving out to show up. When they appeared, long after midnight, the landlord would demand to know what was going on.

Usually, such tenants would sheepishly admit they didn't have the rent and are skipping out. The landlord can then explain the consequences of such action and ask them to sign a statement that they were abandoning the property as of the next day and to give up the keys, which they usually will do.

When the Tenant Abandons but Leaves Furniture Behind

A much trickier situation is when the tenant isn't paying rent and isn't at the property. But the furniture remains there.

As long as furniture is in the rental, you can't assume abandonment. Further, each state has different regulations regarding the removal of personal property such as furniture from an apparently abandoned property.

L a n d l o r d ' s   T a l e

A number of years ago, a young friend of mine, Tony, was renting apartments. One tenant was behind in paying the rent, and whenever Tony went to check up, that tenant wasn't there. But obviously the furniture was. (Tony looked in through a window whose shade was up.)

Weeks went by, then a month. Tony talked to the neighbors, but they couldn't shed light on the situation. Finally, after a month Tony decided the tenant had abandoned the apartment.

Then he called in movers and had the tenant's furniture moved out. He cleaned up the apartment and rented it. A few weeks later, he sold the furniture to an auction company.

Imagine Tony's surprise when a week after that, the tenant showed up, angry as can be, wondering what happened to the apartment and furniture! It turned out the tenant had gone on vacation and mailed the rent check; but it was addressed incorrectly and never arrived. And the tenant was a couple of weeks late getting back

Needless to say, Tony was aggrieved. Ultimately, he gave the tenant a different rental unit, included a month's free rent, and paid for new furniture!

I suggest that in a situation like the one described above, you go back to the rental application in which you asked for the names of relatives or close friends and start calling. Also check with the bank or any other source that may have heard from your tenant. Chances are someone will know where the tenant is, and you can make contact.

If you can't make contact, get in touch with an attorney to advise you on the procedure to follow for abandonment, including notices to give and appropriate waiting times, and for dealing with personal property in such a situation in your state. You might have to get court approval to remove the furniture.

Yes, it's costly and perhaps might be seen as a waste of time. On the other hand, trying self-help can be even more costly and time consuming.

The Tenant Who Dies in the Property

Life goes on and life ends. Sometimes tenants die in your property. If that happens, what do you do?

I'm not sure there are any pat answers, but here are my suggestions. First, be sure that someone in fact did die. I knew of a landlord who would go into an apartment at the drop of a hat, convinced the tenant had died. If the tenant's cat was meowing for a few days, if the rent was a bit late, if she didn't see the tenant three mornings in a row, in she went to check. (Remember, you should have included the right to reasonable entry to the property in the event of an emergency in your rental agreement.) The trouble was, the tenant never died. Usually, the tenant was away on a trip or sleeping late or some such thing.

Sometimes, however, the result's not so nice. Sometimes, the tenant does die. A cat mewling for days, no rent payment, sometimes even a smell can alert you that there's potentially a big problem.

Exercise your right to inspect the property in an emergency. This may mean calling and banging on the door. If repeated attempts fail to gain someone's attention, go back to your applications and see who to call in an emergency and call.

If all else fails and you believe it truly is an emergency, then go inside, preferably with another person to be able to verify that you didn't take or damage anything.

If you find what you believe to be a dead body, stop. Do not proceed. Immediately call 911 or the fire department and report what you believe you've seen. Remember, a person isn't dead until a doctor or medical examiner pronounces him or her dead.

Do not touch anything in the rental nor let anyone else touch anything. At this time you have no idea if the person died of natural causes or if it was a murder. Your apartment may become a crime scene, and the police will be gratified to learn that you didn't mess it up.

Get on the phone and call the tenant's relatives or friends (whose names you get from the application). Try to find out who is the next of kin, so this person can be notified; be as gentle as possible. After all, you may be letting someone know that a loved one has died.

Once the medical examiner has determined that the death was from natural causes (which is probably going to be the case), you may find the next of kin wants to get in to take a suit or a dress needed for the funeral. Although technically you should probably not allow any personal property to be released without legal authorization, common sense and decency tells you to allow this; you may, however, want to accompany the next of kin to be sure nothing else is removed.

There now only remains the matter of the tenant's furniture and personal possessions. It's usually your responsibility to protect and preserve the tenant's personal property, which may mean an accounting of it and storage. Check with your attorney on how to proceed in your state.

Usually fairly quickly, someone will be appointed to take care of the estate, either an administrator (court appointed) or executor (designated by the deceased), who will want you to release the possessions. Be sure that the person is, indeed, entitled to handle the estate. Typically, this person is able to produce court-approved documents to that effect. If you're not sure about the documents, take them to a lawyer or call the court.

On the other hand, if the tenant had few and modest possessions, the relatives may simply not want to bother with the cost and hassle of probate but may instead simply want to take what's there, divide it, and sell what's left. Technically, this should not be done, but as a practical matter, it's done all the time. You can only use your best judgment here. Just be sure that you have legal authorization before you release personal property to the relatives.

Also be sure that you put in your bill for unpaid rent. This includes not only back rent until the tenant died but also any time that the tenant's possessions are in the property and you can't rerent. If there's a sizable estate and a probate proceeding, be sure your bill is included; the administrator or executor will probably have the funds to pay you.

If there are few assets and the relatives are claiming them, give them the bill and explain that rent is due. They usually understand and will want to pay. Most people don't like the idea that the last memory of a loved one is contaminated with unpaid bills.

Of course, there's always the situation in which there are no relatives and the state must dispose of the body and the personal property. Here an administrator will be appointed to oversee the disposal. Get your bill in right away and hope for the best.

Part Four

RULES AND REGULATIONS

23

MAKING REPAIRS

If you don't make needed repairs, your tenants may
and may charge you for them.

It goes without saying that, as a landlord, you're going to have to make certain repairs to the rental property. A dishwasher goes out, a window screen tears, a fence comes down—you need to fix it.

Sometimes a repair is covered by insurance (as is often the case when wind blows down a fence). But most times it isn't, and you have to pay for it. That's when it gets expensive.

It's hoped you've built enough of a cushion into your rental investment that you can afford to make repairs when needed. If you haven't, then you'll have to come up with the money out of your pocket.

The one thing a landlord cannot afford to do, however, is to let things go so that, eventually, a tenant is forced to make repairs. If that happens, you no longer have control over the amount the repair will cost, how it will be done, what damage doing the repair might cause, and where the money to pay for it will come from.

Yet with great regularity, many landlords, by failing to take care of timely repairs themselves, make the mistake of thrusting the burden of repairs onto their tenants.

· Tenants' Repair Rights

Those new to landlording may wonder about tenants making repairs. After all, they're living there; why shouldn't they repair the premises at their own cost? The answer is the difference, of course, between owning and renting. You profit from the repairs, whereas presumably tenants do not.

For this reason many states have now enacted laws allowing tenants to make necessary repairs if you fail to and then to deduct the cost of those repairs from the next rent payment.

The reason for such laws is that, in the past, unscrupulous landlords have rented out premises where there were inadequate water or sanitary facilities or heating or some other necessary item to make the property habitable. The tenants paid the rent but then didn't receive the water or heat or working toilet that they were entitled to. In order to get things working, in the past they might have had to make the repairs themselves out of their own pocket, thus improving the landlord's property. To secure payment from the landlord, they would then have to go to court, where the outcome was always in doubt.

Tenant protection laws of many states, on the other hand, provide that if a landlord does not promptly make repairs that are necessary to bring the property up to a condition fit for human occupancy, tenants can take self-help measures. They can make the repairs themselves and then deduct the cost from the next month's rent.

Usually, however, there are conditions tied to this self-help remedy. Typical constraints on tenant self-help repairs are the following:

- The tenant must have informed the landlord of the problem.
- The landlord must refuse to correct it within a reasonable amount of time.
- The repairs usually must not cost more than one month's rent (or whatever other limit the state imposes).
- The tenant cannot use this self-help method more than once or twice a year.

You should check with your state's department of real estate to find out the exact rules in your area.

Why Not Let Tenants Make Repairs and Deduct the Costs from the Rent?

At first glance, you might wonder what the problem is with having tenants do repairs. After all, isn't the landlord getting necessary work done without the trouble of doing it himself or herself?

L *a n d l o r d ' s* **T** *a l e*

Here's another story about our pal Hal, the worst landlord I ever knew. He ran into this very problem.

Hal had a number of properties, including a small house that he owned and rented out. Fairly late one evening, the tenants called to say the water heater had developed a leak. Water was running out the bottom and into the garage. They had called the gas company, and it had told them the heater was no longer operative and had shut it down. Now, the tenants had no hot water.

Hal, who was home enjoying a ball game with a glass of wine, one of his favorite pleasures, said to the tenants, "Yeah, yeah, I'll get back to you on it." He continued to watch the game and promptly forgot about the tenants.

They called again the next morning, that afternoon, and the following evening. Hal decided they were being pests, particularly as he felt they weren't paying enough rent anyhow. So he ignored them.

A few days passed. The tenants stopped calling, and Hal, involved in other pursuits, promptly forgot about the whole thing . . . until the beginning of the next month, when the tenants sent in the rent—or should have. The rent was $650 a month; the tenants sent Hal a check for $23 and a paid bill for $627 for having a new water heater installed. Needless to say, Hal went through the roof.

He raced over to the property and demanded to know what was going on. He had no intention of paying $627 for a water heater. He hadn't authorized it. Even if he had, he was sure he could get one installed for a couple of hundred dollars. Why, he could install it himself for half that!

The tenants, who had checked with a local real estate agent, calmly explained that they had called him seven times (Was it seven times, he wondered? Could it have been that many?) over a three-day period, but he had not responded.

(continued)

They couldn't live in the property without hot water. So under the laws of their state governing repairs by tenants, they had fixed the problem. Because the tenants felt it was an emergency (they didn't want to wait a week for a plumber's appointment), they called a service person, who came right out and did the work. They told Hal he would be pleased to know that the new water heater was one of the best produced and, of course, one of the most expensive.

What this true story illustrates is the reason you don't want to have your tenants make repairs. Their objectives are inevitably going to be different from yours. They want it done as quickly as possible and cost is no object. You want it done timely, of course, but as inexpensively as possible.

Beware Tenants Who Jump the Gun

Although most tenants may not be aware of their rights in the area of repairs, many are. And a few may want to take advantage of the landlord. They may go ahead and do all sorts of things to the property, such as paint, add new flooring or sinks, or whatever, and then deduct it from the rent. Your only recourse may be to go to court to get the money back from them.

The way to avoid this problem is to make both your and your tenants' responsibilities regarding repairs perfectly clear. You don't want any gray area. To that end, a clause like the one below is often inserted into the rental agreement and then read aloud or otherwise pointed out to tenants at the time they move in. (Note: Have your attorney check over any clauses before inserting them into a rental agreement.)

Repairs and Improvements

Tenants agree not to alter, redecorate, or make repairs to the dwelling, except as provided by law, without first obtaining the owner's (landlord's) specific written permission.

Owner (landlord) agrees to undertake as soon as possible any and all repairs necessary to make the premises habitable and to correct any defects that are hazardous to the health and safety of the occupants upon notification by tenants of the problem. If the owner (landlord) cannot reasonably complete such repairs within three days, he (she) shall keep tenants informed of the work progress.

This sort of language puts tenants on notice that they are not to make repairs by themselves and that they must contact the landlord if any problems requiring repair occur. As soon as the landlord (you) learns of the problem, necessary repairs will be made.

Why let tenants know you're going to promptly take care of work? After all, you may be short of funds when the work is required and may want to let it slip a week or so. The reason is simple: If you don't do the work and the premises become uninhabitable, as noted earlier, tenants may have the right (by state law) to do it themselves and then deduct the cost from the rent (something we've seen that you don't want to have happen).

Of course, sometimes repairs can't be completed immediately (as when parts must be ordered) or cannot be started immediately (as when no workpeople are available). When that happens, the landlord (you) must keep the tenants informed as to what's going on, so they don't assume nothing's happening and attempt the repairs themselves.

What If the Property Becomes Uninhabitable?

One of the implicit requirements of renting is that you provide a property that is habitable. If there's no water, no sewerage, no heat, no light, a broken window, leaking roof, or any other problem that can be conceivably considered to render the premises unfit for human habitation, you can't collect the rent. That's why you've got to fix all serious problems.

L a n d l o r d ' s **T** a l e

A landlord friend had a single-family home rented to a couple who couldn't change a light bulb. They called him for everything.

(continued)

One night they called to say there was a mouse in the house. He said he'd be out the next day with a trap. Before he could get there, he got a panicked call from the tenants saying a big rat was in their bedroom and had them cornered on one side of the bed. They couldn't get out. What should they do?

The landlord drove over only to discover that the rat had disappeared and so had the tenants. They had taken a room at a motel and said the premises were uninhabitable because of vermin.

The landlord put down a couple of traps and then hired an exterminator. Three days later the exterminator explained that some tree rats had gotten into the roof and built a nest. A few baby rats had gotten into the house—no big deal and he was taking care of the problem. But it would be another week or so before he could be sure all of the rats were gone.

The landlord informed the tenants, who said they'd be back a week later. They were and presented the landlord with a bill for the motel costs!

Ultimately, the landlord did not have to pay the motel costs for the tenants, but he lost nearly two weeks' rent plus the cost of extermination. Who's to say how much it would have cost him if he hadn't acted promptly?

Disabled Tenants

In most states, disabled tenants may have the right to modify a unit to meet their special needs. Typically, however, they must first notify the landlord and receive approval. And they must pay for the modifications themselves.

24

SAFETY ISSUES
IN THE RENTAL

*A safe rental means both your tenant and
you will sleep better at night.*

Every landlord should provide a safe rental. That means one in which there are no hazards to the tenant and in which reasonable precautions have been taken to safeguard the property. (See Chapter 12 on environmental hazards.)

Sometimes providing a safe rental is as simple as providing adequate smoke alarms. In other cases, it may mean paying special attention to crime and drug use in the neighborhood. I'll cover these and other safety-related topics in this chapter.

Do You Need a Smoke Alarm?

Most areas of the country now require that at least one smoke alarm be present in all rental properties. In some cases, there must be a smoke alarm in all bedroom areas as well as in hallways and near the kitchen. If you don't have a smoke alarm in a rental and there's a fire, your liability could be enormous. There's no reason not to install smoke alarms in rentals; they are inexpensive, and tenants are usually grateful to have them.

There are at least two different kinds of smoke alarms. One uses a tiny bit of radioactive material in an ion chamber to detect smoke. These are better at detecting rapidly burning fires. A photocell type of detector also detects smoke and is better at sounding the alarm for low-flame, smoldering fires. Detectors that contain both types are available for under $50. Ion chamber detectors are readily available for under $10.

When installing a smoke detector, be sure to check with your local building and safety department to find out whether your local code requires it to be battery operated or hard-wired into the property. Some areas require one type, other areas another; and the code is often strictly enforced.

The only problem here is if you have an existing building that isn't wired for a smoke detector but the code requires it. This can be overcome by having an electrician run an electrical wire from a plug or hot ceiling outlet to a suitable place for the detector, which may cost $100 or more. If the local code requires it, however, you may not have a choice.

If you use battery-operated smoke detectors, be aware that the batteries are usually good for only about a year. It's an excellent idea to have a regular battery replacement schedule that you follow. It also helps to write down the date the battery is installed on a small adhesive label and attach it to the detector, so you'll know how current the battery is.

Be sure you show tenants where smoke detectors are located and how to test them. Also, let tenants know that if the detector starts "chirping," it's not a cricket but a sign that the battery is low; and inform tenants they should let you know about the chirping, so the battery can be changed. For liability reasons, it's important to get a signed statement from tenants that they have a working smoke alarm. (See the end of the book for a sample letter.)

Do You Need Carbon Monoxide Detectors?

Unlike smoke detectors, which sense combustion, carbon monoxide detectors search for an odorless, colorless gas that is produced as a result of incomplete combustion. Carbon monoxide replaces oxygen in the bloodstream and can cause death. Therefore, it's a serious concern, especially in rentals with older heating systems. The following are systems that can produce carbon monoxide:

- Gas furnace
- Oil furnace
- Fireplace

- Gas or kerosene space heater
- Any appliance that produces combustion

The best way to prevent poisoning is to have your heating systems regularly checked by professionals. When a problem is found, correct it immediately.

Although most building and safety departments have been slow to adopt rules on installing carbon monoxide detectors, I would certainly put them in all units.

Should You Have Fire Extinguishers?

A fire extinguisher provides a self-help way for a tenant to put out a small fire (that, incidentally, the tenant may have inadvertently started). Fires most often start in the kitchen, usually as the result of grease burning. Other sources of fires are the garage and any room in the rental with a fireplace.

If you operate an apartment house, the local building and safety department may require that you maintain a fire extinguisher of a certain weight (the weight being the fire retardant material it contains) in hallways and other areas (such as washrooms). You may be required to keep one extinguisher of a certain weight per so many units.

Requirements for extinguishers in single-family to up to four-unit rental buildings are often more lax but may still exist. Sometimes you must actually call the local building and safety department to find out what the fire extinguisher requirements are for your type of rental. Further, there will often be little to no inspection to determine compliance with the rules.

The rub comes if there's a fire. You can be sure that if you didn't provide an extinguisher but one was required, your liability will be enormous. Indeed, if someone should have been seriously injured or, God forbid, should have died, you may become the target of newspaper reporters, who could characterize you as a "slumlord." In fact, you might even face criminal prosecution!

I hope I've scared you enough to consider putting in fire extinguishers when needed. They are relatively inexpensive (often costing less than $20) and can pay for themselves in peace of mind.

Modern extinguishers are rated for different types of fires: "A" is for conventional fires fed by such things as cloth, rubbish, paper, and wood; "B" is for fires fed by grease, paint, oil, and flammable liquids; and "C" is for electrical fires. A good extinguisher for a rental is usually one that is all purpose, that is, it has an ABC rating.

In addition, there's the amount of fire retardant material in the extinguisher. The higher the number associated with a letter, the greater the amount of retardant and the bigger a fire it will cover. Most small fire extinguishers contain three to five pounds of retardant and are enough for a small fire. But this means they only last about ten seconds.

I always have at least one fire extinguisher in each rental unit as required. I also point out to tenants where each extinguisher is located, and I have tenants sign a statement that they know these locations. (See the end of this book for a sample statement.) However, never indicate that the tenant is *expected* to put out fires. Provide an accurate number for the local fire department.

One final word about the charge in an extinguisher: Extinguishers work only when they are charged. The common and least expensive type—dry chemical—cannot be partially discharged; it gets only one usage. Therefore, if you use this type, you should check on a regular basis to see that all are charged. Also affix a label (which usually comes with the extinguisher) showing the last date each was checked.

Most extinguishers carry a claim they can be recharged once used. The trouble is that it's usually only the factory that can recharge them, and the cost of transporting them back and forth and charging them is usually more than the cost of a new extinguisher. It's better to think of them as disposable. However, be sure to instruct tenants not to "test" the extinguisher by trying it out, as that will discharge it. (Virtually all units come with a little gauge that shows if it's charged.)

Pool/Spa Safety

Many times rental units have a pool, a spa, or both. If yours does, be aware of your increased liability. Pools and spas may be bold attractions to hook tenants, but they can also provide terrible complications if someone gets injured in them.

Generally speaking, there are four areas that must concern you with regard to pools and spas: safety at the location, fencing, insurance, and maintenance.

Safety at the Location

Usually you must provide rules and safety precautions located where they can be seen and are easily read in the language(s) most commonly used by tenants. These include such things as who must not use the spa (young children, people with heart problems, etc.), how to revive someone who appears to have drowned, and who to call in an emergency.

Be wary of limiting access to the pool, as that might be considered discrimination. For example, you may be able to say that no one can use the pool after ten in the evening or before eight in the morning. But you probably won't be able to say that children are prohibited from using it. You may not even be able to say that children may not use the pool during certain hours. (Check with Chapter 25 and HUD.)

Fencing

You want only authorized people to use your pool, and that means tenants. You also don't want children to wander into the pool area, accidentally fall in, and drown; and that means you do want to have your pool/spa completely fenced—usually a building and safety code requirement.

Typically, the fence must be at least five feet tall and have a spring-loaded locking gate. Don't let the fence or gate deteriorate to the point that small children can sneak in. If you don't have proper fencing and someone gets into your pool, even if they are trespassing on your property, you could be in more hot water than you ever imagined possible.

Insurance. To cover your liability for a pool/spa in a rental area, you must carry extra liability insurance and be sure that it covers the pool/spa area. Such insurance is not all that much more expensive. I maintain at least a $3 million liability policy, although many landlords feel that $1 million is minimal. These policies are typically obtained by getting an umbrella liability policy on top of your regular insurance policy. Check with your insurance agent.

Maintenance

Spas and pools do not maintain themselves. They must be cleaned regularly, the acid\base balance correctly adjusted, and a cleansing agent, such as chlorine, used to inhibit the development of algae and diseases in the water. You don't want algae (yellow, brown, or black) because it will ruin your pool. You don't want diseases in the water, because these could make your tenants ill. Thus, you need to either maintain the pool properly yourself or hire a service to do it.

If I have a pool at a rental, I always explain proper usage to my tenants and have them sign a statement that they are aware of how the pool should be used and of its inherent dangers.

By the way, if you have a slide or diving board at the pool, I suggest removing it. The chances of someone being injured while using either are enormous; and I don't think it's worth the liability to keep them there.

Earthquake Safety

For those who live in earthquake country (California and most of the West Coast as well as other parts of the United States) there are certain earthquake safety precautions that must be taken, the most common being strapping the water heater.

Water heaters are actually vertical containers of water. They are very heavy when full and normally very stable, but in an earthquake they can sway from side to side and even topple over. When they do, they usually break their water lines as well as the electric or gas lines leading to them and thus can cause a lot of water damage. Even more important, they can cause fires.

To prevent such damage, local regulations often require water heaters to be strapped to walls so that they can't sway in most earthquakes. In California, for example, this is usually a requirement of homes when they are sold; and some communities also require it of rental units. In any event, it's a precaution that's well worth taking by anyone who owns property in earthquake country.

The actual method of securing the water heater is usually spelled out in local or state codes. Check with a good local agent or your building and safety department for details.

I always have my tenants sign a statement that they are aware the water heater has been strapped. (See the end of the book for a sample statement.)

Raising Gas Appliances in the Garage

A funny thing about many flammable gasses—they are heavier than air. This applies to propane, motor vehicle gas, and others.

In a rental, this means that in a garage gas fumes could be escaping from a car's gas tank and lingering close to the ground. A person who is standing might not detect them. However, a water heater, clothes dryer, or other appliance with a pilot light could set off the fumes, causing an explosion.

That's why many local and state governments require any such appliances located in a garage to be at least 18 inches off the floor. Compliance usually means simply buying a wood platform (typically available for this purpose in local hardware stores) and placing the water heater or appliance on it. The cost is often less than $25.

The chances are that a gas explosion in the garage will never happen at your rental. But if it does and you didn't comply with local regulations and have appliances that are not at least 18 inches off the ground, woe unto you.

Peephole Security

Peepholes, also called peepscopes, are optical devices that are fit into doors so you can see who's on the other side without opening the door. They are particularly useful in blind entrances where those inside have no idea who's outside. These commonly occur in multiple-dwelling rental buildings.

Although peepholes may be required in motels and other transitory rental situations, they probably aren't required for single-family up to four-unit rental locations. However, they are a good idea, as they add safety to a property.

A peephole device typically costs less than $10 and is simple to install. (You just have to cut the hole to the correct size.) I would get one that offers a wide range of vision to the person on the inside but is blind to the person trying to look in from the outside.

Lock Security

You want to be sure that you change the locks, or at least change the keying of the locks, for each new tenant. You also want to be sure that the locks hold the doors securely. Many landlords favor a double locking system: a regular door handle lock plus a dead bolt.

There have been cases in which tenants have sued landlords for not providing a secure premises because the locks were inadequate. You don't want this problem.

Also, be sure there are adequate locks on all windows. You don't want the liability that comes from an intruder breaking into a unit because the windows didn't lock properly.

Lighting

It's very important that you provide adequate lighting for common areas at night for your property, particularly if it's a multiple dwelling, for two important reasons. The first is to prevent accidental falls. The last thing you want is a tenant to trip over something and claim that he or she couldn't see adequately because of poor lighting.

The other reason is safety. Bright lighting discourages criminal activity; you don't want crimes committed on or near your property.

Bright lighting today is inexpensive and easy to install. Superbright halogen lights can illuminate the front, sides, and back of buildings with ease. (Be sure to also brightly illuminate parking areas.)

Checking Out Employees

As a landlord, particularly when you have a large complex of rental units, you need to hire employees such as gardeners, handypersons, and rental agents. Be sure that you do a thorough job of checking these people out, including a police records check. (You must obtain their permission to do the latter.) I know several landlords who insist all of their people be bonded, and the bonding company itself requires a thorough check.

Remember, the people you hire will be in close contact with your tenants. They probably have access to the inside of the rental units by means of master keys. The last thing you want is an employee to attack or rob a tenant.

Of course, there's no sure way to protect yourself against an employee who runs amok. But at least a thorough check at the time you hire employees can be used as a defense that you did your best.

Also, keep on checking. If you discover an employee with a problem (such as thievery), get rid of him or her as fast as legally possible.

Responding to Tenant Complaints and Questions

Whenever a tenant complains or questions a security feature of your property—whether the lighting, smoke alarms, or strangers on the premises—take it seriously. Conduct an investigation, correct faulty equipment, and, if necessary, contact local law enforcement.

It's also a good idea to point out any safety features, such as smoke alarms, that your property has to calm a worried tenant. However, avoid any claims that may give your worried tenant an expectation of security. If you emphasize that your property is safe and/or secure, and the tenant should later be a victim of a crime, you can be sure those words about safety and security will come back to haunt you. Remember, in today's world, no property can truly be safe and secure.

It's also a good idea to keep a record of any tenant complaints and questions about security. And make a note of any steps you took to correct the situation. This way, if anything later develops, you have a paper trail to help protect yourself.

If a tenant should be a victim of a crime, take all steps to protect that tenant and others on the property. This includes notifying appropriate law enforcement officials. And it means notifying other tenants of the crime. You don't want to be later accused (if a second crime is committed) of keeping your tenants in the dark about a dangerous situation.

You should also check with local law enforcement about any crime prevention programs available in your area. Neighborhood Crime Watches as well as Multi-Housing Crime-Free Programs may be available. Also check out the Burglary Prevention Council at http://www.burglaryprevention .org.

25

AVOIDING PROBLEMS WITH ANTIDISCRIMINATION LAWS

The best policy is an open policy.

It's been a long time since you could simply refuse to rent your property to anyone for any reason. Times change and, quite frankly, for the better. Today we have antidiscrimination laws in housing that, when you think about it, protect all of us.

For a landlord, however, you have to watch yourself carefully to be sure that you don't discriminate, even inadvertently. The penalties for discrimination can be severe.

According to the Fair Housing Act of 1988, there are a variety of protected classes against whom you cannot discriminate in housing. As discussed in Chapter 9, you cannot discriminate on the basis of the following:

- Race
- Color
- National origin or ancestry
- Religion
- Sex
- Familial status (including children under the age of 18 living with parents or legal custodians; pregnant women; and people securing custody of children under the age of 18)
- Physical disability

Discriminating on the basis of any of the above is illegal according to federal law and applies everywhere in the country, including where you have your rental. This means you cannot take the following actions based on race, color, national origin, religion, sex, familial status, or disability:

- Refuse to rent housing
- Refuse to negotiate for housing
- Make housing unavailable
- Deny a dwelling
- Set different terms, conditions, or privileges for rental of a dwelling
- Provide different housing services or facilities
- Falsely deny that housing is available for inspection or rental
- For profit, persuade owners to rent or deny anyone access to or membership in a facility or service related to the rental of housing

H *i n t*

You may be required to provide a closer parking space in a multiple dwelling unit to someone with a "disabled" permit. Also, you may be required to provide ramps for wheelchairs and special facilities in toilets for the disabled.

If you don't comply, a person can file a complaint with HUD (Department of Housing and Urban Development), and you could be subject to an investigation and, potentially, severe fines.

For more information on the ADA (Americans with Disabilities Act), check http://www.usdoj.gov/cr/ada.

In addition, under the federal Americans with Disabilities Act (ADA), you must allow a visually impaired tenant to keep a guide dog even if you have a "no pets" policy. Further, you cannot limit or discourage occupancy to tenants who have a companion animal required by a medical prescription. This can include not only a guide dog but a variety of other animals that may have been prescribed for a physical or emotional condition. Also, if you offer ample, unassigned parking, you must honor a request from a mobility-impaired tenant for a reserved space near his or her apartment if necessary to ensure access to the apartment.

And if your tenant has a physical or mental disability (including hearing, mobility, and visual impairments; chronic alcoholism; chronic mental illness; mental retardation; AIDS; or AIDS-related complex) that substantially limits one or more major life activities or has a record of, or is regarded as having, such disability, you may not refuse to let the tenant make reasonable modifications to your dwelling or common use areas at the tenant's expense, if necessary, for the disabled person to use the housing. Also, you may not refuse to make reasonable accommodations in rules, policies, practices, or services, if necessary, for the disabled person to use the housing.

Are You Covered?

Certain exemptions to some of the above rules do exist. These involve: an owner-occupied property of four units or fewer; and a single-family house, as long as you don't discriminate in your advertising or use an agent for leasing or securing a tenant. And some senior housing (described below) is exempted only with regard to the age requirement.

I've summarized merely the major points here, but HUD offers free brochures as well as priced books explaining the law in detail through its Fair Housing Information Clearinghouse; the number is 800-343-3442. HUD also offers a free newsletter and online help at http://www .hud.gov. Although designed primarily for tenant use, if you have questions on discrimination, you can call the HUD Housing Discrimination Hotline at 800-669-9777.

In addition, many cities, counties, states, and smaller areas have created local ordinances that add new classes to be protected. You should check with your local housing authority, a local apartment owners association, or a knowledgeable real estate agent who specializes in rentals in your area to find out what these classes are. Some of the ordinances that have been passed have expanded protection on the basis of the following:

- Educational status (can't discriminate because the applicant is a student)
- Sexual preference (can't discriminate if applicants are male, female, or homosexual)
- Occupation (can't discriminate regardless of what the applicant does for a living)
- Medical status (can't discriminate regardless of the applicant's medical condition, for example, a person who has had polio)
- Age (can't discriminate on the basis of age)

Finally, ordinances have also been passed by certain local governments that add special restrictions. Here are some examples:

- Number of occupants per house: bans renting to more than four adults (over 18 years of age) per single-family unit
- Number of cars: bans more than two cars per rental unit

Service Members

Recent legislation gives specific rights to members of the United States armed services when it comes to rentals. These include, apparently, prohibiting, without a court order, the eviction of service members or their dependents from a residence they are occupying. This does not apply, however, if the rent exceeds $2,400 monthly. The landlord may not seize personal property of a service member or his or her dependents to secure payment of any overdue rent.

To evict service members or their dependents, a landlord must go to court. If the service members can show that the military service is materially affecting their ability to pay the rent, the court must postpone the proceeding or may adjust the rent.

Further, a landlord cannot terminate or rescind a lease originated before a service member entered the military. On the other hand, a ser-

---

L *a n d l o r d ' s* **D** *i l e m m a*

With so many antidiscrimination laws on the books, how do you keep out the bad tenants (those who won't pay or might ruin your property) and get the good ones? The good news is that you are free to discriminate in those areas critical to getting a good tenant. Namely, you can reject a tenant who has a bad credit record (has been evicted, is late in paying, has bad credit, etc.), who doesn't have sufficient income to make the payments, who doesn't have enough cash to move in, who has too many members in the family for the size of the property, who has a pet that would damage the property, and so on. Of course, you must apply your policy equally to all.

In other words, you can still go after the good tenants—those who make the rent payments on time and keep the place in good shape.

vice member may terminate a "covered lease" (covering a property occupied by a service member or his or her dependents and used for a
"residential, professional, business, agricultural, or similar purpose"),
provided the lease was drawn before the service member entered military service or the service member receives military orders for a permanent change of station or deployment within a military unit. The lease
must be for at least 90 days.

The exact rules of this legislation are breaking new ground, and in-
terpretations of them can be expected over the next few years. Be sure
to check with your attorney to see if and how they affect you and your
tenants.

How Many Is Too Many?

One area worth a special note has to do with the number of tenants
you allow in your property. Federal law emphasizes that you can't discriminate by refusing to rent to families. On the other hand, local
statutes and common sense might require that you limit the number of
people you can have in your property. What are you to do?

The problem is that there are often no hard-and-fast rules. Building
and safety codes usually state only the maximum number of occupants
per room—and frequently that's as many as half a dozen! (Fire codes
can be more stringent—check with them.)

HUD offers guidelines on occupancy, and these usually translate to
about three per bedroom (two per bedroom plus one).

Unless local codes specify the maximum and minimum number of
tenants you can have in your property, you have to come up with reasonable rules of your own and apply them across the board. As long as you
don't change them for each tenant applicant and they're reasonable,
you may be OK.

Renting to Families with Kids

A word about children is also in order here. The old maxim that
landlords used to live by was "Kids are great—in your place, not mine!"
The reason is that kids are hard on a rental. They tend to mark walls,

H *i n t*

Don't try to charge higher rents to families with children. It may be seen as discrimination. Also, in a multiunit building, don't insist that families with kids live only on the bottom floor or near the playground equipment to cut down noise.

stain carpets, scratch floors and doors, and so on. Many landlords would simply prefer to rent to couples without children.

Even though you can no longer discriminate against a family because it has children, you may be able to limit the number of children you allow based on the size of the rental.

How many kids per rental? As noted earlier, this is a gray area. Some landlords arbitrarily use the guideline of a maximum of two children plus one adult per bedroom. On the other hand, if you have a four-bedroom house, would you want a family with four adults and eight kids living there? There are also considerations of the number of bathrooms, the total living space, the size of the yard, and similar issues.

As noted earlier, you want to be sure any limitations you impose are reasonable. And you also want to apply them across the board. However, keep in mind that your rental policies could potentially have a *disparate impact* on tenants. For example, if you limited tenants to four per household in a rental with three bedrooms, you might be accused of familial discrimination because only small families (with few children) could rent from you.

Nor can you limit the activities of children; those, presumably, are the purview of their parents. For example, you can't have a rule that children may not ride skateboards; you might, however, have a rule that prohibits skateboard riding by anyone. In some states you can also limit the use of pools by children under a certain age unless they are accompanied by adults.

Senior Housing

There are certain adults-only communities where every resident must be, for example, over 62 years of age. Some communities have HUD-approved properties where at least 80 percent of the occupants must be 55 or older. In these communities, the anti-discrimination rules against seniors are exempted.

Create a Written Set of Guidelines

H *i n t*

Be sure your guidelines are available in the language the tenants speak. For example, if they speak Vietnamese, the guidelines should be in that language.

You may go years renting properties without a hassle. But rest assured, one day someone will challenge your rental policies, and you will have to defend them. If you do, your best defense can be a set of written guidelines.

A good analogy here is the workplace. Antidiscrimination, wrongful termination, and harassment (sexual and otherwise) lawsuits are increasingly common. Yet one of the best protections employers can have is a set of written guidelines or rules that they follow scrupulously. If you can demonstrate that you have a clear policy and that you adhere to it across the board, you are one step ahead in any discrimination case.

What does a landlord do for guidelines? Write down exactly what qualification you want for tenants of the property (assuming they don't violate any of the antidiscrimination rules). Take them to your attorney to be sure you haven't left anything out or haven't included anything that is prohibited. Then follow them assiduously. If anyone challenges you, you can whip them out to show you weren't discriminating.

Typical Qualifying Guidelines for Tenants

The following must be applied to *all* tenants:

- Assets in bank—equivalent to two months' rent
- Checking account—established with local bank
- Credit cards—three major cards
- Credit report—one late payment maximum in the past six months
- Income—either a set amount or multiple of the rent (say three times the rent)
- Loud noises—no history of loud parties or noisiness after 10 PM or before 7 AM
- Maximum number of tenants—?
- Personal recommendations—at least two

- Pets—one cat only
- Previous history of rent payments—always on time
- Previous landlord's recommendation—at least "good"
- Smoking—no
- Vehicles—maximum of two cars
- Waterbed—none

Note: check out these or any other guidelines with a local attorney before adopting them.

Gray Areas

What should be apparent is that there are a lot of gray areas in setting qualifying guidelines. For example, can you refuse to rent to a tenant who has a motorcycle instead of a car? The tenant may argue you can't; otherwise, you'd be discriminating on the basis of how a tenant chooses to get around. On the other hand, you might say that motorcycles are all right as long as they are properly muffflered and don't make more than a certain decibel of noise comparable to that of an automobile. (In case you hadn't noticed, many modern motorcycles are elegant, quiet roadsters.)

What you want to aim for is consistency and reasonableness. Follow those two guides, check with a local attorney when in a gray area, and you shouldn't go far wrong.

26

INSURANCE
AND LIABILITY

The thing about insurance is that by the time you need it,
it's too late to buy it.

For a moment, let's ask what is the worst that's likely to happen to you as a landlord? Is it having the rental burn down? Is it not being able to find tenants to rent up the premises? Is it having a tenant who leaves the property a mess?

Actually, although the chances of its happening are very slim, the worst that could happen to you probably is having a tenant sue you for an injury on your property . . . and you're not fully covered by insurance. Your property might be worth $200,000, but you could be liable for hundreds of thousands of dollars or more in damages. This applies whether you own the property or are managing it for someone else. (You can be assured that in any lawsuit, both the owner and the managing landlord—if different—will be named.) Therefore, it behooves you to carry full liability insurance. It covers you for many things related to a property and for which you can be sued.

Thus, the question is not whether you should have liability insurance—you should. It's how much to carry. Many property management firms now say that you should carry at least $500,000 in liability insurance. I think their reasoning stems from the fact that many insurance companies today limit the liability coverage you can get on a single-family rental property to that amount.

However, umbrella policies that cover excess liability are available from many companies. They take over when your regular liability insurance ends, and they go on up. A few years ago I was involved with a condominium rental project that had over 100 units, and we regularly carried a minimum of $15 million in liability insurance.

Although liability premiums are constantly rising, the point to remember is that after you pay your basic premium for the $500,000 or whatever, the umbrella excess coverage is actually relatively cheap. I think the reasoning by the insurance companies is that their risk is greatest for the first $100,000 and decreases dramatically after that. Maybe so, but I suggest you let them worry about statistical risk. To sleep at night, I prefer an umbrella in the millions over me.

Fire Insurance

If you have a mortgage on your property, your lender almost certainly requires you to carry, at minimum, basic fire insurance. This simply means that if the building burns down, your lender gets paid. However, you want to carry enough fire insurance so that you can have your interest in the building protected as well. In other words, you want your equity saved.

In the old days, insurance companies used to offer a form of insurance that would only pay a cash settlement amount. For example, you would insure your property for $100,000 and that's what you would get if the building burned down. If you owed $80,000, the lender would get $80,000, and you'd get the remainder, or $20,000.

Today, however, most insurance polices involve some sort of replacement cost; in other words, if your building burns down, the insurance company will rebuild the property so that you are back to where you started. (Except, of course, that you end up with a brand-new building instead of an older one.) In some cases, the insurance company will also make the mortgage payments during the rebuilding period.

If all this sounds terrific, be aware that there are a lot of pitfalls along the way that you need to be wary of, as explained in the following sections.

Replacement Cost Insurance

To obtain replacement cost insurance, you must buy it. If your policy doesn't specifically say you have it, you may not. Check with your insurance agent.

Be aware that there are several types of replacement cost insurance. Under the standard form, your property is depreciated, and you get only the depreciated value, which may not be enough to actually replace the property. Under the so-called guaranteed form, the insurance company replaces your property regardless of the cost. Guaranteed replacement cost has only recently become available on rental properties from many insurance companies. Also, some guaranteed insurance has limits, say 125 percent of the insured amount. Another thing to check out.

Amount of Insurance Coverage

As a condition of a your mortgage, virtually all lenders require that you carry a minimum amount of fire insurance. Typically, they want you to carry enough to cover the mortgage amount. That, however, may actually be too much coverage!

Today, in parts of the country where real estate values are high, a significant portion of the cost of a piece of property is the land value. In some cases, land values may be 50 percent or more of the total property value. The thing about land, however, is that it doesn't burn. So why insure it? Because the lender demands it.

Perhaps an example will help. You are buying a property worth $300,000, of which the land is worth $150,000. When you purchase it, you get an 80 percent mortgage, or $240,000. Naturally enough, the lender wants you to carry $240,000 worth of fire insurance. That's unrealistic, however, as your building's value is only $150,000. Rest assured the premium on that extra $90,000 is going to cost you a pretty penny. But what can you do if that extra insurance is something the lender requires?

Extended or Homeowners Insurance

If you own and live in your own home, in addition to the standard form fire insurance, you may also purchase homeowners insurance. This covers you for a large number of risks in addition to fire, including damage caused by storms, an aircraft crash, smoke, burst pipes (not the pipes but the damage caused by the water), vandalism, falling trees, landslides, and much more. In the past, this type of coverage was not always available to owners of rental property.

Today, however, extended coverage is available from many insurers, and the cost is often only a small amount over and above the standard policy. Generally speaking, besides the basic coverage, there's also *broad form*, which includes glass breakage and such additional covered areas as loss from the weight of snow or falling objects and some (but not all) water damage. The most extended type of coverage is usually called *special form,* which is like homeowners insurance (albeit not quite as good) for a rental. I suggest that, if available, you definitely carry the best coverage available.

L *a n d l o r d ' s*
C *a u t i o n*

Natural calamity insurance, such as earthquake, flood, and storm insurance, often has strict limitations. It may have a very high deductible, and the total coverage may be limited. Further, a major storm or flood could wipe out an insurance pool's reserves, meaning that you might get only partial payment. It's something to consider.

Earthquake/Flood/Storm Endorsements or Policies

In California you want earthquake insurance. In parts of the Midwest you want flood insurance. In Florida and along the Gulf coast it might be hurricane insurance.

Unfortunately, if you are in a high-risk area, chances are that these kinds of insurance aren't available through the normal channels. Most insurance companies simply won't cover such risks at any price. However, pooled risk insurance may be available, or the federal or a state government may offer risk insurance (e.g., the Federal Flood Program or state-assigned risk programs). Check with a good insurance agent.

The price, when risk insurance is offered, is often fairly reasonable. If for no other reason than your peace of mind, you may want to purchase this insurance.

Other Coverages to Check Out

In addition to the coverages mentioned above that are usually associated with a fire insurance policy, there are other risks you may want to check into. A good policy should cover all of these, although it may not. If they aren't covered, you may want to ask your agent about adding them, or you may want to check with a different insurer who does offer them.

Vandalism. Usually covered under an extended fire insurance coverage, protection against vandalism is becoming increasingly more important. Today, one vandal with one can of spray paint can do thousands of dollars of damage to your property in a few minutes. Broken windows, break-ins, and other forms of vandalism are also increasing. You want insurance to cover you against these.

Inflation guard. This automatically increases the value of your insurance annually and is usually based on some index such as the consumer price index. The idea here is that the same property costs more to replace each year. With this coverage you shouldn't unexpectedly find that you are not fully insured as a result of inflation.

Demolition/Code upgrade. When you have a loss, your property will often be only partially destroyed (although it may be a total economic loss), which means that someone has to come in and bulldoze the wreck. Unless you have a special demolition endorsement, this may not be covered by your policy.

Similarly, if you have an older property, the building code in your area may have been upgraded since your rental was built. It may cost more to replace your property today, simply because the newer building codes are stricter. This type of endorsement pays the additional cost of reconstruction resulting from changes in building codes.

Loss of rents. Although this is added in to many extended coverage policies, you'll want to check to be sure loss-of-rent coverage is in yours. It guarantees that during the time your property is uninhabitable because of fire or another calamity, you receive your rents as if it were fully occupied and thus allows you to continue making your mortgage and other payments.

Glass breakage, equipment, waterbed, mortgage, fidelity, and more. Don't automatically assume that everything is covered in your policy. Many areas may require special endorsements or even separate policies. Of course, there are endorsements available for almost any type of risk. The best bet is to find a good insurance agent and let him or her go over your property concerns with you. You may find you need much more coverage . . . or much less!

Employee insurance. If you have employees, you may also want to get special nonowner auto liability coverage. To protect yourself from a dishonest employee, you may want a fidelity bond.

Also, be aware that there may be a deductible that's fairly high as well as a maximum amount of coverage. These limits, too, can be changed by a special endorsement.

Tenants (or Renters) Insurance

Many new landlords are surprised to discover that their extended coverage policy does not cover the personal property of tenants. If there's a broken pipe, for example, and some of the tenants' furniture is destroyed, your policy may not cover it. This, however, would only encourage the tenants to sue you for damages because of the broken pipe.

In the past it was usually necessary for a tenant to show negligence on the landlord's part to win a lawsuit involving the rental. Increasingly, however, it's becoming the case that the tenants only have to show that there's a defect in the property. This could have important consequences for you if the tenants or their possessions are damaged.

A way for tenants to cover their belongings, however, is with tenants (or renters) insurance, which is widely available and is roughly the sort of insurance you get with a homeowners policy. Extended fire policies are available that usually protect tenants from a wide variety of risks—from fire to their dog's biting someone. But generally speaking, tenants must insure their own belongings.

When they move in, always tell tenants in writing that their belongings are *not* covered under your insurance policy. Encourage them to get their own tenants policy.

Workers' Compensation Insurance

Workers' compensation (workers' comp) pays workers injured on the job. But, you may ask, you aren't hiring anyone, so why do you need workers' comp?

The answer is that you may hire an independent contractor to do anything from mow your lawn to fix your roof. Presumably, that independent contractor carries workers' comp, but if not, and someone working for the contractor is injured on the job while doing work for you, you can almost be certain that the injured person will come to you for compensation—at that point your workers' comp should kick in.

In some states, workers' comp is required to be included on all broad coverage insurance; in others, it is not. Be sure to check your policy and with your agent to see what kind of coverage you have. If you don't have workers' comp, I strongly urge you to get it. The premium is typically not very high for a landlord (or property owner) when added to an extended policy and is usually well worth the expense.

Finding the Right Insurance Company

There was a time when you could have your choice of dozens of insurance companies willing to take your premiums and provide insurance for all the risks you wanted to cover. That's changed in the past few years. What with a host of natural catastrophes blanketing the nation from hurricanes in Florida to floods in the Midwest to fires and earthquakes in California, some insurance companies have been forced out of business by enormous claims at the same time that others, even the biggest, have been forced to cut back. Today, you may find there are only a handful of insurers available, or maybe only one or two, or in some cases none at all!

That means that you may not have a chance to pick and choose just the right insurer for yourself. If that's the case, then you simply have to take what you can get. But if you do have the happy option of selecting among several, here are a couple of points to watch out for:

Ratings. Insurance companies are rated by several firms, probably the most well known being Best's Rating Service. Go for an insurance company with a Best's rating of at least A and preferably A+.

Agents. Check out the agents. Some are independents and can give you quotes from a variety of companies, such as Cigna or Travelers. Others write only for one company, such as State Farm or Allstate. Get several quotes and compare the cost against what you get. And be sure that you're covered! You should demand proof of coverage when you pay your premium, or the agent might delay sending in your policy; if catastrophe strikes too soon, you may not have coverage.

Deductibles. Consider these carefully. Many companies offer significantly reduced premiums in exchange for higher deductibles. For example, you might cut your policy cost in half if you accept a $1,000 deductible as opposed to a $100 deductible. But, you may argue, think of the $900 you could lose in the event of a claim!

That's exactly what I *am* thinking about. By accepting a higher deductible, you are, in effect, self-insuring your property. And this may be a good idea. Consider that you have a claim for $800; you have a $100 deductible, you turn in the claim, the insurance company pays off, and you get $700. But the next time your premium comes along, it may go up. Or you may find that your insurer really doesn't want your business any more.

On the other hand, you have a $1,000 deductible, and you pay the $700 claim yourself. You don't turn it in to your insurance company. Now you have the benefit of a lower premium, plus your insurer loves you because you don't have any claims.

The point here is that you're going to end up paying either way. Only with a higher deductible and self-insurance for small claims, you may save money in the long run and end up with a better insurer and a better policy.

Look for Premium Savers

Most insurance companies offer reduced premiums for certain types of equipment. For example, if you have a smoke detector in the property (often a mandatory requirement of your building and safety code), your premium may be reduced. Similarly, there may be reductions for fire extinguishers kept on the property and for sprinkler or security alarm systems. Check with your insurance company to see how you can save.

Be Careful with Claims

I have a cynical friend who says that the entire purpose of many insurance companies is to collect premiums and deny claims. Don't expect your insurance company to instantly take your word for everything and pay you what you want. You need to document any occurrences, particularly those that involve injury. (Of course, be sure that the injured party immediately receives appropriate medical care.)

Get statements from witnesses, if appropriate. Keep the invoices for all work that you have done. Pay by check, and when you get your canceled check back from the bank, hang on to it as proof that you paid for work done. (Yes, there are still banks today that send back canceled checks if you demand it!) Keep a diary, if possible, recounting all incidents. And report claims promptly to your insurer.

27

KEEPING RECORDS

Never trust your memory; no one else will!

Renting property is a taxing proposition in many ways, not the least of which is dealing with the federal government in terms of recordkeeping. Basically, running a rental is like running a business. You have income (from rents, washing machines, etc.) and you have expenses (mortgage payments, insurance, property taxes, and so on). The only way you can know if you have a profit (or loss) is to subtract expenses from income. If you have a profit, you have to pay taxes on it. If you have a loss, you may be able to apply it elsewhere or, in some circumstances, write it off against your regular income (see the end of this chapter for more on this).

The Internal Revenue Service requires that you keep documentation for all income and expenses so that you can substantiate them, if called on to do so. The last thing you want is for the government to challenge your expenses or income and then not be able to come up with written invoices and receipts to prove what you claim.

The Paper Trail

A paper trail, properly kept up-to-date, will document nearly everything that happens to your rental property. It can be invaluable, not only when dealing with taxation agencies, but also when there is a tenant dispute or when you're providing information to buyers when it comes time to sell.

Of course, if you own one unit, or even a handful of rental units, you don't need a fancy system for keeping records. You can buy a filing box with separators in it and make divisions for each property and headings under different properties. Within each property division, you can keep a separate folder for electrical repairs, plumbing repairs, pool maintenance, gardening, and so forth. You'll also need a folder for each tenant.

For example, you'll have a division for the Rover Street house with half a dozen folders in it as well as a division for the Adams Crest rental with folders in it. As you pay each bill, you put the invoice in the appropriate folder, noting the check number and date you paid it.

As bills come in, they can all be kept in a separate folder marked "To Be Paid." Put new bills in the back and pay from the front, and you'll always be paying your oldest bills first.

And you can keep a ledger into which you record all monies received, from whom, the date, and the purpose. Many accountants advise that you stick all income from your rentals into a single account separate from your personal account to avoid confusion and the chance that someone will later say you failed to properly record rental income.

Armed with your file of documented expenses, your income ledger, and your checkbook (and monthly statements and returned checks), you should be able to withstand an audit as well as be able to keep track of all your monies coming in and going out.

Of course, these days many property management programs are available for your computer. Although those specifically geared to rentals tend to be fairly expensive, you can adapt variations of Quicken and MS Money to do a handy job for you.

Rent and Expense Schedules

If you have only one rental unit, this really isn't important. You can always keep track of who has paid and when in your general ledger.

However, as you add rental units, it becomes increasingly difficult to remember what the money paid was for, who paid it, and so on. A rental income schedule, therefore, with the names of tenants, their addresses,

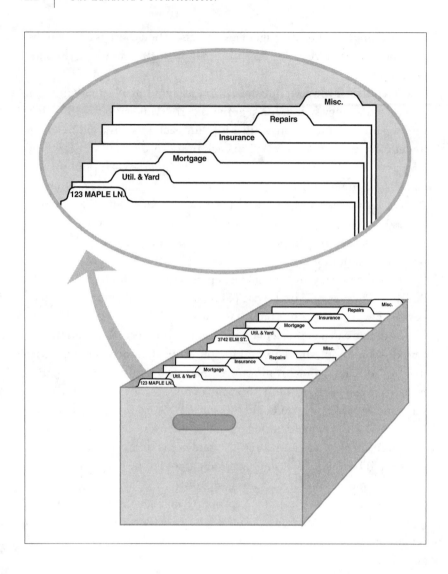

and the date and amount they paid and its purpose (laundry money income is different from rental money income) is helpful. It lets you know
at a glance what money has come in, from where, and for what purpose.

Similarly, a rental expense schedule showing each unit separately
and the expenses paid monthly, such as mortgage, utilities, maintenance,
and so forth, will likewise help you to keep track of where your money is
going from moment to moment.

Tenants' Folders

You should also keep a separate folder for each tenant. In it you will have your copy of the rental application, lease or month-to-month tenancy agreement, disclosures, and all other documents relating to the tenant. You'll update this folder as necessary.

Taxes and Rental Property

As a landlord, you may be responsible for a variety of taxes. The taxes you may need to pay include:

- City licensing and tax fees
- State and county property taxes (both real and personal)
- Local, state, and federal income taxes
- Local, state, and federal capital gains/loss taxes on the sale of your property
- Other taxes that may be levied against you and/or your property

This is a complex and arcane subject beyond the scope of this book. I suggest that you consult with a good tax advisor, CPA, or attorney to find out just how to calculate your tax liability.

H *i n t*

It's important for you to protect your tenants' privacy. Therefore, you should take pains to ensure that no one can come into your rental office and rifle through the folders to gain unauthorized information. You should keep the folders under lock and key; and you may not want to label the filing cabinet (or instead purposely mislabel it) to discourage anyone from breaking in.

RENTAL EXPENSE SCHEDULE

Tenant #	Month					
	JAN	FEB	MAR	APRIL	MAY	JUNE
1	$	$	$	$	$	$
2	$	$	$	$	$	$
3	$	$	$	$	$	$
4	$	$	$	$	$	$
5	$	$	$	$	$	$
6	$	$	$	$	$	$
7	$	$	$	$	$	$
8	$	$	$	$	$	$
9	$	$	$	$	$	$
10	$	$	$	$	$	$
Totals						

Tenant #	Month					
	JULY	AUG	SEPT	OCT	NOV	DEC
1	$	$	$	$	$	$
2	$	$	$	$	$	$
3	$	$	$	$	$	$
4	$	$	$	$	$	$
5	$	$	$	$	$	$
6	$	$	$	$	$	$
7	$	$	$	$	$	$
8	$	$	$	$	$	$
9	$	$	$	$	$	$
10	$	$	$	$	$	$
Totals						

LANDLORD'S FORMS

The following forms are designed to give an overview of the typical forms used in property management. You should be aware that all or part of any form may not apply in your circumstances or may be inappropriate for your state or local area. It is suggested that before using any form, you have it checked out and customized by a competent attorney. The author and publisher assume no responsibility for the legality or appropriateness of use of these forms.

TENANCY AGREEMENT

CAVEAT: *Portions of the following rental agreement may not apply to your circumstances or may not be legal in your state or area. Do not use it as it is. Take it to a competent attorney in your area so that it may be customized for your state and locale and for your particular needs. The author and publisher assume no responsibility for the legality, appropriateness, or timeliness of this agreement.*

TENANCY AGREEMENT
MONTH-TO-MONTH LEASE

THIS DOCUMENT IS INTENDED TO BE A LEGALLY BINDING AGREEMENT. READ IT CAREFULLY.

City _____

State _____

Date _____

_____ Hereinafter referred to as Landlord agrees to rent to _____ hereinafter referred to as tenants _____ the property described as _____ hereinafter referred to as the premises together with the following personal property: carpets, window coverings, light fixtures, built-in appliances, plus the following furniture:

_____

_____

Cross out and initial one of the two following paragraphs that does not apply and fill out and initial the one that does.

☐ LEASE: This tenancy shall commence on _____ 20__ and terminate on _____ 20__ The total rent for this lease period is $_____. The tenants shall pay first and last month's rent in advance. Upon expiration of this agreement, the tenancy shall revert to a month-to-month tenancy at $_____ per month.

☐ MONTH-TO-MONTH: This tenancy shall commence on _____ 20__ and may be terminated by either party by giving a 30-day WRITTEN notice of termination to the other party (unless the law requires a longer notice).

1. RENT: The rent is $_____ per month payable in advance on the ____ day of each calendar month. Tenants to pay rent at the office of the landlord at _____ city _____ state _____ zip _____ or at such other place as the landlord may from time to time designate.

2. BAD CHECKS: Tenants shall pay a $_____ charge for handling of each check returned by the tenants' bank for "insufficient funds." Any dishonored check shall be treated as unpaid rent. It is hereby mutually agreed that if the tenants' bank returns two checks for whatever reason, thereafter tenants shall pay all rent in the form of cash, cashier's check, or money order. Any rent not received by the fifth day after it is due shall be paid only in the form of cash, cashier's check, or money order.

3. SECURITY DEPOSIT

UNDER NO CIRCUMSTANCES SHALL THE SECURITY DEPOSIT BE USED AS THE LAST MONTH'S RENT.

Tenants agree to pay a refundable security deposit of $_____ before occupying the premises. Said deposit shall be refunded within ____ days along with a written accounting of disposition of said deposit after tenants completely vacate the premises provided:

A. No damage, other than normal wear and tear, has been done to the premises, the furniture, or other personal property.

B. Premises are left clean. Landlord may deduct a portion of deposit to pay for certain cleaning if premises are not left clean.

C. All utilities that are the tenants' responsibility have been paid for in full an
d utility providers have been properly notified of the tenants' departure.

D. All keys have been returned to the landlord.

E. All other conditions and terms of this agreement have been satisfactorily fulfilled.

The landlord may use all or a portion of this security deposit as may be reasonably necessary to:

A. Remedy tenants' defaults in payment of rent.

B. To clean premises if left uncleaned by tenants.

C. To repair damages caused by tenants to premises.

If any portion of the security deposit is used during the term of the tenancy to cure a default in rent or to repair damages, tenants agree to reinstate security deposit to its full amount within _____ days of written notice delivered to tenants by landlord in person or by mail.

In addition to the above, tenants also agree to pay a refundable pet security deposit of $_____

In addition to the above, tenants also agree to pay a refundable waterbed deposit of $_____.

4. LATE FEE: It is hereby agreed that if the rent is not paid by the date it is due, tenants shall pay a late fee of $_____ for each day from the rental due date until the rent is paid.

5. INSPECTION: Prior to taking occupancy, tenants agree to inspect the premises and any personal property therein and to execute an inspection sheet that shall become a part of this agreement.

6. ACCESS: Tenants shall allow the landlord access to the premises at reasonable times and upon reasonable notice for the purposes of inspection, making necessary repairs, or showing the premises to prospective tenants or purchasers.
Reasonable means _____ hours _____ days _____ written notice or as required by law.
In the event of an emergency, the tenant agrees that the owner and/or its agents may enter the premises at any time to make any necessary repairs, improvements, or changes. Landlord shall keep a key to the premises. Tenant shall not change lock or keys without landlord's permission.

7. NOTICE: If rent is not paid by the due date, landlord may serve tenants with a ____ day notice to pay rent. If landlord agrees to accept payment of rent in full and late fees after serving notice, tenants shall in addition be subject to a $____ fee for preparing and serving the notice.

8. OCCUPANCY: The total number of adults who may occupy the premises is _____. The total number of children who may occupy the premises is _____. Their names and birthdays are:

_____

_____

_____

No pet (except an animal designated to serve the disabled such as a Seeing Eye dog or as prescribed for a medical condition) shall be kept on the premises without the specific written permission of the owner. The following pet(s) may be kept: _____.

9. VEHICLES: Landlord shall provide ____ covered and ____ uncovered parking areas for tenants. Tenants shall keep a maximum of _____ on the premises. All tenants' vehicles not kept in designated locations must be parked in public areas. Tenants shall park no boat, trailer or recreational vehicle on the premises continuously for more than _____ days without prior written approval of the landlord.

10. DAMAGES AND REPAIRS: Tenants agree to pay for all damages to the premises done by the tenants or their invitees. Tenants agree not to paint, paper, alter, redecorate, or make repairs to the dwelling, except as provided by law, without first obtaining the landlord's specific written permission.

Landlord agrees to undertake as soon as possible any and all repairs necessary to make the premises habitable and to correct any defects that are hazardous to the health and safety of the occupants, upon notification by tenants of the problem. If the landlord cannot reasonably complete such repairs within three days, he (she) shall keep tenants informed of the work progress.

All requests by tenants for service and repairs, except in the case of an emergency, are to be in the form of writing. Tenants agree to keep the premises in good order and condition and to pay for any repairs caused by their negligence or misuse or that of their family or invitees.

It is mutually agreed that it is the tenants' responsibility to repair certain items, such as windows broken or damaged subsequent to tenants' occupancy, at tenants' expense. If tenants are unable or unwilling to repair broken or damaged windows within a reasonable period of time, landlord may make such repairs and charge tenants. The cost of the repairs must not exceed the lowest bid by a competent workman.

As of occupancy, landlord warrants that all plumbing drainage is in good working condition. Tenants thereafter agree to pay for removing all stoppages caused for any reason except for roots, defective plumbing, backup from main lines, or undefined causes as determined by the plumber who clears the line.

11. USE: The premises are to be used only as a residence. No commercial use is allowed. The tenants shall have the right to quiet enjoyment of the premises. The tenants agree not to disturb, annoy, endanger, or incon-

venience neighbors nor use the premises for any immoral or unlawful purpose, nor violate any law ordinance nor commit waste or nuisance upon or about the premises. No waterbed may be used on the premises without the prior written consent of the landlord.

12. UTILITIES: Landlord shall pay for the following utilities _____
_____.

Tenants shall be responsible for opening, closing, and paying all costs for the following utilities _____
_____.

If the tenants are responsible for trash, the tenants shall obtain and maintain trash and garbage service from the appropriate utility company.

13. YARD MAINTENANCE: Landlord shall be responsible for maintaining all common areas. Tenants shall be responsible for maintaining
_____.

With regard to areas tenants are to maintain, they shall be kept clear of rubbish and weeds. Lawns, shrubs, and surrounding grounds shall be kept in reasonably good condition. In the event tenants do not maintain premises in reasonably good condition, landlord at his or her option may provide gardening service at $_____ per month to be paid for by tenants. Landlord shall be responsible for installation, repair, and replacement of all below-ground sprinkler systems.

14. INSURANCE: The landlord shall obtain fire insurance to cover the premises. Tenants are aware that landlord's insurance does not cover tenants' personal property and they are encouraged to secure a tenants' insurance policy.

In the event of a fire or casualty damage caused by tenants, they shall be responsible for payment of rent and for repairs to correct the damage. If a portion of the premises should become uninhabitable due to fire or casualty damage due to no fault of the tenants, they shall not be responsible for payment of rent for that portion. Should the entire premises be uninhabitable due to no fault of the tenants, no rent shall be due until premises shall be made habitable again. The landlord shall reserve the right to determine whether premises or a portion thereof is uninhabitable.

15. HAZARDOUS MATERIALS: Tenants agree not to keep or use on the premises any materials that an insurance company may deem hazardous or to conduct any activity that increases the rate of insurance for the landlord.

16. NEGLIGENCE: Tenants agree to hold the landlord harmless from claims of loss or damage to property and injury or death to persons caused by the negligence or intentional acts of the tenants or their invitees.

17. EMERGENCIES: In the event of an emergency involving the premises, such as a plumbing stoppage, the tenants shall immediately call the landlord at _____ or other phone number as the landlord may from time to time designate and report the problem.

18. DELAY: If the landlord shall be unable to give possession of the premises on the day of the commencement of this agreement by reason of the holding over of any prior occupant of the premises or for any other reasons beyond the control of the landlord, then tenants' obligations to pay the rent and other charges in this agreement shall not commence until possession of the premises is given or is available to tenants. Tenants agree to accept such abatement of rent as liquidated damages in full satisfaction of the failure of landlord to give possession of said premises on agreed date and further agree that landlord shall not be held liable for any damages tenants may suffer as a consequence of not receiving timely possession. If such delay exceeds _____ days from the commencement date, this agreement shall be considered void.

19. SUBLETTING: Tenants shall not sublet, assign, or transfer all or part of the premises without the prior written consent of the landlord.

20. RULES: Tenants shall comply with all covenants, conditions, and restrictions that apply to the premises. The tenants shall comply with all rules of a homeowners association that apply to the premises.

21. ATTORNEY FEES: If either party brings action to enforce any terms of this agreement or recover the possession of the premises, the prevailing party shall/shall not (cross out wording not desired and initial change) be entitled to recover from the other party his or her costs and attorney fees.

22. RESPONSIBILITY TO PAY RENT: All undersigned tenants are jointly and severally (together and separately) liable for all rents incurred during the term of this agreement. (Every member is equally responsible for the payment of the rent.) Each tenant who signs this agreement authorizes and agrees to be the agent of all other occupants of the premises and agrees to accept, on behalf of the other occupants, service of notices and summons relating to tenancy.

23. SUBSTITUTION OF TENANTS: In the event one tenant moves out and is substituted by another, the new tenant shall fill out an application, and tenancy shall be subject to the approval of the landlord. No portion of the cleaning deposit will be refunded until the property is completely vacated.

24. HOLDOVER: If after the date of termination of tenancy, tenants are still in possession of premises, they will be considered holding over and agree to pay rental damages at the rate of 1/30th of their then current monthly rent per day of the holdover.

25. OTHER CONDITIONS: Each provision herein containing words used in the singular shall include the plural where the context requires. If any item in this agreement is found to be contrary to federal, state, or local law, it shall be considered null and void and shall not affect the validity of any other item in the agreement. The waiver of any breach of any of the terms and conditions of this lease shall not constitute a continuing waiver or a subsequent breach of any of the terms or conditions herein. The foregoing constitutes the entire agreement between the parties and may be nullified or changed only in writing and signed by both parties. Both parties have executed this lease in duplicate and hereby acknowledge receipt of a copy on the day and year first shown above. Time is the essence of this agreement.

TENANTS ACKNOWLEDGE RECEIPT OF THE FOLLOWING:

☐ Move-in inspection sheet
☐ Homeowners rules and regulations
☐ Entry key
☐ Community pool key
☐ Remote garage door opener
☐ Security gate card #_____
☐ Lead-paint disclosure statement and booklet
☐ Asbestos disclosure statement

☐ Other disclosure statements
  _____
☐ Drug-free statement
☐ Crime-free statement
☐ Smoke detector in operating condition (tested by tenant)
☐ Door lock notice
☐ Laundry room key
☐ Other _____
  _____

Tenant _____

Tenant _____

Landlord _____

Landlord _____

3-DAY NOTICE TO PAY OR QUIT

TO: _____
_____
_____
_____

You are hereby notified that the amount of $_____ is now due and payable representing rent due from ___/___/___ until ___/___/___ for the property described as _____ along with all storage and garage areas.

Demand is hereby made that you pay said rent IN FULL within three (3) days or quit the premises. You are further notified that if you fail to pay or quit, legal proceedings will be instituted against you to terminate your rental agreement or lease, to recover possession of said premises, and to recover rents, court costs, attorney fees, and damages as specified in your rental agreement or lease.

NO PART PAYMENT OF RENT WILL BE ACCEPTED

Dated this _____ day of _____, _____

Signed_____

Owner or owner's representative

- -

AFFIDAVIT OF SERVICE

State of _____ County of_____

I, _____, declare under penalty of perjury that I served the above notice on the tenant named above on the _____ day of _____, _____ in the following manner:

☐ By handing a copy thereof to the above named tenant.

☐ By delivering a copy thereof to _____,
a person above the age of 18 residing at the above premises.

☐ By posting a copy thereof in a conspicuous place on the above premises, no one being in actual possession thereof.

☐ By sending a copy thereof by certified mail to the tenant at his or her place of residence.

State of _____, County _____

Subscribed and sworn to before me this ___ day of _____, ___

_____Notary Public

Notary Seal   Signed_____

RENTAL APPLICATION FORM

APPLICANT(S):_____

PROPERTY ADDRESS: _____

APPLICANT'S NAME: _____

SOCIAL SECURITY #: _____ DRIVERS LIC.: _____

CO-APPLICANT: _____

SOCIAL SECURITY #: _____ DRIVERS LIC.: _____

NAMES AND RELATIONSHIPS OF OTHER OCCUPANTS

_____ AGE: _____

_____ AGE: _____

PETS:_____

AUTOS: MAKE: _____ MODEL: _____ LICENSE: _____

MAKE: _____ MODEL: _____ LICENSE: _____

HOUSING INFORMATION

CURRENT ADDRESS: _____

  YEARS: ____ MO: _____ REASON FOR LEAVING: _____

CURRENT PHONE #: _____

CURRENT LANDLORD/MANAGER: _____

  PHONE: _____

PREVIOUS ADDRESS: _____

  YEARS: ____ MO: _____ REASON FOR LEAVING: _____

FORMER LANDLORD/MANAGER: _____PHONE: _____

EMPLOYMENT

EMPLOYER: _____ OCCUPATION: _____

YEARS: ___ SUPERVISOR: _____ PHONE: _____

PREVIOUS EMPLOYER: _____ OCCUPATION: _____

YEARS: ___ SUPERVISOR: _____ PHONE: _____

SPOUSE'S EMPLOYER: _____ OCCUPATION: _____

YEARS: ___ SUPERVISOR: _____ PHONE: _____

INCOME AND SAVINGS

MONTHLY GROSS INCOME: _____

SPOUSE'S MONTHLY GROSS: _____

OTHER INCOME: _____

CHECKING ACCT: _____ BRANCH: _____

  #: _____ LENGTH: _____

SAVINGS ACCT: _____ BRANCH: _____

  #: _____ LENGTH: _____

REFERENCES

PERSONAL REFERENCE: _____

  RELATIONSHIP: _____ PHONE #: _____

PERSONAL REFERENCE: _____

  RELATIONSHIP: _____ PHONE #: _____

IN EMERGENCY CONTACT:

  RELATIONSHIP: _____ PHONE #: _____

  RELATIONSHIP: _____ PHONE #: _____

  RELATIONSHIP: _____ PHONE #: _____

CREDIT

MAJOR CREDIT CARD: _____ #: _____ BAL: _____

MAJOR CREDIT CARD: _____ #: _____ BAL: _____

CREDIT REFERENCE: _____ PHONE #: _____

HOW MANY PEOPLE WILL OCCUPY THIS RENTAL UNIT? _____

NAMES OF OTHER OCCUPANTS: _____

HAVE YOU EVER BEEN EVICTED? _____

HAVE YOU EVER FILED FOR BANKRUPTCY?_____

I HAVE READ THIS ENTIRE APPLICATION AND ALL OF THE IN-
FORMATION I HAVE GIVEN IS TRUE AND CORRECT. I HEREBY
GIVE PERMISSION TO LANDLORD TO VERIFY ABOVE INFORMA-
TION, INCLUDING A CREDIT CHECK.

DATE: _____

SIGNED BY APPLICANT: _____

SIGNED BY CO-APPLICANT: _____

PROPERTY INSPECTION SHEET

Date_____

Property Address _____

Tenants' Names _____

_____

Landlord's Name_____

LIVING ROOM, DINING ROOM, FAMILY ROOM, LOFT, BREAKFAST ROOM

(Use separate sheet for each room—circle room to which sheet applies)

Item	Condition on Arrival	Condition on Departing
		Tenants are responsible for damage beyond normal wear and tear and for areas not cleaned.
Floor Coverings		
Walls and Ceiling		
Light Fixtures		
Windows and Screens		
Window Rods and Coverings		
Doors (including hardware)		
Slider and Screen Door		
Fireplace and Equipment		
Other		

Dated _____

Signed Landlord _____

Signed Tenant(s) _____

KITCHEN

Item	Condition on Arrival	Condition on Departing
		Tenants are responsible for damage beyond normal wear and tear and for areas not cleaned.
Floor Coverings		
Cupboards		
Walls and Ceilings		
Windows and Screens		
Window/Slider Coverings		
Doors Including Hardware		
Light Fixtures		
Counter Surfaces and Makeup		
Sink Faucets		
Garbage Disposal		
Stove Burners		
Fan		
Stove Light		
Clock		

Dated _____

Signed Landlord _____

Signed Tenant(s) _____

KITCHEN (continued)

Item	Condition on Arrival	Condition on Departing
Oven Heating Elements		
Broiler		
Light		
Sink Drain		
Dishwasher		
Other		

BATHROOM

Item	Condition on Arrival	Condition on Departing
		Tenants are responsible for damage beyond normal wear and tear and for areas not cleaned.
Floor Covering		
Walls and Ceiling		
Shower and Tub (doors, tracks)		
Toilet		
Plumbing Fixtures Windows and Screens		
Doors and Hardware		

Dated _____

Signed Landlord _____

Signed Tenant(s) _____

BATHROOM (continued)

Item	Condition on Arrival	Condition on Departing
Light Fixtures		
Sink and Counter		
Fan		
Other		

BEDROOM
(Use separate sheet for each bedroom)

Item	Condition on Arrival	Condition on Departing
		Tenants are responsible for damage beyond normal wear and tear and for areas not cleaned.
Floor Covering		
Walls and Ceiling		
Closet, Doors, and Track		
Windows and Screens		
Window Coverings		
Doors and Hardware		
Light Fixtures		
Fireplace and Equipment		

Dated _____

Signed Landlord _____

Signed Tenant(s) _____

BEDROOM (continued)

Item	Condition on Arrival	Condition on Departing
Gas Valve		
Smoke Alarm		
Other		

HALLWAY AND ENTRYWAY

Item	Condition on Arrival	Condition on Departing
		Tenants are responsible for damage beyond normal wear and tear and for areas not cleaned.
Floor Coverings		
Walls and Ceiling		
Closet Doors		
Light Fixtures		
Air-Conditioning and Heating Filters		
Smoke Alarms		
Other		
Utility Room		
Floor Covering		

Dated _____

Signed Landlord _____

Signed Tenant(s) _____

HALLWAY AND ENTRYWAY (continued)

Item	Condition on Arrival	Condition on Departing
Walls and Ceiling		
Light Fixtures		
Gas or Electric Service		
Other		

GARAGE

Item	Condition on Arrival	Condition on Departing
		Tenants are responsible for damage beyond normal wear and tear and for areas not cleaned.
Washer Faucet		
Washer Drain		
Water Softener		
Furnace and Filter		
Air Conditioner		
Light Fixtures		
Floor Type and Condition		
Tools and Equipment		

Dated _____

Signed Landlord _____

Signed Tenant(s) _____

YARD

Item	Condition on Arrival	Condition on Departing
	FRONT	*Tenants are responsible for damage beyond normal wear and tear and for areas not cleaned.*
Sprinklers		
Water Bibs		
Lawn		
Shrubs		
Entry Light		
Walkway And Driveway		
Wall/Fence		
Garage Door		
Door Opener (includes remotes)		
Entry Door		
Doorbell		
Other		

Dated _____

Signed Landlord _____

Signed Tenant(s) _____

YARD (continued)

Item	Condition on Arrival	Condition on Departing
	SIDE	*Tenants are responsible for damage beyond normal wear and tear and for areas not cleaned.*
Sprinklers		
Water Bibs		
Lawn		
Shrubs		
Light Fixture		
Walkway		
Wall/Fence		
Door		
Other		

Item	Condition on Arrival	Condition on Departing
	REAR	*Tenants are responsible for damage beyond normal wear and tear and for areas not cleaned.*
Sprinklers		
Water Bibs		

Dated _____

Signed Landlord _____

Signed Tenant(s) _____

YARD (continued)

Item	Condition on Arrival	Condition on Departing
Lawn		
Shrubs		
Light Fixture		
Walkway		
Wall/Fence		
Door		
Patio		
Patio Cover		
Other		

Dated_____

Signed Landlord _____

Signed Tenant(s) _____

MOVE-OUT INSTRUCTION SHEET

Dear Tenant:

At some point you will be moving from the premises you now occupy. In order to help make that move easier and to avoid confusion, I have prepared the following instructions. They will let you know what's expected of you on move-out according to the terms of your rental agreement.

WHAT IS PROPER NOTICE?

If you have a month-to-month tenancy, you are required by the terms of your rental agreement to give a minimum of ____ days' notice before moving. That notice

1. should be in writing (see the tearout at the bottom).

2. should give the exact date you intend to move.

3. should designate the move-out date; that date should be thirty (30) days from your last rent payment. For example, if you pay on the first, you should plan to move on the first of the following month.

If your plans change and you cannot move out on the day you have designated, please let me know as soon as possible and I will try to make arrangements for you to stay longer. Be aware, however, that in many cases new tenants will be waiting to move in. Also, you will be charged for any additional days you stay.

WHAT RETURNING POSSESSION MEANS

You will not be considered to have moved out and returned possession of the premises until ALL of your personal property (every bit of furniture, clothing, utensils, towels, boxes, and so on) has been removed from the premises including the garage, walkways, utility room, and any other areas you occupy; and you have returned ALL sets of keys. Rent will not stop until all of your property has been removed (assuming also you have given proper notice).

Please call me at _____ at least three days in advance to make arrangements to return keys and to have a move-out inspection.

WHAT IS REQUIRED TO GET YOUR SECURITY DEPOSIT BACK

To get a complete refund of your security deposit you must leave the premises clean and without damage—normal wear and tear excepted—return keys, and fulfill all the obligations of your rental agreement. If you have damaged the premises or left it unclean, a portion of your deposit may be used to pay for repairs, to clean areas that were left dirty (pay special attention to stoves, toilets, tubs, sinks, sills, and floors), and to pay for pet or other damage. Any unused portion of your security deposit will be returned within _____ days along with a complete written accounting of money spent.

If there are marks on walls, please call me first before attempting to clean them, else you could make them worse. Before shampooing carpets or cleaning wall coverings, please call me so that I can let you know which types of cleaning will work on the materials you have and will not cause damage.

YOUR RESPONSIBILITIES

It is your responsibility to call all utility companies to have service discontinued and to turn off phone, trash, and newspaper services. It is your responsibility to leave the premises in a clean and undamaged condition.

- -

Tear off at the dotted line and mail to landlord when you plan to move out.

Tenants' Names _____

Address _____

Day of month rent is paid _____

To:

Landlord's name _____

Landlord's address _____

You are hereby given notice that as per our rental agreement, we are giving you _____ days' notice (_____ days' minimum notice is required) of our intention to move. We understand that we are responsible to pay rent until the end of the notice period.

Date of move-out _____

Signed Tenant(s) _____

NEW OWNER'S/LANDLORD'S LETTER

Date_____

Tenants' names _____

Address _____

Dear Tenants:

As you may already know, I have purchased the property you are renting. I am writing to you by way of introduction so that you will know who I am (I plan to stop by within the next week or so to introduce myself personally) and you will have some idea of what to expect in the coming months.

You will need to change where you send your rent payments. Please make your next and all future rent payments to:

(Name) _____

(Address) _____

Rent can be paid in the form of a personal check, money order, or cashier's check. It is payable on the due date and is considered late thereafter. If you will have to be late for any reason, please contact me as soon as possible. Late rent can result in the institution of eviction proceedings.

I'm sure you're wondering about your security/cleaning deposit. I will be responsible for returning it to you. However, to ensure proper credit, could you please do something for me: Fill out the information requested below and forward it, along with a copy of your old rental agreement, to me. (I use a different rental agreement and soon will be forwarding a copy to you.)

If you have any questions or concerns, please don't hesitate to call me. If not, I look forward to meeting with you in the very near future.

Sincerely,

(Landlord) _____

TENANTS' QUESTIONNAIRE

PROPERTY ADDRESS _____

TENANT'S NAME_____

OTHER TENANT'S NAME _____

NUMBER OF ADULT OCCUPANTS ____

    NAMES _____

NUMBER OF CHILDREN _____ AGES _____

NUMBER OF PETS _____ TYPE _____

NUMBER OF CARS ____ TYPE _____ LICENSE _____

                            TYPE _____ LICENSE _____

EMPLOYER? _____

    PHONE AT WORK _____

CURRENT RENTAL RATE $_____

DATE RENT IS DUE _____

DATE RENT CURRENTLY PAID TO _____

DATE MOVED IN _____

DATE LEASE ENDS (UNLESS MONTH-TO-MONTH) _____

AMOUNT OF LAST MONTH'S RENT PAID $ _____

REFUNDABLE SECURITY DEPOSIT PAID $_____

OTHER DEPOSITS PAID $_____

    PURPOSE _____

ARE ANY OF THE FOLLOWING APPLIANCES OR COVERINGS
YOUR OWN PERSONAL PROPERTY? ☐ stove ☐ washer
☐ dryer ☐ refrigerator ☐ carpeting ☐ wall coverings
☐ other _____

NOTIFY IN CASE OF EMERGENCY _____

      PHONE_____

YOUR PHONE_____

SIGNED _____

PREVIOUS OWNER'S/LANDLORD'S LETTER

Date_____
To Tenants:
Name(s) _____
Address _____
_____

Dear Tenants:

This will serve to inform you that I have sold the property you are currently renting. The anticipated date of title transfer is _____.
Please contact the new landlord/owner for needed repairs after that date.
Until then, you may continue to reach me at (phone) _____.

I will be transferring your security/cleaning deposit in the amount of $_____ to the new landlord/owner who will be responsible for refunding it to you, assuming you fulfill your rental agreement obligations upon move-out. If you have questions about this, please contact the new landlord/owner immediately.

The new landlord/owner is _____ who can be reached at _____, phone _____.

Sincerely,

(Previous Landlord) _____

TENANTS' LETTER OF RECOMMENDATION

Date_____

To Whom It May Concern:

This will recommend (insert tenants' names here) to you. (Tenants' names) have been my tenants from _____ to _____.
During that time the rent was always paid promptly, there was no damage done to the premises, the yard was well kept, and there were no unusual problems. When they moved out, the property was left in a clean and undamaged condition.

I consider (tenants' names) to be excellent tenants.

Sincerely,

(Landlord) _____

LANDLORD'S RECORD OF
TENANT RENTAL PAYMENTS

PAGE ONE—TENANT RECORDS

TENANT #1
TENANT NAME _____
TENANT ADDRESS _____
TENANT PHONE _____
RENTAL RATE $ _____
DEPOSITS HELD $ _____
MOVED IN _____

TENANT #2
TENANT NAME _____
TENANT ADDRESS _____
TENANT PHONE _____
RENTAL RATE $ _____
DEPOSITS HELD $ _____
MOVED IN _____

TENANT #3
TENANT NAME _____
TENANT ADDRESS _____
TENANT PHONE _____
RENTAL RATE $ _____
DEPOSITS HELD $ _____
MOVED IN _____

PAGE TWO—RENTAL SCHEDULE

Tenant #	Month					
	JAN	FEB	MAR	APRIL	MAY	JUNE
1	$	$	$	$	$	$
2	$	$	$	$	$	$
3	$	$	$	$	$	$
Totals						

Tenant #	Month					
	JULY	AUG	SEPT	OCT	NOV	DEC
1	$	$	$	$	$	$
2	$	$	$	$	$	$
3	$	$	$	$	$	$
Totals						

REQUEST TO VERIFY EMPLOYMENT

Name_____

Company_____

Address _____

_____

Date_____

Dear Employer:

_____ (tenant's name) has applied to rent a house (apt./condo) from me and has given you as his/her employer. He/she says that he/she has worked for you for the past _____ years/months at a weekly salary of $_____.

I would very much appreciate it if you would verify this for me so that I can proceed with qualifying _____ (tenant's name) for the rental. Please phone me as soon as possible at _____. If you are unable to phone, please fill out the area below and return this sheet to me.

Sincerely,

Landlord

- -

☐ Verified as given   ☐ Temporary   ☐ Permanent

☐ Not verified

Comments _____

Employer _____

30-DAY NOTICE OF RENT INCREASE

Tenant: _____

Address: _____

_____

_____

Dear _____:

It has been _____ years since we last changed your rent.

As I'm sure you're aware, during that time rental rates have increased significantly in our area. And we have personally experienced increased costs for maintenance, taxes, and repairs, not to mention inflation.

Therefore, we are now forced to increase rents for the dwelling you occupy.

Effective date of change:_____

New rent:_____

We value you as tenants. If you feel you have special circumstances that you would like to discuss with us, please call our office.

Sincerely,

(Landlord) _____ Date _____

NOTICE TO PERFORM

Tenant: _____

Address: _____

_____

_____

TO: _____

_____

You are hereby notified that you are in violation of the following term(s) of your lease/rental agreement:

In violation: _____

_____

_____

You are hereby requested to correct the above violation within _____ days. If you fail to perform as directed, landlord may elect to begin legal proceedings to recover above premises and to secure damages as provided by your lease and as allowed by law.

Note: This is NOT a termination-of-lease notice.

(Landlord) _____ Date _____

NOTICE OF INTENT TO ENTER

Tenant: _____

Address: _____

_____

_____

According to your rental/lease agreement, the landlord/owner or de-signees may enter the property you are renting after giving a reasonable notice of at least 24 hours in advance.

You are hereby notified at least 24 hours in advance that the landlord/ owner or designees intend to enter the premises you are renting at the address noted above for the purpose of:_____

Approximate time of entrance: _____

Estimated duration of stay: _____

If you will be available at the above time, please let the landlord know. However, it is not necessary that you be available on the premises at the time of entry. Landlord/owner or designees, after knocking to deter-mine if anyone is home, will use a passkey to gain entrance.

Change of Lock Notice: If the landlord/owner or designee is unable to enter because tenant has changed or rekeyed locks, landlord will use a locksmith to open door and locks will be rekeyed. A new key will be given to tenant who will be charged for the service.

Signed: _____ Date: _____

Delivered in person by:

Signed: _____ Date: _____ Time: _____

RECEIPT FOR KEYS

Tenant: _____

Address: _____

_____

_____

Tenant acknowledges receipt of _____ keys to the above premises. Loss of any keys should be reported immediately to the landlord.

It is understood that tenant will not make any additional keys without the landlord's specific permission. It is further understood that if the tenant rekeys or adds/changes the locks, a set of new keys will immediately be given to the landlord.

Tenant acknowledges receipt of a copy of this statement.

Signed Landlord _____ Date _____

Signed Tenant _____ Date _____

NOTICE OF SMOKE DETECTOR

Tenant: _____

Address: _____

_____

_____

Tenant is hereby notified that the above premises has _____ operating smoke detectors as approved by the state fire marshall and installed in accordance with regulations of the state fire marshall and local ordinances that may apply.

Tenant acknowledges that he/she has been shown location of smoke detectors and has tested them to determine if they are in working condition. Tenant will immediately notify landlord if battery on smoke detector runs down (usually accompanied by a "chirping" sound).

Tenant acknowledges receipt of a copy of this statement.

Signed Landlord _____ Date _____

Signed Tenant _____ Date _____

NOTICE OF FIRE EXTINGUISHERS

Tenant: _____

Address: _____

_____

_____

Tenant is hereby notified that there are _____ fire extinguishers at the above premises. Fire extinguishers are located at:

_____

_____

When using a fire extinguisher, stand at least six feet from fire and spray in short bursts at base of flame.

Tenant acknowledges receipt of a copy of this statement.

Signed Landlord _____ Date _____

Signed Tenant _____ Date _____

DISCLOSURE OF INFORMATION ON LEAD-BASED PAINT AND/OR LEAD-BASED PAINT HAZARDS

Lead Warning Statement

Housing built before 1978 may contain lead-based paint. Lead from paint, paint chips, and dust can pose health hazards if not managed properly. Lead exposure is especially harmful to young children and pregnant women. Before renting pre-1978 housing, lessors must disclose the presence of known lead-based paint and/or lead-based paint hazards in the dwelling. Lessees must also receive a federally approved pamphlet on lead poisoning prevention.

Lessor's Disclosure

(a) Presence of lead-based paint and/or lead-based paint hazards (check (i) or (ii) below):

    (i) _____ Known lead-based paint and/or lead-based paint hazards are present in the housing (explain).

    _____

    _____

    (ii) _____ Lessor has no knowledge of lead-based paint and/or lead-based paint hazards in the housing.

(b) Records and reports available to the lessor (check (i) or (ii) below):

    (i) _____ Lessor has provided the lessee with all available records and reports pertaining to lead-based paint and/or lead-based paint hazards in the housing (list documents below).

    _____

    _____

    (ii) _____ Lessor has no reports or records pertaining to lead-based paint and/or lead-based paint hazards in the housing.

Lessee's Acknowledgment (initial)

(c) _____ Lessee has received copies of all information listed above.

(d) _____ Lessee has received the pamphlet *Protect Your Family from Lead in Your Home.*

Agent's Acknowledgment (initial)

(e) _____ Agent has informed the lessor of the lessor's obligations under 42 U.S.C. 4852(d) and is aware of his/her responsibility to ensure compliance.

Certification of Accuracy

The following parties have reviewed the information herein and certify, to the best of their knowledge, that the information they have provided is true and correct.

Lessor _____ Date _____ Lessor _____ Date _____

Lessee _____ Date _____ Lessee _____ Date _____

Agent _____ Date _____ Agent _____ Date _____

RENT RECEIPT

Receipt #____

Received from:_____

As rent payment for premises commonly known as:

_____

City   State   Zip

From:_____

To:_____.

NOTICE: There will be a $_____ service charge for all checks returned unpaid. Late rent payment charges may also be applied on returned checks.

TENANT INSURANCE NOTICE

Tenant: _____

Address: _____

_____

_____

Tenant is hereby notified that while landlord carries fire and casualty insurance on the property, this covers only the premises and not the tenant's possessions. Should tenant wish to insure his/her possessions against loss from fire, water, or other source, he/she must secure his/her own tenant's policy. These are available from most insurers.

Sincerely,

(Landlord) _____

Date

A

Abandoned property, 210–14
  late rent and, 210–11
  personal property and, 211–12
  tenant death and, 213–14
Abbreviations, in ads, 74–75
Accountants, 9
Accredited Residential Manager, 36
Active/passive tax rules, 39
Advertising
  bulletin boards, 69
  hook, 75
  Internet, 69–70
  neighborhood flyer, 67–68
  newspaper. *See* Newspaper
    advertisements
  signs, 66–67
Age, discrimination and, 235
Agent, 8–9
  inventory statistics and, 18
  rental listings, 70–71
  as resource, 8–9
Allergic reactions, 108
Amenities, 74
American Lung Association, 105,
  106, 107
Americans with Disabilities Act, 66,
  234
Antidiscrimination, 65–66, 78, 82,
  233–40
  citizenship status and, 98–99
  income qualification and, 92
  rental applications and, 88
  senior housing and, 238
  verifying rental application
    information, 89

Apartment buildings, 12–13
Appliances, 142, 163
  buying property with, 49
  raising gas appliances in garage,
    229
Application, rental. *See* Rental
  application
Arbitration clauses, 134
Asbestos contamination, 105–7
Attorneys, 9, 133
  evictions and, 200–201
  rental agreements and, 127

B

Background check, 98
Bad checks, 189–90
Bathrooms, 14, 56, 141
Bedrooms, 55–56
Best's Rating Service, 248
Black mold, 107–9, 149
Boltlocks, 139
Bonded firms, 36
Bounced checks, 189–91
Broad form insurance coverage, 244
Bulletin board(s)
  ads, 69
  cable access channels, 70
  online, 69–70
Burglary Prevention Council, 232
Business tasks, of landlords, 8
Buying rental property, 46–53
  considerations, 46–47
  giving notice of ownership
    change, 49–50
  increasing rent, 51–52
  keys and, 53

Share the message!

Bulk discounts
Discounts start at only 10 copies and range from 30% to 55% off
retail price based on quantity.

Custom publishing
Private label a cover with your organization's name
and logo. Or, tailor information to your needs with
a custom pamphlet that highlights specific chapters.

Ancillaries
Workshop outlines, videos, and other products are
available on select titles.

Dynamic speakers
Engaging authors are available to share their expertise
and insight at your event.

Call Dearborn Trade Special Sales at 1-800-621-9621, ext. 4444,
or e-mail trade@dearborn.com.

Dearborn™
Trade Publishing
A **Kaplan Professional** Company